Chinese Martial Arts

From Antiquity to the Twenty-First Century

In the global world of the twenty-first century, martial arts are practiced for self-defense and sporting purposes only. However, for thousands of years, they were a central feature of military practice in China and essential for the smooth functioning of society. Individuals who were adept in using weapons were highly regarded, not simply as warriors but also as tacticians and performers. This book, which opens with an intriguing account of the very first female martial artist, charts the history of combat and fighting techniques in China from the Bronze Age to the present. This broad panorama affords fascinating glimpses into the transformation of martial skills, techniques, and weaponry against the background of Chinese history, and the rise and fall of empires and their governments and armies. Quotations from literature and poetry, and the stories of individual warriors, infuse the narrative, offering personal reflections on prowess in the battlefield and techniques of engagement. This is an engaging and readable introduction to the authentic history of Chinese martial arts.

Peter A. Lorge is Assistant Professor of History at Vanderbilt University. He is the author of *War, Politics and Society in Early Modern China, 900–1795* (2005) and *The Asian Military Revolution: From Gunpowder to the Bomb* (2008).

Chinese Martial Arts

From Antiquity to the Twenty-First Century

PETER A. LORGE

Vanderbilt University

CAMBRIDGE
UNIVERSITY PRESS

CAMBRIDGE UNIVERSITY PRESS
Cambridge, New York, Melbourne, Madrid, Cape Town,
Singapore, São Paulo, Delhi, Tokyo, Mexico City

Cambridge University Press
32 Avenue of the Americas, New York, NY 10013-2473, USA

www.cambridge.org
Information on this title: www.cambridge.org/9780521878814

© Cambridge University Press 2012

First published 2012

Printed in the United States of America

A catalog record for this publication is available from the British Library.

Library of Congress Cataloging in Publication data
Lorge, Peter Allan, 1967–
Chinese martial arts : from antiquity to the twenty-first century / Peter Lorge.
p. cm.
Includes bibliographical references and index.
ISBN 978-0-521-87881-4
1. Martial arts – China – History. I. Title.
GVII00.7.A2L67   2011
796.815′5—dc22 2011012674

ISBN 978-0-521-87881-4 Hardback

Contents

Preface and Acknowledgments

I was not born a warrior. I am not tough, strong, fast, agile, or brave, so I have none of the natural gifts necessary to be good at martial arts. Despite these limitations, I have loved martial arts for as long as I can remember, and I have actively practiced various arts since the age of fifteen. This book therefore has more personal significance for me than other academic work I have done. It also means that I have more than just an intellectual debt to acknowledge in the writing of this book; I have a debt to all of my martial arts teachers as well. Though I cannot claim intellectual or scholarly gifts any greater than my physical or spiritual ones, I do offer this study as some measure of recompense for the many teachers who did their best for me over the years.

In the intellectual realm I owe a vast debt to Stanley Henning. His article, "The Martial Arts Encounters Academia," is a model of clarity and rigor and should be the starting point for anyone beginning to write on Chinese martial arts. Beyond his many valuable articles, Stan has been a real mentor to me in this field, through e-mail and phone calls, supplying me with critical insights and citations. One day I hope to meet him in person.

Matthew Polly, whose excellent book on the modern Shaolin monastery has received so much well-deserved praise, kindly answered several technical linguistic questions of mine and supplied me with a few choice anecdotes. Unlike him, however, I have no intention of getting into a ring for a real fight. Ralph Thaxton made his research on post-1978 China available to me, vastly improving my coverage of the late twentieth century. Brian Kennedy kindly helped me find materials during a visit to Taiwan. My colleague Ruth Rogoski supplied me with several critical citations. Yuh-fen Benda greatly facilitated my research, on one occasion turning what would have been a week and a half of work into little more than an hour.

My editor at Cambridge, Marigold Acland, has once again proven herself a brilliant midwife of academic research. The anonymous readers greatly helped my thinking and writing. The intellectual thrashing they gave me was all to my benefit, even if it probably hurt more than the lessons of my martial arts teachers.

I have been very fortunate in martial arts teachers over the years. All of them were far more patient with me than I had any right to expect. In chronological order, to the best of my recollection, I must thank Sensei Louis Neglia (Brooklyn), Sam Um (Austin), Komizu Sensei (Austin), Kanetsuka Sensei (Oxford), Sifu Jack Shamberger (New York), Wu Shifu (Taibei), Sensei Peter Hobart (Philadelphia), Wang Shifu (Beijing), and my current teacher, Shawn Hammonds, and all the guys at Nashville MMA.

Finally, and most important, I must thank my family, from my parents who supported me in studying martial arts as a teenager and studying Chinese and Chinese history in school, to my wife and children, who have accepted my physical and mental absence as I researched and practiced martial arts. All of them (particularly my mother) resolutely accepted the odd dings and dents incurred when an incompetent clod tries to learn how to perform complex and elegant maneuvers.

Just as this volume was completed my Classical Chinese teacher, Yang Youwei, passed away in Taiwan. I have therefore dedicated it to his memory.

Introduction

Chinese martial arts has a written history and is part of the society in which it developed. One of the greatest myths about Chinese martial arts as a whole is that it has no written record. Many people assume or assert that the only source of knowledge about its origins and development is the tradition orally transmitted from martial arts teachers. Adding to the misunderstanding of the past, this imagined oral tradition seldom places the martial arts in the broader context of Chinese history or, when it does, uses a simplistic, static, and inaccurate description of that past. In fact, the amount of available written material on martial arts in Chinese history is enormous. As a first step in confronting such a vast body of information, this book will describe the origins and development of the Chinese martial arts across Chinese history. I will argue that these arts are the developed physical practices of armed and unarmed combat, which must be understood primarily as military skills, not methods of self-cultivation or religious activity.

That said, although the martial arts stemmed from military requirements and related activities like hunting, these skills took on added meaning as markers of status and of certain mental or spiritual qualities. Warfare and hunting were important in the identity of early Chinese aristocrats, for example, and their class was closely associated with chariot-borne archery. Aristocrats not only fought with certain weapons but they also fought under specific rules of combat that reinforced their shared sense of class. As time went on, changes in society and technology undermined the military, economic, and political basis for these chariot-riding aristocrats. Armies grew in size and improved in armament, thus spreading the skills of warfare further out among the common people. Government officials were expected to lead in wartime, and farmers were expected to become soldiers when needed. In unstable and war-ridden times the martial arts were thus widely practiced throughout Chinese society.

As Chinese society grew in size and complexity, individuals developed greater and greater specialization. While most of society, of course, remained farmers, and the government continued to require them to perform military service, some men specialized in martial skills, from hand-to-hand combat to leading armies. With the decline of the aristocracy, the lower ranks of the elite, the *shi* 士, gentlemen or knights, were able to rise to the upper ranks of government through their skills and knowledge. Some of these gentlemen, like Confucius (551–479 BCE), sought to reform government and society through their ideas. Failing to find a sympathetic ruler, Confucius became a teacher, instructing men in the manners of gentlemen and inculcating them with his ideas of proper governing. Other men specialized in military skills, working as generals, officers, bodyguards, and duelists. There was still considerable crossover, as even Confucius had students with martial skills and was himself trained in the basic skills of a gentleman, such as archery.

While the *shi* of Confucius' time were certainly trained in the martial arts as part of their basic education, it was extraordinary for men who would call themselves *shi* fifteen hundred years later to be similarly trained. Chinese society and culture were not static, and as they changed, the practice of martial arts and the meaning of this practice also changed. Even within a given time period, the individuals who practiced martial arts, and their sex or ethnicity, could produce dramatically different meanings. Some women were practitioners, and certain martial arts were primarily, if not exclusively, associated with particular ethnic groups. The various steppe groups were generally superior horse-archers, even while many Chinese warriors also maintained these skills. Martial arts also played a role in gender construction, though the gender connotations of martial practice in China, among the Chinese and among other ethnic groups, differed significantly from Western traditions. War was a highly gendered activity, and therefore the majority of people practicing martial arts were men, but this was not exclusively so even among the Chinese.

As in Europe, some religious orders became closely associated with martial arts. Most of these associations in China were developed, or at least amplified, by fiction in the form of plays, literature, and eventually film. Fiction is a powerful force in assigning meaning within culture, and it has played an important role in defining martial arts in China, particularly from the second half of the imperial era until the present. At the same time, however, the represented world of fiction frequently deviates sharply from the real practice. While this book makes some use of fiction in the discussion of the martial arts, it focuses primarily on the reality of its practice.

The modern understanding of martial arts as only unarmed fighting skills for self-defense, abstracted movements for self-cultivation, or the wielding of archaic weapons for aesthetics or improved health is a modern perspective inconsistent with most earlier practice. By contrast, the performance of martial arts for entertainment and even ritual is fundamental and original to their practice. Nevertheless, the modern understanding of Chinese martial arts is not wrong because it differs from its earlier place in Chinese society; it is simply an example of how things change. And indeed it is hard to fix martial arts into a single meaning in the modern era since Chinese society is itself currently in flux.

The reader should therefore be clear that Chinese martial arts is a vast and complex subject with not only continuous change over time but also dramatic regional, ethnic, gender, and functional differences. This book is an attempt to provide a survey of martial arts in Chinese history without any pretension of comprehensiveness. Before beginning the chronological history in Chapter 1, I will therefore deal with a few general issues in the remainder of the introduction. First, I will define what I mean by "martial arts," presenting a broader explanation of this term than is commonly used, justifying this for the reader. Second, I will discuss the problem of authenticity, including some of the modern issues of styles and values. Finally, I will present a technical philological explanation of the terms used in Chinese and English to refer to martial arts. I will leave for the conclusion a more general discussion of some of the issues that the study of martial arts raises.

DEFINING MARTIAL ARTS

In this book, I define "martial arts" as the various skills or practices that originated as methods of combat. This definition therefore includes many performance, religious, or health-promoting activities that no longer have any direct combat applications but clearly originated in combat, while possibly excluding references to these techniques in dance, for example. Admittedly, the distinctions can be muddled as one activity shades into another. In addition, what makes something a martial art rather than an action done by someone who is naturally good at fighting is that the techniques are taught. Without the transmission of these skills through teaching, they do not constitute an "art" in the sense of being a body of information or techniques that aim to reproduce certain knowledge or effects.

Stanley Henning pointed out to me on several occasions that the practice of martial arts is extremely individual. Every practicing martial artist is aware that a person's own performance of the skills that a teacher is imparting is biased by both the teacher's and the student's natural inclinations. These biases come in addition to the particular art's own body of skills, which are necessarily selective rather than comprehensive. There is no such thing as a single art or "style" that contains every possible martial skill. Many martial artists therefore study under multiple teachers to both broaden their skill base and mitigate the biases of a given teacher. As a consequence, there is an inherent tension between what an individual does and what an individual teaches, or has been taught. Martial arts as a living tradition is like any craft tradition in that skills must be taught, learned, and performed by individuals who innovate even while reproducing the tradition. I will return to this issue later.

There are many skills, techniques, practices, and traditions that would fall under my definition of martial arts. Consequently, throughout this book I use the term in two ways. It is used first in the singular, referring to the complete group of skills covered by my definition. The second sense of the term, which I use much less frequently, is as a plural term for the disparate arts, styles, and practices at a given time or place. Martial arts styles appear quite late in Chinese history, by the Ming Dynasty (1368–1644) or possibly slightly earlier; before that, martial skills were not grouped together into distinct named sets. At most, a student learned the martial art of a particular teacher. Those arts descended from a teacher, or sometimes associated with a location, defined themselves in lineage terms traced back to a founder. Founding teachers were often mythical or were provided with legends that made them the unique source of skills (which actually stemmed from the ongoing martial practices of the founder's time).

This definition of martial arts has several advantages: first, it is not specific to any culture and therefore emphasizes the universality of trained forms of combat in different places and times. Second, it ties practices back to their original intent, that is, to improve the performance of violence. Third, it includes all combat techniques, not just Asian empty-handed fighting. Fourth, it eliminates our contemporary and entirely erroneous perspective on these practices in China that defines them in terms of peace, self-defense, and religion.

All cultures have martial arts; highly developed fighting techniques are not unique to East Asia. It is merely a modern construction that consigns boxing and wrestling, for example, to the realm of sports (and Olympic competition) and extremely similar East Asian fighting techniques to acceptable activities for middle-class Westerners. Even fencing, shooting, and archery qualify as sports, albeit not very popular ones, while East Asian forms of fencing, archery, or other weapon use are martial arts. There are historical reasons for these constructions of the meaning of martial arts in contemporary English, but they create an artificial and distracting barrier to understanding Chinese martial arts in its real social historical meaning. What makes Chinese martial arts distinct is not that China has them and other cultures did not and do not, but the particular forms and meanings of the practice.

At root, martial arts is about skill with violence. Even in its purely performative manifestation, the movements of martial arts are about effective violence. It is because effective violence can be physically elegant and aesthetically pleasing that it has taken on such a broad and long-standing place in theater and film. Martial arts is visually compelling to many people, and watching it became a form of entertainment. Its connection to the power of violence is what makes it different from a dance constructed on purely aesthetic grounds.

Martial arts performance and the critical military core of martial arts practice emphasize the use of weapons. It is better to be armed in a fight, and learning to use weapons is and has been basic to martial arts training for most people in history around the world. We must include learning to use firearms in this category as well. There is no heuristic reason for excluding weapons (including firearms) from the consideration of martial arts, except to effect an artificial and misleading demilitarization of East Asian martial arts. It is logically challenging, though obviously not impossible, to construct Chinese martial arts practice with swords and other weapons into a nonviolent practice. But for most of Chinese history, archery, with a bow or crossbow, was the primary martial art; firearms were added to the list of martial skills as they became available. The current emphasis in the West on empty-handed martial arts speaks to the Western ideas of China (which have seeped back into China) and to the nature of Western society.

It is a modern perspective, both inside China and abroad, that Chinese martial arts is only about self-defense and self-cultivation. This connection to nonviolence is further enhanced by a vastly distorted connection between religion and the martial arts. Martial arts preexisted both religious Daoism and Buddhism and was mostly practiced outside the religious context. Only by excluding soldiers and militiamen, who constitute the vast majority of martial artists in all time periods including the present, and focusing on the relatively tiny number of civilian martial artists can we make self-defense the main goal of martial arts training. An even smaller group of martial artists practiced martial arts, mostly archery in the Confucian tradition, primarily for self-cultivation. The use of martial arts to promote health alone is likely no older than the nineteenth and possibly even the twentieth century.

AUTHENTICITY AND REAL KUNGFU

A history of Chinese martial arts has to confront the issue of authenticity because history is frequently used to authenticate these skills. A related question concerns "secret" teachings and "real" martial arts transmitted through "true" masters. While these questions do not naturally arise from the historical sources prior to the sixteenth century, they do emerge as issues in the sixteenth century and continue to the present day. The twenty-first-century martial artist and the historian of martial arts often seem to be in a perpetual search for a true or authentic martial art that is in some way "real" and effective in ways that inauthentic martial arts are not. Somehow the acquisition of this true martial art would confer invincibility and enlightenment on its practitioner. Since by this definition the art so acquired would make its practitioner superhuman, no ordinary teaching could achieve this. Thus, the teaching must be a secret passed from master to select disciples by direct transmission and seldom written down.

The standard for what would constitute an authentic martial art is therefore both impossibly high and extremely compelling. There are few, if any, reliable objective markers of someone attaining such perfect skill in a perfect art. Some martial artists argue that their success in dueling or tournament performance clearly demonstrates their attainment of great skill and the superiority of their style of the arts. Others counter that the parameters of these contests are so artificial and the scope of the skills required for success in them so narrow that they are meaningless as a marker of true martial arts skill. Worse still, the artificial confines of the event and the competitive attitude of the participants are directly contrary to any true martial art. A further problem is that tournament fighting is almost exclusively a forum for the young – in itself a guarantee of shallow understanding of profound arts.

Authenticity is an argument for the value of a particular practice or way of practicing rather than a historical artifact. There is no established authority that determines what is or is not authentic, even though particular organizations may set their own standards and declare any deviation from those standards to be wrong. A good comparison would be Chinese food. Who determines what is authentic Chinese food? If a Chinese person in China adds a new ingredient to her cooking, does that make it inauthentic? Europeans introduced chili peppers into China from South America, and they are now a standard and accepted part of many regional Chinese cuisines. Therefore any food using chili peppers is not authentic by pre–Ming Dynasty standards. And what of the individual? If a Chinese person (however understood) cooks a Chinese recipe poorly, is the resulting dish more authentic than the same recipe cooked well by a non-Chinese? There is no clear answer to these questions in either cooking or martial arts.

Both contemporary and premodern practitioners of the martial arts often lay claim to ancient origins for their techniques. As with the histories of many physical practices before the age of video recording, it is functionally impossible to compare an earlier with a contemporary practice. We are forced to compare descriptions and static drawings with current practice, leading to ambiguous results. Douglas Wile has attempted to find broad connections between Ming Dynasty martial arts and more recent Taiji forms as a way to lengthen Taiji's history.[1] Wile wisely treads carefully around the defining legends of Taiji, choosing to downplay their tendentious and entirely fictional construction. For many practitioners, the legends, though they see them as truth and not fiction, validate their martial art, giving it a greater value than its purely physical and mental benefits alone.

The Shaolin Buddhist Temple serves a similar function, authenticating martial arts by direct or indirect association. Meir Shahar's book, *The Shaolin Monastery*, provides a great deal of scholarly information about a key facet of the modern understanding of Chinese martial arts; it does so, however, without directly stating that the evidence the author presents does not support the idea that Shaolin was important for martial arts before or after the Ming Dynasty.[2] Even during the Ming Dynasty, Shaolin was only one part of a vast landscape of martial arts practice. And of course martial arts was practiced in China for thousands of years before Shaolin was founded. Buddhism did not bring martial arts to China, though large Buddhist institutions, like other large landowners, employed armed, trained security forces.

Common to all of the arguments about authenticity is competition in the marketplace for martial arts students and legitimacy. Someone interested in learning martial arts must not only choose a teacher or style but must also justify that choice. This was true in the Ming Dynasty when Qi Jiguang (1528–88) surveyed a number of martial arts styles to determine the most effective techniques to teach his soldiers, and it is true for martial arts teachers today. Some schools stress their pragmatic value in self-defense, disparaging other schools for flowery and impractical techniques. Other schools argue that their martial art is deeper than just self-defense and will yield greater personal benefits than merely combat effectiveness. Every school tries to prove its case with a very limited set of arguments: practicality, pedigree, a teacher's accomplishments, and disparagement of the competition. All of it distills down to "they are bad, we are good."

A claim to ancient pedigree can in a positive way be seen as an attempt to substantiate the effectiveness of a technique through its continued practice. Thus, for something to have been used and maintained by generations of practitioners is proof that they found it useful. Unfortunately, no currently practiced style of Chinese martial arts can reliably trace itself back more than a few centuries, and most much less than that. This is not to say that the individual techniques making up any current style are inauthentic or in some way false, but that the particular organization and theory of a designated style cannot be legitimated by an ancient pedigree. Most of the techniques used in current martial arts are much older than any style, and many may well be ancient.

It is the techniques and skills that are "authentic" in Chinese martial arts, not particular schools or styles. This authenticity, if we even allow such a fraught concept, comes from these techniques being practiced as martial arts for combat or performances over centuries and even millennia in China. To say, as some martial arts teachers currently do, that modern Wushu is not the real Kungfu has no historical or truth value; it is merely marketing. Just as the meaning of practicing martial arts in Chinese society has changed as Chinese society has changed, so too does the meaning or value of martial arts vary widely with each individual practitioner.

The site of martial arts practice is the individual, and the value of this practice can be judged only in relation to that person. A soldier may learn techniques that worked for others in combat, yet fail in battle himself, without invalidating the use of those techniques. Most people who learn martial arts for self-defense will never actually use it. Those who practice a martial art to improve their well-being succeed only if they actually feel better for doing it, regardless of the pedigree of the style. At some point a practice may stray so far from earlier techniques as to no longer qualify as martial arts, or be so badly taught or performed that it fails in its intended effect. Authenticity is in the eye of the beholder, but also in the marketing campaigns of many schools.

KUNG FU, GONGFU, QIGONG, AND CHINESE TERMINOLOGY IN ENGLISH

Like the Chinese martial arts themselves, the terminology used in Chinese to discuss the martial arts has changed over time. To add to the confusion, many Romanization systems – and sometimes no discernible system at all – are used to render Chinese pronunciation into Western alphabets, making very unclear just what is being discussed. This is particularly true when different dialects are involved. Movies and twentieth-century popular culture have further garbled transmission. Yet there is more at stake in questions of terminology than simple clarity. When a new term is introduced in Chinese, it is important to know whether it denotes a new practice or style, or if it is a new name for something older. Since newness is not usually prized in the martial arts, new practices often claim old pedigrees, whether specious or not.

The *Oxford English Dictionary* incorrectly defines "Kung-fu" or "kung-fu" as the Chinese form of karate. It is perhaps on firmer ground in referring to a 1966 article in *Punch* as containing the first attested mention of the term in English.[3] (This might have to be modified, however, as Bruce Lee used the term "gong fu" in an unpublished essay in 1962.) Nevertheless, clearly its use in English began in the twentieth century. "Kung-fu" is the Romanization for the Chinese characters 功夫 in the Wade-Giles system, and "gongfu" in the Pinyin system that is currently the most widely used, though "gongfu" has thus far not entered English dictionaries. In Classical, Literary, and Modern Chinese, the term is not specific to the martial arts, however, meaning effort, skill, accomplishment, or a period of time.[4] But by 1984, "gongfu" was indeed used in the particular sense of martial arts in a Mainland Chinese newspaper.[5] The use of Kung-fu or gongfu in English may be due to a misunderstanding or mistranslation of modern Chinese, possibly through movie subtitles or dubbing.[6] In any case, it was not a word used in Chinese to refer directly to the martial arts until the late twentieth century. Chinese speakers seldom use the term gongfu, except when speaking English, where it seems to accord with contemporary English usage.

Modern Chinese speakers usually refer to "wushu" 武術, literally "martial arts" or "martial techniques" when discussing the martial arts as a whole. The term first appeared in the early sixth century in the *Wen Xuan* 文選. (The *Wen Xuan*, or *Anthology of Literature*, was compiled by Xiao Tong (501–31), the Crown Prince of the Liang dynasty, and became a basic reader for Chinese literature from the Sui dynasty until the end of the Qing dynasty.) A slightly earlier term "wuyi" 武藝, also literally "martial arts," was also generally used from the early third century, though it has not continued into Modern Chinese (the "yi" of "wuyi" is the same "art" used in the Confucian "Six Arts"). The emergence of these two terms, wuyi and wushu, may indicate the development of a new mental category of activities that had not been separated out before. The Confucian Six Arts encompassed the set of skills necessary for a gentleman, most of which had martial applications – indicating that a gentleman was supposed to be able to lead in peace and war. Most recently, the Chinese government has established wushu as the international term for its competitive sports version of Chinese martial arts.

The earliest term, however, was "Jiji" 技繫, "boxing," which is attested in the works of the philosopher Xunzi (313–238 BCE).[7] Many different words were used to refer to Chinese martial arts and the individual skills that comprise it over China's long history. We cannot, therefore, insist upon a single term for martial arts during all of Chinese history, though wushu comes quite close; this is even more true when we move into the realm of English, or other foreign languages. "Kungfu" in all its spellings now seems to be the English term for Chinese martial arts, however constituted. I have chosen not to use kungfu in that way in this book, however, because its use in English is so recent.

Chinese usage has clearly changed in the last decades of the twentieth century, if not somewhat earlier. In *American Shaolin*, Matthew Polly tells of a Shaolin martial artist who states: "Everyone knows that *laowai* are no good at kungfu."[8] Polly clarified this for me: "So when Coach Yan said to me, 'The Laowai are no good at kungfu,' [h]e meant 'gong fu.' White boys weren't good at the deeper aspects, the Ch'an of it. Or the fighting of it. And I remember this distinctly because there was a challenge match on the line. And in such a context, the term 'gong fu' would always be used instead of 'wushu.' So while wushu may be the category, 'gong fu' is something special."[9]

Another term that has become prominent recently, and is subject to considerable confusion, is "qigong" 氣功. Although a recent study found the earliest use of this term in 1934, current practitioners usually described it as an ancient discipline. Here we are faced with a fundamental problem in proving or disproving the existence of specific physical or mental practices based on written descriptions that use different terminology. This problem is further exacerbated by language that is sometimes deliberately vague and describes esoteric or even secret teachings. Modern practitioners of qigong may imagine that they recognize the root of a contemporary technique in an ancient description, but it is impossible to prove that these techniques are the same.

Wang Guangxi asserts that while the term qigong came into use at the end of the Qing dynasty (1644–1911), it had been practiced for thousands of years under the name "xingqi" 行氣 or "daoyin" 導引. He is only able to make sense of this by defining qigong on the one hand as the secret teachings of internal practices possessed by all martial arts, and on the other as meditation. It is the latter definition that allows him to connect the terms *xingqi* and *daoyin* to *qigong*, and to directly tie *qigong* to the most ancient textual and epigraphic records. Wang presents no evidence for this tie, however, or even a strict definition of what *xingqi* or *daoyin* were, beyond asserting that there were three distinct versions of this practice: Confucian, Daoist, and Buddhist.[10] It seems the only connection *qigong* has to any earlier practices is the mention of "qi" 氣, breath, life force, soul-stuff, or some other vague philosophical discussion of *qi*.

In the absence of any clear, modern definition of qigong, there is no way to connect contemporary practice to earlier practice. We are thus left without either a linguistic or a functional means to discuss qigong before the twentieth century. Nor is it certain that qigong should be included in a study of martial arts. If it is simply some kind of moving meditation or a directed practice of breathing, then physical and mental exercises of this kind were probably included in many martial arts. Yet it is also probably true that many other arts – calligraphy, for example – might have these exercises. At the same time, it would clearly be inaccurate to subsume the martial arts, whose main function is not breathing or meditation, under the category of *qigong*. Given all of these linguistic, functional, and historiographical problems, this book will not discuss qigong before the chapter on the twentieth century.

CONCLUSION

The chapters that follow trace Chinese martial arts in a conventional chronological narrative, from about 1200 BCE to the present, thus emphasizing the historically embedded and changing place of martial arts in

China. Many scholars of China, both Chinese and foreign, have accepted the myths and fictions of the martial arts without serious challenge. Others have simply assumed that these physical practices were never written about. However, a growing body of Chinese language scholarship on martial arts has opened up a field that was hitherto quite obscure. One of my goals here is to bring the fruits of this Chinese scholarship to the attention of Western scholars.

Ignorance about martial arts is profound, particularly as practiced in China. Unlike Japanese and Korean martial arts, Chinese martial arts has only recently become well known in the West. The scholarly study of these arts, with the exception of a few pioneering Chinese scholars of the early twentieth century, really began in the 1980s. We are thus confronted with a most ancient and fundamental practice that is at the same time quite new in the realm of history writing. Rather than start from the myths and try to deconstruct them, this book starts at the beginning in the hope that history itself will take care of the myths.

From the Stone Age to the End of the Spring and Autumn Period

The bow and arrow was for savagery what the iron sword was for barbarism and fire-arms for civilization – the decisive weapon.

Friedrich Engels (1820–95)[1]

WOMEN IN WARFARE

One of the first named martial artists in Chinese history is a woman known as Fu Hao. She was, of course, not the first martial artist in China; that distinction is lost to our records, but Fu Hao is the first person for whom we have a name, an account of her military exploits, and an intact tomb. Her particular importance is due to the fortunes of archaeology, though it is clear from what we know of her that she was a woman of considerable significance in her own time. Her tomb was discovered in 1976 at Anyang and was the only undisturbed royal tomb from the Shang dynasty (ca. 1600–ca. 1045 BCE) royal cemetery complex, dated to approximately 1200 BCE (Fu Hao's tomb itself has been dated to 1180–70 BCE). Lady Hao was a consort of the Shang king Wu Ding, and when she was buried, her tomb was filled with a staggering array of bronze, jade, stone, ceramic, and bone objects. These ranged from exquisitely carved knickknacks, to large bronze food vessels, to real bronze weapons. And yet despite this immense display of wealth, her tomb was actually one of the smaller ones.

By itself, Fu Hao's tomb would have been simply sensational, even if the presence of weapons, both real and ritual, in a woman's tomb might have been a problematic curiosity. But among the thousands of oracle bones recovered at Anyang, over a hundred inscriptions relate to Lady Hao, with twelve specifically concerned with her military activities.[2] On one occasion, for example, she led some 13,000 troops in an attack on the Qiang. The oracle bones themselves, usually turtle plastrons or ox scapulae, were used in divination by the Shang kings to seek guidance from divine sources on many topics, including hunting and war. First recognized as ancient writing in 1899, these bones were eventually traced back to Anyang, where the first excavations were done between 1929 and 1937. Anyang is the birthplace of Chinese archaeology, and it is important to note that the history of warfare, and thus martial arts, in China is present in the earliest extant writings.

We know that Lady Hao led troops in battle, but not whether it was unusual for a woman to do so, or even whether leadership required her to take part in hand-to-hand fighting or simply to act in a supervisory role. It is difficult to place her in a larger context of women and warfare beyond noting that, contrary to our modern assumptions, a woman did participate in battle some 3,000 years ago. From our modern perspective, we automatically question whether a woman really led troops in battle despite all the evidence that she did, and even though we would never raise such a question of a man with similar archaeological evidence. Fu Hao's prominence, problematic though it may be, does highlight a number of important themes in the history of martial arts. Specifically, Lady Hao's place as royal consort, general, warrior, and mother alerts us to the changing place of martial arts in Chinese culture and society. Over three millennia ago, the sort of woman who could become a king's consort was also capable of supervising a military expedition and even, perhaps, taking part in the fighting. Her ability to participate in warfare directly was a marker of her aristocratic status. This changed in later times, and most, but by no means all, aristocratic Chinese women would move increasingly away from the physical performance of violence. Some upper-class Chinese women continued to participate in war, as did aristocratic women from the steppes, but as time went on skill in martial arts ceased to be a marker of high status for women. In later periods, skill in certain kinds of martial arts would instead become, for women in particular, a marker of ethnicity.

Even in Lady Hao's time, of course, the majority of participants in war were men. Most of the oracle bone inscriptions related to war discuss men, and most of the real weapons found in tombs are in men's tombs. And as far as we know, the commoners who also participated in battle were exclusively men. In all likelihood then, Lady Hao was not representative of Shang women, or even Shang aristocratic women. Early Shang battles were fought on foot, with axes, spears, *ge* (or dagger-axes), and bows. Aristocrats in the Shang who fought on foot had better quality, and more complete, outfits of arms and armor, though even these high-born warriors maintained martial skills similar to those of their low-born counterparts. Unlike the commoners, the aristocrats were able to practice and maintain their skills through regular hunting. Hunting required individual skill with weapons, particularly the spear and bow, and the ability to coordinate the activities of a group of hunters. In China, as elsewhere, hunting and warfare were related activities. Weapons were practical tools of violence, and the goal of fighting, like hunting, was to kill one's target.

CHANGES IN WARFARE IN THE SHANG DYNASTY

Warfare changed over the course of the Shang dynasty, in some ways more dramatically than it had from the Stone Age to the Bronze Age. While many early Shang weapons were improved bronze versions of earlier stone weapons, the introduction of the chariot in the mid to late Shang would subsequently transform warfare. Archery also changed, as more powerful composite bows were developed by perhaps the late Shang. These developments speak to a growing differentiation in society and an increasing specialization of martial skills within different groups. Martial skills became not only socially stratified but also increasingly gendered by the time of the Zhou dynasty (ca. 1045–256 BCE). Men fought and women did not; at present we know of no Zhou dynasty counterpart to Fu Hao.

The introduction of chariots into China changed aristocrats from better-armed infantry, to mobile missile-armed warriors. Both archery and chariot driving required a lot of practice to be done well; effective archery from a moving chariot must have required years of training. Thus, both the specific tools of aristocratic warfare and the time required to use those tools effectively limited participation in battle to men of wealth and their supporting troops. From the first half of the Zhou, called the Western Zhou (ca. 1045–771 BCE), through the Spring and Autumn period (770–476 BCE), clusters of poorly armed and trained infantry supported these aristocratic chariot archers, though the infantry's role in massed chariot battles is unclear. The putative number of infantry accompanying a chariot also rose from the late Shang to the Zhou, from ten to twenty-five, the reason for this being similarly obscure. Overall army size increased, requiring more widespread martial skills. The number of chariots participating in battle grew as well, extending the aristocratic mode of warfare into the knightly class.

Specialized martial arts spread to broad segments of the population during the Spring and Autumn period. It is also in this period that we begin to have actual historical records, however laconic and uneven in reliability. With respect to military matters, most citations simply mention that state A attacked state B, or that person C led an attack on city D. All we can learn from these reports is that the constant raiding and warfare of the aristocracy was considered worth recording. Our knowledge is also enhanced by the existence of large bronze vessels, cast with self-commemorating inscriptions on them extolling the exploits of some individual. Martial accomplishments thus formed an essential part of the aristocratic identity. War was important, and given that war in this period required the personal participation of commanders in battle, martial arts prowess was also important.

The extensive recording of military feats performed by the aristocracy, along with the regular inclusion of chariots and weapons in elite tombs, makes it clear that martial arts were a fundamental part of the function and identity of the ruling class. Bronze weapons were manufactured in large numbers with consistent forms, demonstrating knowledge of a common set of martial skills. Martial arts would have been ordinary skills for Shang and Zhou aristocrats. As we turn now to the consideration of those individual weapon skills, we must keep in mind that their association with nobility would directly affect the subsequent generations' attitudes toward the martial arts. This also includes the related ritual aspect of martial dances, a critical spiritual and disciplinary part of the martial arts in China.

ARCHERY

The earliest archaeological evidence for archery in China, a flint arrowhead found at Shiyucun in Shanxi province, is some 28,000 years old.[3] Arrow shafts and bows have crumbled over the centuries, leaving only the arrowheads made of stone, bone, and later, bronze. While bows and arrows may have been most frequently used for hunting, there is also ample evidence that they were used to kill other people. Neolithic skeletons, for example, have been excavated with bone arrowheads still embedded in them. Other remains have been found with multiple arrowheads closely grouped in the torso. These groupings of arrowheads indicate that the arrows were lodged in the body when it was buried, since they were not stuck in the bones, and that the victim had been ritually killed by archery. One female victim may have had her hands tied in front of her when she was killed.[4] It was not simply a matter of killing a victim; it had to be done in a particular way to be meaningful.

Archery seems from the earliest times to have developed a particular spiritual or symbolic value quite beyond its pragmatic use as a means to kill at a distance. We cannot know from archaeology why it made sense to execute a prisoner with a volley of arrows rather than simply dispatching the person with a hand weapon. We also do not know the social status of those executed. Were they important people killed in a manner that emphasized their status, or were they ordinary people slain by archery for some ritual or otherworldly reason? Many high-status Shang tombs included the skeletons of sometimes hundreds of sacrificial victims. Ritual death by archery seems to have disappeared by the time of the Shang, however, at least around high-status tombs. Funerary sacrifice of humans continued through the Zhou dynasty and even into the Han dynasty, though not apparently by archery.[5] Archery continued to fulfill an important ritual function through highly formalized competitions for the aristocratic and knightly class. The Zhou construction of formal archery would resonate throughout the rest of imperial Chinese history as a spiritual and social act demonstrating self-cultivation. This point will be taken up more fully in the following chapter, when we turn to Confucius and several of the other great thinkers of the Warring States period.

Chinese and Central Eurasian bows were originally simple wooden staves with animal gut strings, evolving later into composite recurved bows, made of bone, sinew, and wood glued together to form short, powerful weapons. It took considerable skill to manufacture such a weapon, and one of the reasons for associating aristocrats with archery in the Zhou dynasty may well have been the expense of the bow. Economic, and thus social, status may have dictated the kind of bow, and even the kinds of arrows, one used in warfare. Higher-status people used better bows and arrows, and used them more regularly outside of warfare. Hunting became a purely elite pursuit when most commoners became farmers, though a certain amount of low-level hunting likely persisted in the general population in the less agriculturally developed areas.[6] Certainly in later times, and possibly in the Shang and Zhou as well, the government was careful to control the manufacture and possession of weapons. By the Warring States period (475–221 BCE), a military storehouse was one of the three necessary facilities of a ruler's palace.[7]

The association of archery with warfare and hunting also connected it to manliness and virility. On one occasion, when two men sought the hand of the same woman, it was agreed that the woman would decide. The first man presented himself in fine clothes and made proper ritual presents of jade and silk. The second man chose, instead, to demonstrate his prowess as a warrior by driving up in a chariot, leaping out, firing his bow in either direction, and then leaping back on his chariot and departing. This second demonstration was seen as a sign of true manliness (and won over the woman in question).[8] It was not that the first man was incapable of the same sort of martial display, but he had not thought to use such a demonstration of his battlefield skills in courting a bride – and thus he lost her.

Finally, archery's importance in hunting was critical to the social bonds of the aristocracy. Sharing meat taken in hunts was a basic medium of social, and therefore political, intercourse. Portions of animals killed by an aristocrat were distributed both up and down the social hierarchy in carefully prescribed amounts. This was also a ritual of warfare, one among a highly formalized set of practices established to reinforce aristocratic culture and identity. Hunting was primarily dependent upon archery, and so, in a sense, the aristocratic social structure was based upon the martial art of archery.

THE DAGGER-AXE (*GE*), AXE, AND SPEAR

While Stone Age Chinese made extensive use of axes for work and warfare, they also produced a weapon unique to China: the *ge* or dagger-axe. The dagger-axe was a dagger-like stone, and later bronze, head affixed to a pole at a right angle. This may have developed out of the sickle, a common agricultural tool. Unlike the axe, however, the dagger-axe was only useful as a weapon of war. In this sense, it is the first non-dual-use tool of violence in Chinese history. The dagger-axe was designed to kill other men and is as ubiquitous in Stone Age and Shang tombs as arrowheads (and thus bows). If there is an original martial art in China that was only concerned with fighting other men, it was the skill of using a dagger-axe in battle.

The dagger-axe is a curious weapon. It appeared long before cavalry or even chariots took the field in China, but certainly after simple wooden spears. This chronology tells us that it was not designed, as some might otherwise guess, to drag down a horse-rider or chariot passenger. Dagger-axes evolved in form over time without changing the essential concept of a blade fixed perpendicular to a shaft. The shaft itself could be short, for close combat like a hatchet or tomahawk, or much longer, closer in size to a spear. At least based upon current archaeology, the dagger-axe was a much more important battlefield weapon than the spear in the early Shang.

While large numbers of bronze spearheads have been excavated for the late Shang, the dominance of the dagger-axe makes it clear that the infantry battles of the early and middle Shang were fought in fairly open formation. Dagger-axes needed to be swung to be effective, and a tightly packed group of men would have rendered the weapon unusable.

ILLUSTRATION 1. Axe head, Shang Dynasty, Laufer Collection. Courtesy of the Field Museum and Ernest Caldwell. Photo by Ernest Caldwell.

A significant caveat to this characterization of early Shang formations is the discovery in an early Shang tomb in Hebei of a *ji*, a weapon that had both a spearhead and a dagger-axe. Before this find in 1973, the *ji* was believed to be a Western Zhou weapon. No such combined weapon has been found at Anyang or in any other high-ranking tombs, so the predominance of dagger-axes in the early Shang, and their continuing importance into the late Shang, still seems to hold.

Dagger-axes continued to be the most widely used close combat weapon through the Western Zhou, though *ji* were now becoming more widespread. The *ji* would push out the dagger-axe entirely in the Warring States period and become a standard infantry weapon in the Han dynasty (202 BCE–220 CE). Spears were still not used in great numbers in the Shang, Western Zhou, or Spring and Autumn period. In terms of martial arts, the conservatism in weapon design and manufacture alerts us to a similar conservatism in combat skills. Century after century, despite other kinds of weapons being available, combat in China was limited to archery and dagger-axe fighting.

The persistence and ubiquity of the dagger-axe in combat was not reflected in a concomitant symbolic importance. In the symbolic realm it was the axe that assumed supreme importance for a general or a ruler. Very few axes were used in combat, but axes were used to behead inferiors who transgressed against the authorities. Fu Hao's tomb, for example, contained two large, finely cast bronze axes, one of which had her name cast on it. These axes were too heavy for combat at 8.5 kg each, and rather were used as symbols of military command. When a general was sent on a campaign in the Spring and Autumn period the ruler charged him with his duties and gave him either a bow or an axe.[9]

Lady Hao's burial with a pair of axes is explained by a much later, Warring States period text, the *Liutao*:

The ruler personally took the ax by its head and presented the handle to the commander, and then said, "From here upward to Heaven you shall regulate it." He took a second ax and presented the handle to the commander and said, "From here downward to the [Yellow] Springs [realm of the dead] you shall regulate it."

Having thus received the symbols of authority from the ruler, the commander made a request:

I desire that you grant one more charge to me, and if you do not agree then I will not dare to command. I will obey your commands but all orders will come from me. When I meet the enemy and decide to fight, I will have an undivided mind. In this way then I will have no Heaven above, no Earth below, no enemy in front, and no prince behind.[10]

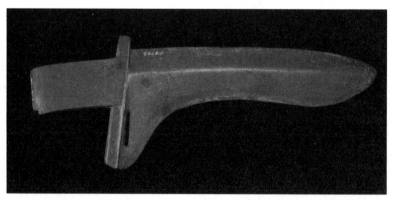

ILLUSTRATION 2. *Ge* halberd head, late Western Zhou to mid–Warrring States period, Laufer Collection. Courtesy of the Field Museum and Ernest Caldwell. Photo by Ernest Caldwell.

We cannot know whether such a ceremony with these particular concerns took place before Lady Hao went out on her campaigns, but the presence of the dual axes in her tomb is suggestive of a similar bestowal of authority from a ruler to a field commander. A ruler had the power to execute an inferior as punishment for a failing. He transferred this power to a commander who acted for him in leading troops in combat. Executing someone with an axe was quite different from killing the person in combat with a dagger-axe. The twin axes in Fu Hao's tomb argue for a ceremonial differentiation of politically endorsed violence, as opposed to an unregulated clash of arms unsanctioned by the state.

A commander's authority to regulate the army under her or his control, as distinct from the ruler's authority over his subjects under ordinary circumstances, describes a separate martial realm of different rules and values. Lady Hao's axes indicate that Shang dynasty aristocrats were keenly aware of this separate arena and that her importance and role in that realm could be indicated and instantiated by burying her with the tools of command. The weapons in her tomb, the dagger-axes, arrowheads (and presumably bows along with them), knives, and the like argue that she was a warrior. She knew how to fight because she was an aristocrat. The pair of axes showed that she was also a general.

Dagger-axes and axes thus represent different aspects of the martial world when used as funerary goods. A man's status as a warrior and member of the aristocracy was marked by burial with a bronze dagger-axe. A commander's status was indicated by the inclusion of a pair of noncombat axes. At the same time, combat axes and symbolic jade dagger-axes were placed in tombs. Fu Hao's tomb contained a jade and bronze spearhead, even though spears do not appear to have been very important weapons symbolically or in combat at that time.[11] Her tomb also included forty jade dagger-axes, one of which was inscribed: "The Lufang submit five dagger-axes as tribute."[12] The Lufang were a tributary state of the Shang and sent jade dagger-axes to maintain their relations with the Shang court.

A practical weapon was rendered symbolic when it was made out of a precious material like jade, or made too large or heavy to be wielded effectively in battle. These physical goods achieved their symbolic goal by divorcing themselves from the possibility of combat. By standing outside the realm of martial arts, they took on another meaning despite being rendered in the form of weapons. There were many other funerary goods, particularly in the highest-status tombs like Fu Hao's, which also indicated the wealth and importance of the occupant. Yet, in addition to the enormous bronze vessels and jade knickknacks, aristocratic male tombs and even a female one

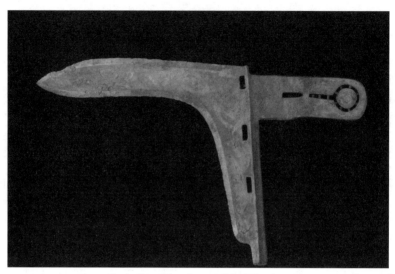

ILLUSTRATION 3. *Ge* halberd head, possibly Warring States period, Laufer Collection. Courtesy of the Field Museum and Ernest Caldwell. Photo by Ernest Caldwell.

included weapons. The dagger-axes in tombs, both combat and symbolic, are markers of the close association between Shang, Western Zhou, and Spring and Autumn period aristocrats and warfare. These men and women were steeped in combat and identified themselves with fighting and martial arts through the regular burial of particular weapons with their dead. This extended even to circulating symbolic weapons made of precious materials as a means of exchange within the aristocratic class.

CHARIOTS

Chariots were mainly markers of royal status rather than instruments of war during the Shang dynasty. Edward L. Shaughnessy has argued that the chariot arrived in China in a mature form about 1200 BCE from Central Eurasia.[13] Over time, it changed from a prestige item that functioned as a command platform (in the Shang) to a central vehicle of battle (in the Western Zhou) and then declined until it became a clumsy anachronism. Shang oracle bones record far more instances of enemies using chariots against the Shang than Shang forces using chariots themselves. The Shang adoption of chariots was therefore an adaptation of a foreign technology, whether as a necessary response to defend against chariots or simply to take advantage of a new device. A similar process of adopting a foreign military practice would occur with the advent of cavalry at the end of the Spring and Autumn period.[14]

Chariots were expensive machines to build and maintain, and they were challenging to operate. Over time, the expense and difficulty of manufacturing and driving a chariot became not only an accepted part of aristocratic life but also a symbol of high status. Chariot driving became a martial art, a necessary skill for aristocratic participation in warfare. The way one participated in battle was a status marker. Aristocratic men in the Western Zhou and Spring and Autumn period fought from chariots with bows in the same manner that they hunted for game, and low-born men fought on foot. Even within the three-man team who rode a chariot into battle, one's rank relative to the rest of the team determined one's role. The lowest-ranked man drove the chariot, the next higher-ranked man wielded a dagger-axe or spear, and the highest-ranked man employed a bow. Most aristocratic men would have been trained in all these skills – chariot-driving, wielding the dagger-axe, and shooting with a bow.

Chariot-to-chariot warfare among the aristocrats not only framed the social status of the important participants in battle but also dictated where, when, and under what conditions that battle could take place. Just as the Ancient Greeks had to agree upon a battlefield for their infantry battles, so too did ancient Chinese chariot-riding aristocrats have to find a proper space for their chariot battles. Battles required flat, open spaces; took place during daylight hours (presumably starting early enough in the day to complete the fight); and needed dry weather. A large-scale battle could not take place on a muddy field where all the chariots would bog down, though we hear of several instances of individual chariots getting stuck in the mud. Fighting was a highly constrained and formalized event, not outwardly dissimilar to a modern sporting event. The goal of an aristocrat was to fight and defeat another aristocrat.

This is not to say that warfare was not a deadly business. The participants were actively trying to kill each other, and in the Shang dynasty, at least, captured enemies could be sacrificed to one's ancestors. Thus, dating just after two brief divinations mentioning chariots in warfare by Shang enemies, we have a long inscription on a bovine scapula recording a Shang victory from around 1100 BCE:

Minor Vassal Qiang allied and attacked, capturing Rou of Wei ... 24 men, 1,570 (men) of Er, the Earl of Fan ... horses, two chariots, 183 shields, fifty quivers, and ... arrows. We (used =) sacrificed Earl Du of You to Da Yi, (used =) sacrificed Earl Mao of Shen to ... Fan to Ancestor Yi, and (used =) sacrificed Rou to Ancestor Ding.[15]

Here too it is the enemy that uses chariots in war, and not the Shang. Warfare was extremely lethal, and while we have no idea of the number of casualties inflicted during the actual fighting or the fates of the captured ordinary soldiers, the aristocratic enemies were clearly killed in a ceremonial fashion for the benefit of the Shang ancestors. Moreover, many wounds that were not immediately lethal during battle would have resulted in a subsequent death given the poor state of medicine at that time. Despite any superficial resemblances, warfare was not a sport.

Chariots were widely used by the Western Zhou, and the Zhou king bestowed elaborate chariot accoutrements on favored individuals. Yet these were also practical weapons of war and were subject to the pragmatic need to succeed. Thus chariots were not used against the Huai Yi in the many battles the Zhou fought against them because the terrain involved was marshy. This continued into the Spring and Autumn period, where the succeeding states located in the same region, Wu and Yue, faced the same constraints. Chariots were a weapon of the Central Plains of China, making them part of the Northern Chinese tradition of martial arts.

Massed chariot battles, supported by infantry, became a feature of warfare in the second half of the ninth century BCE. A number of inscriptions on bronze vessels record victories in battle in northern China resulting in the capture of dozens, and sometimes over a hundred, chariots. These larger tallies of chariots were acquired fighting the Zhou's northern competitors, showing once again that the direction of military technology and martial techniques flowed from Central Eurasia into northern China. At the same time, Zhou successes demonstrate that Chinese aristocrats had developed considerable skill in chariot warfare themselves.

The northern tribes drove the Zhou out of the Wei River valley in 771, forcing the Zhou rulers to reestablish their main capital to the east at modern-day Luoyang. During the Spring and Autumn period, which was the first part of the Eastern Zhou (770–256 BCE), the individual states or fiefs that comprised the Zhou measured their military strength in the number of chariots they could field. Battles between these states involved hundreds of chariots. The state of Jin, for example, brought some 700 chariots to the Battle of Chengpu in 632 BCE. While the states were measuring their strength by the number of chariots they could field, they also began to employ forces of infantry armed with crossbows or spears. Large infantry armies primarily composed of commoners would eventually be the backbone of Chinese armies, though that was centuries in the future. Chariot warfare remained dominant in the Central Plains of China until the advent of cavalry toward the end of the Spring and Autumn period. In other words, a change in battlefield technology would result in a later shift in martial arts practice. This change in martial arts practice would, in turn, have important social effects.

New technology in the form of chariots, and possibly composite bows, may have been responsible for the defeat of the Shang dynasty at Muye in 1046. Shaughnessy suggests, in contrast to previous scholars, that the Zhou forces defeated the Shang army not because of superior virtue, or revolutionary social development, but because they had a large chariot force and the Shang did not. He is careful to note that "nowhere in the historical record is there any mention that the Shang army facing them used chariots to any extent."[16] This carefully worded explanation, accompanied by mention of improved Zhou dagger-axes, better stabbing swords, and perhaps composite bows, presents a fundamentally martial arts–based argument for the Zhou overthrow of the Shang.

The Zhou military did not have a massive technological advantage in the sense of possessing weapons beyond the understanding of the Shang. What the Zhou did have was a different understanding of fighting. It would not have been enough to have simply manufactured large numbers of chariots, new dagger-axes, and possibly swords and composite bows and to have distributed them to the Zhou army. Changes in both the numbers and types of weapons used in battle require a wholesale shift in training. Even if Shaughnessy is only partially correct, we still have a major political and cultural shift directly connected to a change in martial arts practice. A large-scale deployment of chariots required more men trained in their use than the upper aristocracy alone could supply. New weapons similarly would have created the need for a systematic recruitment and training of men to use them. Although we do not know who these men were, whether they were retrained Zhou soldiers or newly recruited from Zhou subjects or allies, the new centrality of chariot warfare would mark the society, culture, and martial arts of the next few centuries.

MARTIAL DANCES

Up until this point I have concentrated on the modes of warfare, and martial skills that can be reconstructed based upon archaeology. There is an additional area concerning martial arts that is intimately related to warfare, spirituality, and social hierarchy: the martial dance. Martial dances are hard to distinguish from drilling in martial arts since they are formalized movements that replicate movements used in combat, invoke otherworldly attention and assistance for combat, or attempt to induce a particular mental state useful in combat. Dance as a whole is a challenging subject for historical study because, unlike weapon skills, it leaves almost nothing in the way of artifacts to prove its existence. The earliest textual descriptions of dance are from the Warring States period, though several of these sources claim that they have reproduced or transmitted documents from earlier times. Dance itself impinged upon two other extremely important interrelated areas, music and rites, which were of particular interest to the followers of Confucius.

The ceremonial importance of dance as a whole distinguished it from other semi-martial activities like football and hunting. It nevertheless was similar to these other group pursuits in requiring individual and unit coordination of movements and in being heavily constrained by formal rules and social functions in addition to its martial value. Of equal importance to the history of martial arts, dances, martial or otherwise, were public displays. The performative aspect of Chinese martial arts is thus tied very directly to martial dances and is a very early characteristic of martial arts in China. This is distinct from martial contests in which participants directly fought each other with a variety of martial skills. Martial dances were the earliest displays of martial skills that did not serve a competitive purpose, but rather an aesthetic and spiritual one. This aesthetic and spiritual function involved both the performer or performers and the audience.

A Han dynasty dictionary would directly connect martiality, *wu* (武), with dance, *wu* (舞): "Martiality means 'to dance'; the movements of an assault are like the drumming out of a dance."[17] This definition postdates the period currently under discussion, but it shows how a possibly specious definition could arise from a homophonous relationship between words and the more reasonable connection between music and dance, and music and war. A later account of the Battle of Muye asserts that the Zhou army performed a war dance the night before combat that terrified the Shang forces. The dance itself was recapitulated at the Zhou court, along with a formalized recreation of the victory itself. This was part of the musical tradition of the Zhou.[18] Given the central position of the Battle of Muye in the founding of the Zhou dynasty, it is not surprising that the Zhou court would regularly revisit the event in performance.

Music and dance were extensively used in military preparations because drums and gongs were one of the only effective ways to communicate with large numbers of men during a battle. Men wearing helmets and engaged in fighting would be unlikely to hear verbal commands, no matter how loudly projected, from any distance. The sound of drums carried much farther and served to directly connect the commander to his men. As army size grew it became increasingly difficult to coordinate bodies of men moving even fifty or a hundred yards away from the overall commander, let alone a much greater distance. Music also aroused the emotions, something Confucius noted, and prepared men to fight. Dance was an outward demonstration of the coordination of the emotional states of a large group of men by music, as well as a practical process for teaching them to act as a unit. This last effect of music and dance is particularly important to questions of individual versus group behavior.

We see in some early poetry the subjection of the army to the general through the medium of musical instruments:

Fang Shu came to take the command. His chariots were three thousand, with a host of well-disciplined warriors, Fang Shu led them on. With his jinglers and drummers, He marshaled his hosts and addressed them. Intelligent and true is Fang Shu, Deep rolled the sound of his drums; with a lighter sound he led the troops back.[19]

The general is empowered through the use of music to order the troops. They respond directly to his signals, a sure sign not only of his qualities as a leader but also of their discipline. Even through the exaggerated medium of poetry we can see that army organization and control are products of music and drill.

The earliest physical evidence of any sort of dance is a drawing on a Neolithic pot depicting several figures with linked arms. Whether this is in fact a dance, we do have mentions of dance on Shang oracle bones. Why these dances are performed is unclear, particularly whether they had any relationship to martial arts. The Shang military mostly fought on foot, as we have already discussed, very likely in an open formation that allowed them to use their dagger-axes to best effect. During the succeeding Zhou dynasty larger numbers of chariots and infantry fought coordinated battles. Most infantry still used the dagger-axe, but increasing numbers used *ji*, which may have allowed for more compact formations that relied upon the spear point rather than the hacking point. Disciplined units of spearmen would have been able to fend off chariot charges. Thus, Zhou emphasis on martial dances may have been due to greater emphasis on training and unit coordination. This is speculative, of course, but worth considering as we try to connect changes in technology, martial arts, and society.

Zhou dynasty martial dancers are reported to have held bows, arrows, spears, axes, and dagger-axes when performing. On the one hand, this affirms the connection between these dances and the actual skills of the battlefield. All the performance weapons were the sorts of weapons in actual use. On the other hand, however, the inclusion of bows and arrows argues that many of the dances were abstractions that represented battlefield weapon use rather than performances demonstrating weapon skills. Any Zhou court performance would have provided an audience of aristocratic martial artists trained in precisely the weapons on display. The martial dance to them must have been an invocation of martial spirit as well as a tribute to previous victories. Martial dances commemorated past battles as a physical reminder of history for a largely illiterate audience and emphasized their connection to their ancestors.

Martial dances served a historical as well as a cultural function. Through music and dance, a past event was connected to a particular set of emotions and imprinted on succeeding generations who then shared a common understanding of history. The performance of these dances in the Zhou court or before a battle legitimized the authority of the audience by affirming their connection to successful ancestors, or by tying the group together through the shared emotional bonds of a common experience. Political legitimacy was derived from seeing the dance performed in exactly the way it had been performed before by all previous courts. This was true for other dances and ceremonies as well. Exact repetition was a sign of orthodoxy, and variation a sign of heterodoxy. We see similar concerns today over the correct transmission of a martial arts form from a founding teacher to the schools of his students. Martial dances in the Zhou were a physical, unwritten system for demonstrating political, social, and cultural identity.

Although I have discussed the military and social facets of martial dances, I have thus far only alluded to the spiritual aspects of dance and music. Dance and music were performed in court in honor of past rulers. It is debatable whether these dances contained a spiritual or religious component. They clearly involved emotions, rather than simply the intellect, but defining them as "spiritual" or "religious" depends upon one's definition of those terms. If by "spiritual" we mean connecting to some emotional, nonintellectual human need, or connected to the otherworldly spirits of the ancestors that Shang and Zhou aristocrats believed were present in their world, then these dances were indeed spiritual. To the extent that the dances were for the benefit of those spirits, then they were also "religious" under some definitions. More to the point, Chinese martial arts from the earliest times fulfilled a role beyond training for violence. This role existed before any of the Warring States schools of thought were formulated, and far in advance of the arrival of Buddhism in China (indeed, long before even the inception of Buddhism in India).

The performance aspect of martial arts has always been present in China, and it is important to understand that this went beyond simple contests of skill. Explicitly military demonstrations complete with weapons and music were critical ceremonial events in the Zhou court. Martial dances instantiated political legitimacy by reminding the audience and participants of the battlefield victories that had created the dynasty. Martial dances were also connected to military drill and the coordination of large units of soldiers. When large numbers of men were trained together in weapon skills as part of their military training, they became part of a regular martial dance that allowed their individual martial arts skills to be inspected. The repetition of these skills in a particular pattern, a formal, ceremonial dance, also reiterated a particular teaching or political lineage. In China, martial arts cannot be separated from the formal performance of those skills as an intentional display outside of combat.

VIOLENCE AND SOCIETY

Before this chapter is concluded, some mention should be made of the place of violence in the political and social order of Western Zhou and Spring and Autumn period China. This discussion can help to explain the changes that took place during the Warring States period covered in the next chapter. Martial arts are not a politically or socially neutral set of skills. Unlike certain purely technical skills – like making pottery, for example – the performance of violence has profound implications for societal organization and political authority. Licit and illicit violence are culturally defined through a number of institutions, both formal and informal. As I have discussed above, martial skills and the performance of violence defined certain classes in Chinese society. Mark Edward Lewis's classic study, *Sanctioned Violence in Early China*, describes the evolution of a number of linked violent practices connected to changes in political authority and social organization.

The context of violence is fundamental to understanding its significance. During the Western Zhou and the Spring and Autumn period, aristocrats defined themselves by the performance of particular kinds of violence. Hunting, warfare, and violent inter-clan feuding were not just struggles for power but were assertions of identity. An aristocrat was someone who regularly used violence in defense of honor, or to prove his martial skills, or for any number of other reasons. The identity of the entire group of aristocrats was based upon the individual use of violence, and thus, martial arts. The political value of a given violent event was usually less important to the majority of participants than their own inclusion and performance during the event. In short, an aristocrat was expected to be a violent person.

Our modern standards of violence are very different from those of three thousand years ago. There were no police forces available to maintain order, and "justice" was not an absolute concept whereby all people shared certain theoretical rights unmitigated by power and privilege. Indeed, power and privilege defined a person's place in society and framed the meaning of any interpersonal act. Violence among aristocrats was part of the system of manners of their intricate social network. Fighting another aristocrat in the open field from a chariot in the prescribed fashion was a noble and praiseworthy act. Stabbing another aristocrat from behind in an ambush with a knife might not be. We know nothing of the relationship between violence and commoner society. This effective separation between the aristocrats and commoners was possible when a relatively high percentage of battlefield participants were aristocrats, and when their weapons and skills gave them a distinct advantage over the commoners.

As army size grew during the Western Zhou and into the Spring and Autumn period, more commoners took part in war, and their martial skills improved. At the same time, the political ramifications of continual inter-aristocrat violence became unsustainable. An increasing cycle of violence was spreading martial arts and weapons to a greater part of society and changing the significance of violence within culture. Unrestrained martial arts performed as part of aristocratic identity was becoming a threat to social order. The Spring and Autumn period would be the last time in Chinese history that the political authorities accepted the idea that the private use of violence did not concern them.

CONCLUSION

This chapter has laid the groundwork for succeeding chapters in several ways. First, I used the example of Lady Hao to highlight the importance of martial skills in aristocratic identity and also to show that women could and did fight and lead troops in battle from the earliest times. Martially capable women arose with some regularity throughout Chinese history, though the ethnicity and class of women who did so changed over time. Martial arts in China, though always gendered and strongly biased toward men, has also always maintained a place for women. Second, I placed archery at the forefront of martial arts skills. Archery would retain this preeminent position in martial arts long after firearms became important on the battlefield. For the Zhou aristocrat, it was not just archery, but archery from a chariot that set him apart from the commoners on the battlefield. Third, I emphasized the significance of martial dances. Martial dances were not just physical training but also emotional, mental, and spiritual training as well. They served to legitimize certain groups by creating lineages of practice, or physical histories, through the regular repetition of orthodox martial arts patterns. All of these three aspects of martial arts were present from the earliest times and have persisted in one form or another until today.

Another characteristic of martial arts, even at this early stage, is conservatism in skills. This conservatism is not surprising. The archaeological and historical record argues extremely consistently that martial arts are a conservative practice. Dagger-axes were ubiquitous from the Stone Age until the Warring States period. Chariots came into use for practical reasons and then continued in use some time after they had been rendered obsolete. Even as they faded from martial practice, chariots continued to be used in literary expressions throughout imperial Chinese history (an unsurprising linguistic or cultural conservatism). This conservatism is not particularly characteristic of Chinese martial practice; it is inherent in all martial arts, on and off the battlefield. Martial arts is a taught practice, and when the legitimacy of a skill is based upon its proven, rather than proposed, efficacy, the past is the best guide to what works. At the same time, any new weapon had to become widespread enough, and someone had to figure out how to exploit its qualities in battle, before it could challenge the established matrix of weapons and martial arts.

Martial arts did change from this early practice, while retaining the general characteristics outlined earlier. The dagger-axe and the chariot disappeared, the sword and spear came into use, and cavalry took the field. Even as the weaponry and skills changed, however, their meaning within Chinese culture still retained a memory of their past. As we will see in the next chapter, the association of chariot driving and archery with the upper class would create a long-lasting connection between these particular skills and noble character. The teachings of such foundational thinkers as Confucius, who was of the knightly class and looked back to earlier times as a golden age, would permanently legitimize archery as an ennobling practice. These thinkers would place an enduring stamp on the Chinese understanding of martial arts as they used examples of martial skills to explain moral concepts to other members of the knightly class, while at the same time arguing that moral development was more impressive and important than martial skills.

2

The Warring States Period

A villager from Daxiang remarked sarcastically, "How great is Confucius! He is so broadly learned, and yet has failed to make a name for himself in any particular endeavor."

When the Master was told of this, he said to his disciples, "What art, then, should I take up? Charioteering? Archery? I think I shall take up charioteering."

The Analects[1]

Spring and Autumn period aristocrats were organized into kinship lineages focused on ancestral temples. Warfare was part of the service to these temples, a way in which an individual could win glory for himself and his lineage. Indeed, the jealous and violent defense of one's honor, and that of one's lineage, was a cultural tie that bound the aristocracy together and separated them from the commoners. Lineages existed apart from the putative political authorities, and all aristocrats shared a similar status, making the organization of power within the aristocracy flatter culturally than would be found in the more hierarchical political structure. As the Spring and Autumn period wore on, however, the incessant warfare, feuds, and vendettas among the aristocracy began to destroy it. The old political order crumbled to be replaced by a new, more hierarchical system in the Warring States period.[2]

The new political order that emerged in the Warring States period developed gradually. Not only was the aristocracy destroying itself but the changes in warfare (and martial arts), new political ideas, and a host of other technological changes began to appear and would affect many aspects of society over several centuries. The culmination would come in 221 BCE with the triumph of the Qin dynasty and the creation of the imperial Chinese political order, discussed in the following chapter. Chinese culture, particularly in the area of thought or philosophy, flourished during the Warring States period, providing the intellectual foundation for the rest of Chinese history. Confucius, Mencius, Laozi, Zhuangzi, Sunzi, Xunzi, to list only a handful of thinkers, struggled to make sense of the constant, large-scale warfare and perceived moral decay of their time, and to propose some means either to improve on the situation or to accommodate oneself to it and remain moral.[3] A key problem in Warring States Chinese society was the function, scope, and frequency of violence.

Martial prowess had served to distinguish the Spring and Autumn aristocrats, but as the violence that their culture demanded became widespread and frequent, aristocratic society had functionally destroyed itself. Obviously, the scope and frequency of violence had to be diminished, but in the process the function of warfare and violence also changed. Technological changes in weaponry, including changes in individual martial skills and unit tactics, prevented any reconstitution of the aristocratic class, and permanently altered the relationship of commoner society to the martial arts. At the same time, the ideal of what a "noble man" 君子 was continued to hark back to an earlier, mythical ideal of a moral, cultivated warrior.[4]

Warring States thinkers were, with the possible exception of Mozi, members of the knightly class, and some, like Hanfeizi, were of even more elevated background. These men were therefore well acquainted with the martial arts because of their stations in life, and directed much if not all of their efforts at communicating their ideas to rulers of states and other members of their own class. Martial metaphors permeated many of these thinkers' works. What emerged was not just martial arts–inflected rhetoric but also a clear awareness of the possibilities of martial arts for self-cultivation. Martial arts required a clear and focused mind, something valuable beyond the realm of actual fighting. Yet this use of martial metaphors was also tempered by the need to discredit violence as an appropriate instrument of rule, and, connected to this, the argument that moral cultivation was harder to achieve and more valuable than martial arts mastery.

The martial arts backgrounds of the great Warring States thinkers are often ignored when considering their works, with the exception of Mozi. Mozi, it has been suggested, may have been of the merchant or artisan class, but he created and led a highly disciplined, militarized school. Part of Mozi's solution to the problem of interstate warfare was the philosophically intriguing, but strategically bankrupt, idea of everyone only fighting defensively. His school backed up his ideas by offering its services and disciples as defensive experts to states under attack. While the primary skill they offered was in defensive siege craft, their martial capabilities likely included close combat as well. The Moist disciples were also highly militarized in their obedience to command hierarchy and willingness to die in the pursuit of their ideals.

With the collapse of lineage ties for warriors and expansion in the number of people involved in fighting, questions of loyalty became prominent. It was no longer clear to whom one owed one's loyalty, under what circumstances it should be pledged, or under what circumstances revoked. This was particularly problematic for the knightly class who had hitherto stood on the lowest rung of aristocratic society. Chariot warfare had drawn more members of the elite, including the knights, into warfare during the Spring and Autumn period, diluting to some extent the distinction of fighting from a chariot. Of even greater significance, however, was the shift toward specialization in skills among the elite. Exactly when and why this began is unclear, but by the Warring States period, more professional generals and administrators were working for the various states in roles formerly filled by favored nobles or family members of the court. In general, these specialized professionals came from the knightly class.

Skills became more important, or were more salable, in the Warring States period. Confucius' remark that "The gentleman is not a vessel,"[5] or what we would currently understand as "an instrument," was a rejection of the notion that a man should be employed for his specific skills alone and not for his moral qualities. But of course his rejection of this practice arose because that was precisely what was happening. Confucius argued that rulers should hire moral men who had cultivated themselves through study. These good men would be better able to run a government and assist a ruler than men whose only qualification was skill in a particular job. A good ruler would employ good men, and the positive effects of this configuration of leadership would spread throughout society to its great benefit.

Most rulers of individual states seemed more concerned with pragmatic survival or expansion in a very competitive environment and less with moral development. That effectively meant developing a strong military and a strong domestic economy. In this environment, men with martial skills could find a place at a lord's court as a retainer. Rulers as a whole also took pains to take control of the legitimate use of force. The political authorities no longer accepted violence as a marker of class; violence now had to serve the political purposes of a state. An aristocrat was not supposed simply to start a fight to prove that he was a legitimate aristocrat. He should fight when he was told to do so by his ruler. This notion progressed even further as army discipline and coordination increased. Every warrior now had to fight only when his duly assigned commander ordered him to, and not before, and to subordinate himself to the army's military and political goals. War and martial arts fully became an instrument of the state. To act otherwise was to become an outlaw and to be punished.

Just as thinkers and other sellers of skills roamed about trying to find a place at a ruler's court to practice their trade, some individuals rejected or functioned very much outside the new bounds of authority. We see for the first time a new sort of man, a righteous hero who is neither bound by political authority nor by fear of death. This "knight-errant" acted violently and without restraint, using his martial skills to avenge wrongs or insults. In another form, he was also an assassin, that ultimate outsider to carefully constructed political authority. Where in the past such violent behavior had been simply a part of aristocratic culture, in the Warring States period it was the action of an outlaw.

Knights-errant and assassins were valorized in history and fiction in response to the subordination of individuals to the state. For the rest of Chinese history, in fiction if not in fact, righteous heroes always found themselves at odds with the state. Although Confucius argued for the supreme value of the moral man over the warrior or functionary, he was himself of the knightly class and trained in its skills. He did not, therefore, reject the martial arts, or even denigrate them, so much as he wanted to put them in their proper place. Confucius respected, for example, the traditional archery contest and all the values that went with it. Archery would repeatedly come up in the works of other thinkers, demonstrating its central conceptual place as the ultimate martial skill and marker of martial arts. This would remain true despite the emergence of new weapons, like the sword, the advance of the *ji* (halberd), and our first mentions of unarmed combat.

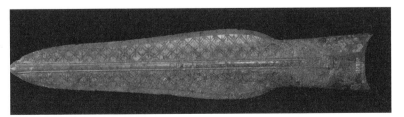

ILLUSTRATION 4. Mao spear head, Warring States period, Laufer Collection. Courtesy of the Field Museum and Ernest Caldwell. Photo by Ernest Caldwell.

The place of the martial arts changed in the Warring States period from a skill exclusively of the elite to an instrument of the state. Try as the many states, large and small, might, however, they could not fully subordinate martial skills to their will. The martial arts were a threat to state authority unless they were part of that structure. Like other skills, martial arts could be bought and sold by anyone. Having escaped the bonds of culture and class, martial arts were now broadly available, and beyond control. There would thus always be a certain tension between the government and the martial artist because martial artists possessed a skill that could threaten the state's authority but could not be entirely controlled by the state.

Straight, double-edged bronze swords 劍 (*jian*) were developed during the Western Zhou, but were initially quite short; they probably functioned as weapons of desperation rather than for offensive fighting, much like the curved, single-edged bronze knives 刀 (*dao*) found earlier. It is nevertheless important that these stabbing weapons emerged in the same period, though over centuries, as halberds, with their stabbing spear head. Slowly and subtly, it seems, warriors were learning to become point fighters, rather than edge or dagger-axe fighters. This new orientation in weapons design must have reflected new martial arts. The short, eleven- to eighteen-inch-long blades, of the Eastern Zhou period lengthened to about twenty-two inches by the late Spring and Autumn period. These longer swords developed in the southern Chinese states, particularly in Wu and Yue, probably because fighting in the south was more infantry based.[6]

The level of workmanship on Chinese bronze swords from this period could be stunning. One of the most famous swords was made for Jiu Qian, the king of Yue, also known as Goujian. Not only was it finely decorated, with designs on the blade, inlaid blue glass on the hilt, and an inlaid gold inscription but it was also treated with sulfide to prevent corrosion. Other fine blades of a similar nature have also been found, though these weapons are the finest of their kind. Most warriors would have fought with much plainer swords. These were personal weapons for close combat and of little use from a chariot.

At least for some warriors, swords replaced short-hafted dagger-axes for close combat by the late Spring and Autumn period. Swords are far more flexible in combat, allowing for a much greater range of attacks and defenses. Their use increased across the Warring States period, as production responded to demand for the new weapon. The other great advantage for swords, apart from their ability to stab, was their portability. A sheathed sword could be hung from a warrior's belt or girdle, allowing him to keep a very effective weapon always at hand (an important point which will be illustrated in the story of the assassination attempt on Qin Shihuangdi in the next chapter). Swords could also be used inside or in confined quarters, where dagger-axes could not. Before the sword, one could only carry a dagger for personal protection. But the sword was a real battlefield weapon that could be carried everywhere.

Steel swords also appeared toward the end of the Spring and Autumn period. Steel, an alloy of iron and carbon, was produced in China by the sixth century BCE (steel is harder than wrought iron and less brittle than cast iron). It was not until the middle and late Warring States period, however, that iron and steel implements, including armor and weapons, were produced in useful amounts. Bronze weapons still predominated, vastly outnumbering the iron weapons found in tombs, but the advantages of iron were apparent. Iron swords were longer than bronze swords, averaging 80–100 cm, with the shortest equal in length to the longest bronze swords.[7] Iron weapons are lighter and stronger than bronze weapons, though more subject to corrosion.

The spread of iron furthered the development of the sword and probably changed the way it was used as well. Weapons were manufactured from a wide variety of materials in the Warring States period, with tombs yielding arrowheads of bronze, iron, and bone mixed together, and swords of bronze and iron, but the use of iron was critical for the sword. Unlike spears, dagger-axes, or bows, the reach of a sword depended upon the material it was made of. Iron and steel made swords more effective, allowing them to be constructed to the specifications that experience proved most advantageous or preference chose as the best balance between length and weight. Iron and steel allowed swords to be made to the specifications of the martial artist.

A final aspect of the development of the sword from bronze to iron is the distinct regionalism of initial production. Like the chariot, which spread from the steppe, to China's Central Plains, and then on to the south, swords began as regionally idiosyncratic weapons. Wu and Yue in the south were renowned for their bronze swords, and this has largely been borne out by archaeology. High-quality iron swords were initially thought to come from the states of Chu, Han, and Yan. Lower-quality swords were available in other places, but the highest-quality arms were made in very particular places. Swordsmanship presumably followed the same course as swords, with the art developing alongside the weapon, and then spreading as it was adopted across China. At this early stage we hear of places famed for their swords, but no famous swordsmen. Most famous martial artists in the Warring States period were archers.

ARCHERY AND ARCHERY CONTESTS

Archery remained a central preoccupation of Chinese elites in the Warring States period. Not only was it a practical skill for hunting and war but it also carried ceremonial and spiritual power. As a consequence of this, many thinkers used archery analogies to explain their larger points about morality. The audience for these thinkers was other members of the elite who were intimately familiar with archery. Archery became the first martial art directly connected to mental cultivation, that is, to a distinct mental focus transcending ordinary concerns. The archer as martial artist projected the practice of a means of violence into a number of realms that we would recognize today. Archery was a practical skill of war, it was a performance skill, it demonstrated proper attitude and deportment, and at its highest level it developed an improved mental state. It would even figure in many early legends, written down during the Warring States period, and seemingly possessed magical qualities.[8]

The practical skill of archery used to kill men or animals is widely attested in texts from the Warring States period. Aristocrats shot from chariots just as they had during the entire Zhou dynasty, using thumb rings for a Mongolian release. Most tomb finds that include quivers have no more than two or three dozen arrows accompanying the chariot. If this is even somewhat representative of the amount of firepower the average chariot archer possessed in the field, then he could hardly sustain combat for very long. Given the limited stamina of the chariot horses, this was probably just as well. This does make it clear, however, that the aristocratic chariot archers were not firing enormous coordinated volleys of arrows. Most of the aristocratic archery would have been directed at other aristocrats – that is to say, carefully aimed shots more in the form of a personal duel.

Chariots diminished in effectiveness across the Warring States period even before true cavalry appeared. Although the trend is clear, it is difficult to parse the various factors and designate the primary reason for the shift. From the perspective of archery, chariot archery would have had little effect against disciplined, massed, armored infantry with shields. Infantry archers, when available, would have had more firepower than a chariot archer or even a group of chariot archers. Added to this was a new archery weapon, the crossbow, which appeared in the late Spring and Autumn period.[9] The crossbow was slower than the bow but easier for less trained troops to use, and it had greater penetrating power. But infantry archers did not require the addition of the crossbow to outshoot the chariot archers. In the Mediterranean world, the Mycenean chariot-riding aristocrats were defeated by the massed infantry of the "Sea Peoples," though the exact course of that defeat is unknown.

Disciplined, massed infantry could have rendered the chariot ineffective regardless of changes in archery. The crossbow was not a revolutionary weapon; it may well have been that the growing size and improved command and control of the infantry finally allowed the mass of commoner soldiers to defeat the aristocrats. This changing military environment was profoundly disturbing to the political and social order. The aristocratic archer was no longer the master of the battlefield. His martial mastery disappeared, or was rendered moot, by new forms of combat. The great flourishing of thought in the Warring States period was partly caused by the tumultuous changes in almost every area of life. And while the crossbow trigger mechanism would become its own metaphor for timing and holding force in abeyance for a devastating strike, the elites turned to the memory of archery as an aristocratic pursuit for reassurance.

The aristocrats of the Zhou dynasty practiced extremely formal archery ceremonies. From the descriptions in the *Record of Ritual*, the major test for the participants was their deportment, not their accuracy. Interestingly, like other major rituals, music played an important part, in some sense connecting this ceremony to martial dances. The participants were paired according to seniority and ability. Although charioteering and wrestling contests were also regular parts of the Zhou performance events, archery was used to rank the participants for court posts. The goal in this formal setting was not military effectiveness. As Confucius described it:

The Master said, "It is said, 'In archery, one does not emphasize piercing the hide of the target, because people's strengths differ.' Such is the ancient Way."[10]

Here Confucius is detaching the function of archery in battle or hunting from its performance as simply a performance. This passage was later explained by Zhu Xi (1130–1200 CE) to indicate that archery contests were used to measure virtue:

The ancients engaged in archery in order to observe a person's virtue, and therefore were concerned with hitting the center of the target rather than piercing its hide . . . . [T]he saying in the *Record of Ritual*, "After King Wu defeated the Shang, he demobilized his troops and held an archery contest outside the city walls, and the practice of shooting to pierce the target came to an end," refers precisely to this. Once the Zhou declined and ritual fell into disuse, however, the various states turned again to military strife, and the practice of shooting to pierce the target was revived. Hence Confucius' lament.

Edward Slingerland, the translator of these passages points out that Zhu Xi paraphrased them from the "Record of Music." In the "Record of Music," King Wu marks his shift to civil administration and culture by not only putting away the chariots and armor, inverting the shields and spears, appointing his generals to civil feudal positions, and swearing not to fight again, but also by demobilizing the troops and holding an archery contest where the officers put on civilian clothes, took off their swords, and, while shooting to ritual music, no longer sought to penetrate the hide of the target.[11]

King Wu's archery contest is described as a demilitarization of archery, and, as a result of this, a rejection of war. This is an odd construction of events, to say the least. While King Wu probably never rejected war, he may well have ceremonially indicated that his war against the Shang was over by putting away the implements of war and changing out of battle dress. He could not do away with archery contests entirely, however, and the only way to somewhat diminish the lethal aspects of archery was to assert that the practical effect of a given shot was no longer the main point. The skill of hitting the target, also part of the lethal requirement of archery, presumably remained. Obviously before King Wu's change in practice both accuracy and penetration were critical. Archers were measured by their ability to hit the target with a strong enough shot to inflict damage. As we have already discussed, this skill with archery and the competition were a central part of elite interaction.

Zhu Xi, for his part, inferred a considerable amount from the passage. Confucius says nothing about accuracy, only the divorcing of archery contests from the question of strength. I will discuss the issue of strength in martial arts later, but here it is important to note that Zhu Xi inserts the notion of accuracy as equated with virtue, something that is not indicated by Confucius. For Confucius, the ceremonial aspects of the archery contest served to distinguish the higher cultural mores of gentlemen and to reinforce their group solidarity:

The Master said, "Surely archery can serve as an illustration of the fact that the gentleman does not compete! Before mounting the stairs to the archery hall, gentlemen bow and defer to one another, and after descending from the hall they mutually offer up toasts. This is how a gentleman 'competes.'"[12]

The gentleman Confucius referred to was not in a struggle with other gentlemen to win the contest; at most this was secondary. Two areas important to the gentleman were demonstrated in his performance in the archery contest: ritual capability, and internal cultivation. Ritual puissance was critical, of course, but the physical display a gentleman made during the contest was indicative of his internal mental state. That state, and the centrality of archery within the lives of Warring States period elites, connected archery metaphorically to the pursuit of virtue. Thus we see that Zhu Xi's later interpellations regarding Confucius on archery were in fact connected to his reading of the later Confucian scholar Mencius (372?–289? BCE). Two passages in Mencius use archery as an analogy for benevolence and self-cultivation:

Benevolence is like archery: an archer makes sure his stance is correct before letting fly the arrow, and if he fails to hit the mark, he does not hold it against his victor. He simply seeks the cause within himself.[13]

Here Mencius assumes that the archery being practiced is in a contest, not in battle or a hunt. Success in archery is entirely within the archer and does not depend upon outside events or people. Archery for the Confucian scholar became a measure of personal development. It is a skill that one practiced, and whose success or failure was the result of the archer's own discipline in repeatedly reproducing the correct form, just like correct behavior. It is also something that has no connection to his competitor, also just like correct behavior. The archery contest thus became a competition with oneself.

Martial arts has always been a highly individual and personal practice, as I noted Stanley Henning observing in the introduction, and which Confucians like Mencius also clearly recognized. Wisdom, for Mencius, was something that could be developed, just like martial arts:

To begin in an orderly fashion is the concern of the wise while to end in an orderly fashion is the concern of a sage. Wisdom is like skill, shall I say, while sageness is like strength. It is like shooting from beyond a hundred paces. It is due to your strength that the arrow reaches the target, but it is not due to your strength that it hits the mark.[14]

The skill of archery, like any skill, martial or otherwise, can be developed if one puts effort into it. Mencius has offhandedly separated strength and skill, following Confucius' own comments separating the skill and correct ritual practice of archery from the strength to penetrate the target. The emphasis on skill and deportment over skill, deportment, and strength, directly attacked the warlike emphasis on archery that was probably practiced during the Warring States period. Minus the question of strength, a much broader sector of elite society could effectively participate in archery contests, including those who now specialized in civil skills.

Confucian stress on correct form over effect or function proceeded from an acceptance of the continued importance of archery contests in elite circles, and the desire to downplay the value of strength alone. How many cultivated men were forced to participate in archery contests where they were beaten by uncouth, sloppy archers with poor form but great power and accuracy? The objective, external demonstration of archery skill, which included the ability to penetrate the target, made these uncultivated men seem better than the Confucian gentlemen. Getting the form correct showed internal cultivation, rather than the mere external strength of the warlike archer. The Confucian struggle over the value and meaning of archery contests was part of its larger project to influence cultural values. As the premier martial art, archery was the symbol, metaphor, and site of the struggle for the meaning of martial skills.

The final aspect of archery that emerges with the focus on individual performance in contests is the idea that true mastery of a skill requires a transcendent mental state. This is different from the focus and discipline the Confucians stressed. While they saw the correct performance of the form of archery as a reflection of proper upbringing and cultivation, they did not consider the practice of archery itself a route to a higher mental state. The idea that the practice of archery to the level of true mastery would lead to a superior, or even superhuman, mental state emerged in the Daoist writings of Zhuangzi and Liezi. The same story of Liezi's archery practice is recorded in both texts:

Liezi wanted to show off his skill of archery to a friend. He drew his bow and placed a cup of water on his left forearm. Then he notched an arrow and let it fly. Before the first arrow hit the target, he had let off the second and the third. When he saw that all three arrows hit the center of the target, Liezi was quite pleased with himself. So steady was his hand and so focused was his concentration that the water in the cup did not spill.

His friend, however, was not impressed. He said to Liezi, "What you showed me was merely the skill of eye and hand, and not the state of mind of the true archer. Let's go up to the mountains and stand on the edge of a cliff. If you can shoot accurately under those conditions, then I shall be convinced of your mastery in archery."

The two went up to the mountains, and when they reached the top of a peak, Liezi's friend walked toward the edge of a cliff that dropped a thousand feet below. Standing with his back to the drop and with half of his foot over the edge, he invited Liezi to join him.

Liezi was already trembling when he saw his friend walk toward the edge of the cliff. Now, at the thought of standing with his back to an abyss, he fell on his face and broke into a cold sweat.

Liezi's friend then said, "The master archer can fire an arrow under any condition. Whether he sees the clear sky or faces the yawning abyss, he can still shoot with the same state of mind. He is not affected by conditions of life and death, for nothing can move the stillness of his mind. Look at yourself now. You are so scared that you can't stand up or look straight. How can you even begin to demonstrate the art of archery?"[15]

Liezi's form on the field is clearly perfect, but it is his state of mind that is flawed. Here we have one of the first indications of the awareness that the practice of martial arts, though this passage surely applies to all skills, can lead to an elevated state of mind where perfection of the skill creates perfect mental focus. It is noteworthy that this idea appears in China many centuries before the invention of Chan Buddhism, before Buddhism even reached China.

Moral and intellectual performance is and will always be more important to thinkers than physical performance. Martial artists, or any performer of physical skills, must always question the enduring value of their skills. Particularly for martial artists, where age eventually diminishes the abilities of any fighter or performer, physical perfection is temporary. If the only value produced is the simple correct repetition of a task, then it has taught the performer nothing. Archery was the means to make these points, both moral and physical, because it was central to the elites of the Warring States period. The premier martial art embodied every important aspect of martial arts in Chinese society at that time – practical, performative, and spiritual.

HALBERDS (*JI*) AND SPEARS

The dagger-axe had been the main close combat weapon well into the Zhou dynasty, when it began to be replaced by the sword and the halberd (*ji*). Composite versions of the halberd had developed early on by placing a bronze spearhead with a dagger-axe head on the same pole arm; this was replaced in the Spring and Autumn and Warring States periods by single piece iron heads that included the two points at right angles to each other. Even as the halberd proliferated, so too did the spear, at least judging by the archaeological record. Spears would ultimately take over completely as the pole arm of Chinese armies for the rest of Chinese history. This raises the question of whether the dagger-axe part of the pole arm persisted in use purely because of tradition. It is hard to find other armies in any time or place with a similar weapon. Even Swiss halberds soon gave way to the pike in medieval Europe (except in their current, symbolic, use at the Vatican). It is possible that the Chinese halberd was a hybrid or transitional weapon between the dagger-axe and the spear.

Weapon design and choice is not an esoteric archaeological question with respect to the martial arts. I have already discussed the fundamentally conservative nature of martial arts and, by extension, weapons. We do not know how these weapons were actually used in combat, but their design and the trajectory of weapons use is suggestive. While the infantry were shifting to halberds and spears, for example, chariot-borne warriors carried longer hafted dagger-axes with multiple heads for a swiping attack. This might be an indication that chariots were searching for a new way of fighting infantry, or perhaps for fighting other chariots. As battles grew larger and longer, continuing beyond an individual chariot's arrow supply, some new effective combat system had to be created if the chariots were to retain any relevance.

Once battles were no longer duels between aristocrats, the chariot archer's days were numbered. Even long hafted halberds or dagger-axes would have been ineffective against massed infantry. Close combat for chariot-borne warriors was now conducted with swords, not dagger-axes, and took place after the fighters dismounted from the chariot. It would have been nearly impossible to strike someone with a sword while leaning out of a moving chariot, if for no other reason than concerns about tilting the vehicle and overturning it. A spear would also be mostly ineffective from the moving car of a chariot for reasons of reach and recoil. Even if one could spear someone to the side as one passed, the shock might knock you from the chariot. The main function of a spear for a chariot-borne warrior would be to fend off infantry who tried to approach. Changes in weapons, army composition, and tactics, left chariots struggling for relevance.

The shift from dagger-axe to sword, and dagger-axe to halberd and then spear, was a remarkable shift in martial arts. Masses of infantry could fight effectively standing in close ranks using the spear point facing out, where before they would have needed more space to wield dagger-axes effectively. Soldiers were now trained to fight with the points of their weapons rather than by hacking at an individual. Hand-to-hand combat may have shifted from a more individual practice to a more group-oriented practice. The vestigial dagger-axe point was now a holdover from a different mode of fighting and a different class of warriors. Dagger-axes harked back to individual fighting between aristocrats.

Halberds and spears marked the rise of mass warfare and the departure of aristocratic dominance of the battlefield. War became the activity of commoners and the knightly class, rather than an arena for proving aristocratic identity. At least in the Warring States period, the halberd and spear were the individual weapons of soldiers fighting en masse, not the individualistic weapons of an outstanding warrior. We have no mention of anyone fighting an individual contest with a halberd or spear, in sharp contrast to battle descriptions of aristocrats shooting at each other with arrows. The halberd itself soon disappeared from the battlefield, leaving only the spear, and, in the future, a few fleeting literary references to it (see Chapter 4).

UNARMED COMBAT

Many modern martial artists are primarily concerned with unarmed combat, though this was of much less significance, judging by the extant sources, than armed combat during the Warring States period. Some form of unarmed combat likely developed well before the Warring States period, but it is only in writings from the time that we have positive evidence for it. There are three aspects of unarmed combat to consider: weight lifting, wrestling, and striking. The first of these may seem out of place to the modern eye, but sheer physical strength was directly related to martial prowess during the Warring States period. Wrestling was also quite important and shared ritual practice with archery and charioteering. Unarmed striking, by contrast, does not appear to have been very important. All of this should alert us to the predominant use of martial arts at that time as a means of violence. Weapons were the easiest way to improve the effects of violent actions.

Sheer physical strength was understood in the Warring States period to be a marker of martial prowess.[16] This association would continue for most of the rest of Chinese history, changing perhaps only with the advent of bodybuilding and the sport of weight lifting in the twentieth century. While the majority of the Chinese population was involved in hard physical labor in their daily life, men of truly extraordinary strength were still noteworthy. In a time of human-powered weapons, a stronger fighter could inflict more damage and even shoot arrows farther. Stronger fighters could also bear up better under the weight of armor and had an advantage in wrestling and unarmed combat. Physical strength went beyond the simply martial, however, indicating a general vitality and overall power. No less a person than Confucius was reputed in a number of texts (*Lüshi Chunqiu, Liezi, Huainanzi, Lunheng*) as able in his youth to single-handedly raise the door bar on a city's gate.

The main test of strength in the Warring States period was tripod lifting. The tripods used were the massive bronze vessels used for food and symbolic purposes, some weighing hundreds of pounds (the largest found thus far, the Simuwu tripod from the late Shang, is 800 kg). Two methods for tripod lifting were the two-man lift and the one-man lift. In either case, the lifters involved had to be tremendously strong and skilled. Mistakes made during lifting could be fatal, as when the Qin King Wu engaged the strong man Meng Shuo in a tripod-lifting contest when they arrived at the Zhou court in 307 BCE. The Qin King dropped a tripod and broke his leg, leading to massive blood loss and death. Meng Shou was executed for his involvement.

The Qin kingdom was particularly known for its strongmen, and apart from the unfortunate Meng Shuo, we also know of a Niao Huo, who was made a general, and a Ren Bi, who also obtained a position because of his strength. This was no mere fetish of the Qin court, however, as the military writer Wuzi declared that the strongmen in the army were absolutely critical to its success. Strength was a critical component of martial capability and was recognized as such.

Wrestling is a very ancient art, which also must have long predated the written record. The *Record of Ritual* includes wrestling, with archery and chariot driving, as part of the activities performed for the ruler: "[In the first month of winter] the Son of Heaven orders the generals and commanders to instruct on martial [matters], practice archery, chariot driving and wrestling."[17] Wrestling may have included striking, but practiced as a military skill for soldiers, unarmed strikes would have been of limited use. We must keep in mind that soldiers expected to fight armored opponents, against which hand or foot blows would have been ineffective. An armored opponent could, however, be wrestled to the ground. The other attraction for wrestling as a demonstration of martial arts was that it highlighted physical strength and was possibly less harmful to the participants in a time without padded gloves.

The distinction between wrestling and unarmed striking was far from clear in early China. This is another example of how our modern categories of martial arts do not adequately describe past practice. The first evidence for unarmed striking or boxing *shoubo* 手搏 comes from the *Gongyang Commentary* on the *Spring and Autumn Annals*, which records an incident in 682 in which Zichang Wan, an official of Duke Min of Song, became angry and "struck Duke Min, breaking his neck."[18] Another text, the

Xinxu, records the same incident in more detail: "Wan got angry, so he struck Duke Min in the jaw, teeth fell from his mouth, his neck was broken and he died."[19] In both cases the term translated here as "struck," *bo*, is defined in the commentary to another story of unarmed fighting in 659 in the *Guliang Commentary* as "*shoubo* 手搏."[20] In that story the defeated boxer returned to kill his opponent with a knife. The *Zuozhuan* similarly records a boxing match in 632 between Chu Zi and Meng, the Marquis of Jin: "Meng, Marquis of Jin and Chu Zi boxed."[21]

The common thread in all of these descriptions of unarmed striking combat, and several more stories could be added, is the effectiveness of a skilled fighter. There was also nothing extraordinary about a contest between two boxers beyond the particular results of bouts recounted in the texts. These were not wrestling or grappling contests, or duels with weapons. Moreover, it is clear that a trained fighter could deliver devastating, and sometimes lethal, strikes, indicating a high level of training in a mature and sophisticated martial art. Wrestling bouts were seldom as dangerous. The empty-handed striking arts were well developed at a very early time in China, and they had practical uses. What we do not know is the relationship between these skills and martial dances; there is no indication of how boxers trained.

KNIGHTS-ERRANT AND ASSASSINS

The subordination of martial arts to political control gave rise to a new sort of martial artist, the knight-errant or assassin. Any martial artist not acting in the service of the state was by definition an outlaw. Bandits had, of course, always existed; no society has yet been able completely to eradicate the scourge of thugs using force to steal, rape, or murder. What changed in the Warring States period was that a martially capable man could act contrary to the political order, using his skill as a means of self-definition, rather than class or group definition. That is, by continuing to be loyal to a dead superior or assassinating a political figure for someone else, the knight or assassin proves his own qualities as a human being. The contest is between the political order and the moral, ethical, or cultural order, with the lone martial artist asserting a calling above political order.

Sima Qian (fl. ca. 135–86 BCE) created the biographical category of "Assassin-Retainer" in the *Shiji*, or *Records of the Grand Historian*.[22] This category was not retained in other histories, and it may speak to Sima Qian's concerns about overbearing political authority. Sima concluded his chapter: "Of these five men, from Cao Mei to Jing Ke, some succeeded in carrying out their duty and some did not. But it is perfectly clear that they had all determined upon the deed. They were not false to their intentions. Is it not right, then, that their names should be handed down to later ages?"[23] All but one of them, Cao Mei, was killed while carrying out his plans.

The examples of two, Yu Rang and Nie Zheng, describe the range of martial arts capability and some of the motivations of this sort of man. I will return to this category, and the most famous assassin, Jing Ke, in the next chapter. Yu Rang was an unrecognized retainer serving first one family and then another until he entered the service of Earl Zhi. Earl Zhi treated Yu Rang extremely well, and after the Earl was defeated, killed, and his clan wiped out, Yu determined to requite his earlier good treatment: "A man will die for one who understands him, as a woman will make herself beautiful for one who delights in her. Earl Zhi understood me. Before I die, I will repay him by destroying his enemy! Then my spirit need feel no shame in the world below."

Yu tried and failed on two occasions to assassinate Earl Zhi's nemesis. On both occasions he went to extremes to place himself in a position to assassinate his target. Indeed, he explicitly rejected the idea of falsely accepting employment with his target in order to get close to him. To do so would have been a disloyal and morally unacceptable act, whereas trying simply to get close enough to kill the man was otherwise fair play. He was caught and pardoned on his first failed attempt, but after being caught on the second, he was killed. His exemplary loyalty to Earl Zhi, however, marked him as an extraordinary man, and he was given his target's cloak to stab with his sword before he died.

Nie Zheng was hiding out as a butcher after having killed a man in his native village. He was sought out by Yan Zhongzi, who wanted to hire someone to kill the prime minister of Han, Han Xialei, who was also the uncle of the Han ruler. Nie resisted all requests and gifts while his mother was still alive, but after she died, he accepted. Nie chose to go into Han Xialei's office alone with just a sword and kill him. Although the prime minister was surrounded by armed guards, Nie walked in and murdered him. Nie then killed thirty or forty of the guards, before peeling off his own face, gouging out his eyes, and disemboweling himself so no one would know his identity. Nie was motivated by the kind treatment of Yan Zhongzi.

While it is difficult to determine the martial competence of Yu Rang, it seems clear that Nie Zheng was quite skilled as well as bold. A man who could kill several dozen armed men by himself must have been extremely skilled. There is a certain measure of exaggeration to these stories, of course, but they are indicative of a conception of the heroic martial artist. Unlike a dismissed government official, the exemplary martial artist could try to take revenge or prove himself against the political order. At least in the textual remains of the past, the martial world began to emerge as a counterpoint to the authority of the civil bureaucratic state. Martial arts empowered resolute men to resist the subordination of society to political control. The martial hero was born as a counterpoint to the state's monopoly over the licit use of force.

CONCLUSION

In the Warring States period, martial arts completely broke loose from its function as a marker of the aristocratic class and became a tool of state authority. Many of these skills, particularly archery, continued to retain a positive association with nobility, however, and were connected to the idea of self and group discipline, order, and self-cultivation. Warring States armies were trained and controlled instruments of violence for the state rather than chaotic assemblages of hotheaded, independent-minded warriors. Concomitant with that, military law was far harsher than civilian law because its function was to order and direct the expression of violence rather than simply suppress it. Where the martial world had previously been part of the aristocratic milieu, it was now an officially separate environment where controlled violence in service to politics was acceptable. War and the martial arts were no longer ennobling, however, when war was largely the province of commoners. A new ideology emerged, arguing that serving the state through licit violence was a sign of morality and self-control.

The controlled use of violence was necessary to create an orderly society, but it created a basic tension within martial artists. A conscripted soldier was usually reluctant to leave his civilian life, learn martial arts, and participate in the dangerous activity of war. His main concern was to leave the army and the practices of fighting as soon as possible and return to his former life. Most soldiers were conscripted from the ranks of the farmers, and the ideal of the farmer-soldier, the man who did not want to fight, remained the ideal for the rest of imperial Chinese history. Yet reluctant farmer-soldiers did not make the best martial artists or soldiers. Conscript armies were led and bolstered by specialized warriors and commanders. These specialists were necessary for teaching martial arts, directing large bodies of men, providing combat leadership, and generally forming conscripts into effective armies.

The decline of aristocratic power with respect to the state was accompanied by an increasingly specialized, or perhaps even "professionalized," society. Within this milieu, martial arts became one of a number of skills that someone could make a living practicing, the definition of a profession. This should not be taken too far for the Warring States period. Society was still understood to be divided into four classes: knights 士, farmers 農, artisans 工, and merchants 商, with the knightly class serving as government officials in peace and officers in war, and the farmers serving as soldiers in wartime. The knightly class maintained a set of skills (the six arts): archery, charioteering, mathematics, music, calligraphy, and rites (in the Confucian context, "rites" encompassed manners, customs, and ceremonies). Confucius was described by Sima Qian as "teaching the six arts." Most of these skills had direct or indirect martial as well as non-military uses. It is also clear that while Confucius taught these arts, he was not a proponent of specialization in any one of them, or of selling oneself based upon those skills. Nevertheless, many gentlemen sought advancement through their accomplishments in one or more of those arts.

Martial arts spread throughout Chinese society as armies grew and conscripted tens of thousands of ordinary farmers into military service. This growth in armies was accompanied by the large-scale production of iron weapons. Mass armies and constant warfare militarized swathes of society and valorized the profession of arms. Many thinkers struggled against the enthusiasm for martial arts and warfare, particularly among the rulers. When Mencius suggested to King Xuan of Qi that submission to another state was the best way to promote good relations, the King replied:

Great are your words, but I have a weakness. I am fond of valor.
  I beg you not to be fond of small valor. To look fierce, putting your hand on your sword and say, "How dare he oppose me!" is to show the valor of a common fellow which is of use only against a single adversary.[24]

Mencius continues in the passage to advocate righteous anger and waging war against injustice, something that is the correct orientation for a ruler. He explicitly denigrates the sort of personal valor that interests the king as being beneath him. Of course, this was precisely the kind of valor expected of Spring and Autumn period aristocrats, and it had not entirely disappeared as an aristocratic norm or cultural ideal in the minds of Warring States period elites. Mencius also asserts a difference between personal martial arts practice and war, a distinction Spring and Autumn period elites would not have supported.

In the Warring States period we see for the first time, though it may have begun earlier, a slight separation between war, and the skills and tools of war. This separation was not great in the Warring States period, nor was the separation marked between government official and army officer, or soldier and warrior. Weapons were still a central part of court ritual, as martial dances accompanied by music enforced and reinforced aristocratic and political identity. The composition and weapons of armies changed, however, and we do not know whether the weapons used in those court rituals also changed or simply became archaic. At the same time, the new weapons were being issued to large numbers of soldiers who were all being trained in martial arts to use them. The rituals no longer matched the military reality in terms of men, meaning or, perhaps, technology.

Martial arts made even commoners dangerous in ways they had not hitherto been. Training could make anyone an effective fighter. A capability that threatened the security of the state and society had to be controlled by every means available – political, legal, cultural, and social. But the martial arts were also necessary for the protection of society and the state, and for the expansion of political authority internally and externally. The martial arts now permeated society as a whole, changing the aristocracy's relationship to war and society, and calling into question many previous political assumptions. What Confucius and many other thinkers sought to do was to justify elite rule through moral superiority – an intellectual project increasingly necessary since they no longer held a monopoly on the martial arts.

The martial arts were central to the state's control over violence, both in peace and war. A new culture and ideology developed in the Warring States period to accommodate this situation, and it involved both redefinitions of previous social structures and the invention of new ones. The martial arts were not unique in this, of course, as the Warring States period was a golden age of Chinese thought in every area. Disciplined soldiers replaced aristocratic warriors, and the interconnected martial arts that linked aristocrats through ritual, military practice, and culture were separated into individual functional categories. People saw new uses and functions for the martial arts.

Archery in the Warring States period became perhaps the first martial art promoted for the positive effects it had on the practitioner. This was not just the instantiation of social harmony through the ritual reinforcement of cultural hierarchy urged by Confucius, but also the development of a superior mental state suggested by Liezi and Zhuangzi. A true archer achieved a higher order of functionality that transcended the mere physical performance of shooting. Other texts indicate that a similar state could be achieved through mastery of any physical skill, so the idea was not restricted to archery. But archery was deeply tied to the elites, to violence, and to a certain spiritual power that went beyond ritual correctness. Unlike the master butcher in Zhuangzi the archer possessed the power of life and death over other men. Practicing a lethal skill was understood to develop the archer, in addition to its martial uses.

The martial arts, like so many other areas of Chinese culture, were transformed during the Warring States period. But the open and dynamic environment of interstate struggles came to a close in 221 BCE. The rise of the Qin kingdom and its eventual conquest of all of the other Chinese states changed the trajectory of Chinese history. Later Chinese historians would come to read that change as the inevitable result of developments in the Spring and Autumn and Warring States periods. As we shall see in the next chapter, there was no clear sign of inevitability at the time. Martial arts were central to the intense wars of conquest waged by the Qin, and part of Qin success was due to its highlighting of certain martial qualities. The impact of those practices continued into the succeeding Han dynasty, where the martial arts and their place in society and culture shifted again and again.

3

The Qin and Han Dynasties

My strength uprooted mountains,
My power covered the age.
But the times do not favor me,
And Piebald cannot gallop fast enough.[1]

The territorial and symbolic unification of China in 221 BCE under the Qin ruler was the result of decades, if not centuries, of warfare. The Warring States period was ended by a series of wars and campaigns that had militarized virtually all of Chinese society, spreading martial skills throughout the population. All of the states fighting for power or survival required military service from their adult male subjects, and much of a given government's functions were involved in mobilizing resources and men for war. While the great thinkers were read and discussed by some educated men, moral suasion played little role in reducing the overall level of violence. The Qin state defeated its rivals and imposed real temporal central authority over the Chinese ecumene for the first time.

Later historians gave much of the credit for Qin's victory, and subsequent collapse, to the policies instituted by Lord Shang (390–38 BCE). Lord Shang's policies were part of an intellectual tradition usually translated into English as "the Legalists." The Legalists believed that the best way to run a state was through the establishment and ruthless application of rules and regulations. In the case of the Qin, those rules were designed to maximize military power and food production. Rewards were given for taking enemy heads in battle, and punishments were imposed for military failure. There was, of course, more to the success of the Qin than its harsh system of laws or its ruthless centralization of power in the hands of the ruler. All of the other states had their own systems for mobilizing enormous armies from their populations.

Having created China's first empire, the Qin government had to shift its efforts toward internal consolidation and demilitarization of the population. A massive collection and melting down of weapons was squarely aimed at preventing insurrection. Demilitarization was a new problem for a Chinese government; all previous governments had either restricted most military training to the ruling class or sought to train their subjects for war. The Qin government had to diminish any internal threats to its power while maintaining enough force to put down rebellions and continue outward expansion. It failed in these efforts, and the new empire broke down soon after the death of the first emperor in 210 BCE. In the fighting that followed, two main contenders for power emerged: Xiang Yu, an aristocrat from Chu in the south, and Liu Bang, a farmer from Pei county in Jiangsu.

Although Liu Bang would eventually win out and establish the Han dynasty (206 BCE–220 CE), it is in the person of Xiang Yu that we see the conflicting emotions and skills of an aristocratic Chinese man in third century BCE China. Xiang Yu abandoned book learning because he thought it beneath him, and then abandoned fencing because it was a skill restricted to defeating only a small number of men. He then turned to military thought as a skill useful for great accomplishments, but he dropped that as well. Yet despite his stunted education, he personally slaughtered an office full of officials and clerks at the start of his career and went on to win battle after battle.

The Han dynasty that Liu Bang founded would last for some four centuries. And just as the Qin dynasty had been challenged to adapt to new political circumstances and military requirements, a challenge it was unable to meet, the Han dynasty also faced important political and military changes. Politically, the Han imperial government sought to complete the interrupted defeudalization of the Qin, breaking down the fiefs of imperial relatives and the descendants of the founding generals. This process took decades but was eventually successful. Militarily, particularly with the centralization of power in the hands of the central court, the most important problems facing the imperial army shifted to the borders. Border threats required longer serving, more specialized troops rather than militia. The standing army was increasingly composed of professionals, convicts with commuted sentences, and steppe cavalrymen.

The final blow to the Warring States/Qin military system that the Han inherited was the rebellion and establishment of the New Dynasty of Wang Mang from 9 to 23. Wang Mang temporarily overthrew the Han dynasty by deposing the child emperor he was regent for. An army composed of the household forces of local powerful families, led by a member of the imperial clan and bolstered by the militia, defeated him. After the reestablishment of Han rule, militia service was abolished to prevent future would-be rebels from gathering significant bodies of trained soldiers from among the farmers.[2] The average farmer was demilitarized, though of course powerful families continued to maintain their own household security forces as before. Indeed, as we shall see again and again throughout Chinese history, powerful families, merchants, and religious institutions always maintained considerable military force at their disposal. All of those forces were trained in martial arts and well armed.

As Han society evolved away from widespread military service, attitudes about the place of martial arts changed as well. The significance of the changes in government policy, specifically the demilitarization of the Han farmers after Wang Mang was defeated, have been overstated by some.[3] Chinese society as a whole likely became less militarized as farmers were no longer expected to demonstrate certain minimal martial skills. Fighting became less of a skill and more of a profession; that is, martial arts were skills learned by people who intended to make their living practicing those skills. Society became more specialized, leaving farmers to farm and soldiers to fight. This should not be taken too far, however, as most of these central government policies were imposed slowly, incompletely, and in dramatically different ways in different parts of China. Local circumstances – living near the border, for example – might override the government's general interest in demilitarizing farmers.

Powerful local families continued to raise, train, and arm their own forces. Many of these forces were primarily their tenant farmers, with some additional professional fighters to train and lead those men in emergencies. People with land and goods to protect hired their own security forces, since one could not rely upon the government for protection.

The Qin and Han dynasties responded to the problem of widespread martial arts knowledge in Chinese society in different ways. Both dynasties recognized that it was unwise and functionally impossible to abolish martial arts entirely among the commoners – unwise because both dynasties recognized that the populace as a whole was a vast reservoir of military power when properly drafted, trained, and directed. The dynasties could not give up access to that power or allow it to drift into the hands of local elites and power holders. Yet even if they had wanted to remove the martial arts from the populace, it would have been impossible. The government's tools of control were insufficient to the task, its reach very limited; there were too many groups with exceptions to the prohibitions, and the martial arts were too firmly embedded in society. One of the main entertainments was martial arts performances.

The Qin response was not to prohibit martial arts but to prohibit the private ownership of weapons, to cease regular military reviews at the local level, and to promote wrestling. These practices were aimed at deflecting the martial arts into less government-threatening routes. In a certain sense, this was the first time that the martial arts, in the form of wrestling, were officially separated from the military. Previously, all martial arts had had a direct connection to war and hunting. This policy was tied to strong central control and defeudalization. It was as short-lived as the Qin itself.

The Han did not continue the Qin policy and returned to a system of militias more characteristic of the Warring States period. Only in the second half of the Han dynasty, after the Wang Mang interregnum, were ordinary farmers no longer trained in martial arts. Perhaps as a direct result of the Han retention of widespread martial arts training, Han entertainments also went beyond wrestling to include fencing, boxing, and other martial arts as well as dancing and many nonmartial performances. This would give rise to the Han dynasty "Hundred Events," and through that to the foundations of theater in China.

The shift of military reviews toward wrestling and other martial arts performances for entertainment was simply part of a succession of changes in the martial arts. Shang and Zhou aristocrats had hunted and fought together to demonstrate their prowess and status, and then had watched martial dances at court to recapitulate political legitimacy by recalling actual battles. As martial arts moved out into the larger population, reviews of troops sought to ensure that farmers were practicing martial arts for state service. At the same time, the knightly class fetishized archery contests to demonstrate their superior status and moral qualities through formalized martial practice. All of these skills had practical uses on and off the battlefield, but just as consistently, they were used in performance. By the Han dynasty, then, it is clear that performance and battlefield martial arts were fundamentally interlinked.

It is often difficult clearly to explicate martial arts practice on the battlefield because of the nature of the sources. We are more fortunate in the sources with respect to individual combat and the place of martial arts in Chinese culture. This chapter therefore begins with the first emperor and his would-be assassins, and then turns to Qin dynasty wrestling, the contest between Xiang Yu and Liu Bang that resulted in the founding of the Han dynasty, and finishes with the development of martial arts alongside the Hundred Events.

THE FIRST EMPEROR AND HIS WOULD-BE ASSASSINS

The Qin creation of a unified Chinese empire faced considerable opposition both from the kingdoms it ultimately destroyed and from individuals who sought to derail the rise of a despot. Of course, the Qin was not unique in either of these areas, as attested by the constant warfare and frequent assassinations of individual rulers during the Warring States period. When the Qin king became the first emperor of China, however, he also became a symbol of harsh, despotic rule. This association of the Qin king, usually referred to as Qin Shihuang or Qin Shihuangdi (the First Emperor of Qin), continues today. Thus the stories of the men who attempted to assassinate him portray individual resistance to despotism rather than the simple effort of someone to murder a ruler.

The most famous assassin in Chinese history is Jing Ke. Jing Ke was described as loving reading and fencing, a significant juxtaposition of interests that set him above the ranks of mere violent thugs. Sima Qian's account of Jing includes two incidents in which he withdrew in the face of an aggressive and angry interlocutor. In the first instance, Jing Ke was discussing fencing with a man named Gai Nie. When Gai Nie became angry and glared at Jing, Jing withdrew and immediately departed the town. Gai regarded this as a sign of his own ferocity and Jing's timidity. He thought he had thoroughly intimidated Jing with a glare.

In the second instance, Jing was playing a board game with Lu Goujian. When Lu got angry and shouted at him, Jing left, never to return.[4] Jing's response to angry, rude, and confrontational behavior was connected to his interest in reading. Although Jing would prove himself to be the bravest man of his time, and a skilled swordsman, he refused to respond in kind to unpleasant aggressive men who could neither discuss fencing nor play a board game without losing their temper. Gai Nie's self-satisfaction with having intimidated Jing, as he believed, was not only a way for Sima Qian to demonstrate Jing's superior character but also to denigrate the sort of loud-mouthed, overly aggressive behavior of the common martial artist. The truly great warrior and martial artist was not a chest-thumping thug.

Sima Qian's biography of Jing paints him as humble, erudite, and unpretentious. When Jing reached the state of Yan, he began habitually to hang around the marketplace with a dog butcher and a dulcimer player, Gao Jianli. Jing spent time with men of low standing and also associated with worthy and powerful men during his travels. Sima Qian repeatedly refers to Jing's love of reading, reinforcing his intellectual strength and making it clear that Jing's interest in reading carried through into his adult life, rather than being an aspect of his upbringing that he subsequently dropped (as a counterexample, see Xiang Yu, discussed later).

Jing Ke was enlisted in a plan to assassinate the Qin king by Tian Guang, while Jing was living in the kingdom of Yan. Tian was summoned to consult with Dan, Heir of Yan, about Dan's desire for personal revenge against the Qin king. The motivation for assassinating the Qin king was not noble, and Dan demonstrated his lack of character in his interaction with Tian Guang. Tian had formerly been a man of daring and wisdom, but he was now past his prime and recommended that Dan contact Jing Ke. As Tian was leaving Dan to inform Jing Ke, the Yan Heir warned Tian not to speak to anyone else about the matter they had discussed. Tian asked Jing Ke to see Dan, but he warned him that Dan was not of good character:

I have heard that the actions of a man of honor do not cause other men to doubt him. Today the Heir told me "What we have spoken of are crucial affairs of state, I beg you not to let them be known, Venerable Sir." Thus the Heir doubts me. When his actions cause other men to doubt him, this is no high-principled gallant.[5]

Tian Guang urged Jing Ke to see Dan and inform him that Tian had killed himself so he could not speak of the matter. He then cut his own throat. The contrast here between men of high character and those of low character is striking. Good men trust others and are therefore trustworthy; they respect the wisdom of good men to know what is and is not correct. When Dan admonished Tian Guang to keep quiet, he directly insulted Tian, either feeling he was too foolish to know he should keep quiet or incapable of doing so. The only way to prove his own trustworthiness was to kill himself. Tian Guang's suicide was a direct expression of a severe ethical code that prized honor and reputation above all else.

This willingness to kill oneself to prove one's honor was then recapitulated and advanced by Fan Wuqi, a Qin general who had offended the Qin king and fled to the sanctuary of Yan. Jing Ke agreed to assassinate the Qin king and was showered with gifts from Dan, but he pointed out that he would be unable to get close enough to kill him without a significant token. Jing suggested using as tokens General Fan's head, since the Qin king had placed a bounty on it, and a map of a particular piece of Yan territory. Presenting the map was a symbol of surrendering that land, and it would provide a place for Jing to conceal a poisoned dagger. Dan refused to violate the sanctuary he had given General Fan, however, so Jing went directly to the general and explained the situation to him.

General Fan cut his own throat to enable Jing Ke to get close enough to the Qin king to kill him. Again, we see a warrior who is willing and able to cut his own throat to accomplish his goal, be it preserving his honor or furthering a plan to kill his enemy. Jing Ke did not, however, seem to have imagined his mission as a one-way trip. He angrily upbraided Dan when the Heir questioned his delay in setting out while waiting for his assistant: "One who sets off without considering his return is a whelp!"

In any event, Jing's plan succeeded up to the point where he pulled out the hidden dagger and grabbed the Qin king's sleeve with his left hand to stab him. The Qin king was able to pull away before he got stabbed. Jing then chased him around the upper audience chamber while his attendants panicked. The Qin court physician struck at Jing ineffectively with his medical bag. All of the armed guards were in the lower chamber, and could only be summoned by the Qin king. The Qin king was too busy trying to free his long sword from its scabbard while evading Jing. Once the long sword was free, he quickly wounded Jing, who in a last ditch effort threw the dagger at the King, missing him and striking a bronze pillar. (Jing was later executed.)

It took the Qin another five years to conquer all of China, and in 221 BCE elevate the Qin king to the new title of emperor "*huangdi* 皇帝." After this all of Jing Ke and the Yan Heir Dan's retainers were pursued. Gao Jianli, the dulcimer player and old friend of Jing Ke's, went into hiding. Eventually he revealed himself, and through his skill as a dulcimer player was brought to Qin Shihuang to perform. The emperor had pardoned him, but also had had him blinded with acid. Gao placed a piece of lead in his dulcimer, and when the emperor drew close to him as he played, he tried to strike Qin with the weighted dulcimer. He missed, and was executed.

Sima Qian completes his portrait of Jing Ke by inserting a comment by Lu Goujian, the man Jing had backed away from when he shouted at him during a board game. Having heard of Jing's failed assassination attempt, Lu lamented: "Alas, what a shame he did not study carefully the method of assassination with a dagger! How profound has been my failure to understand men! When I shouted at him before, he must have thought I was not [his kind] of man!"[6]

The attempts of Jing Ke and his friend Gao Jianli to kill Qin Shihuang were not the last. After the first emperor's encounter with Gao Jianli, he made sure to keep men from the states he had conquered away from his immediate presence. Later in his rule, however, his party was attacked while touring Bolangsha. The two assassins mistakenly attacked his attendants' carriage and then fled. One of the would-be assassins was a man named Zhang Liang, an aristocrat from the conquered kingdom of Han; to assist him in the attack he had enlisted the aid of a man renowned for his strength.

The weapon he provided for this strongman was an iron staff weighing 120 catties (about 160 pounds). Although we hear nothing again of the strongman after the failed attempt, Zhang himself went on to become a key strategist and general for Liu Bang, who would found the Han dynasty.[7]

QIN DYNASTY WRESTLING

Once the Qin created the first Chinese empire, the new emperor attempted to demilitarize Chinese society to some extent. Private martial arts practice was forbidden, as was the possession of weapons, particularly among the aristocracy of the conquered kingdoms. The main threat to the state was a large group of armed subjects resisting government authority. Without weapons, however, even a group of well-trained martial artists was not a threat. As Zhang Liang's assassination attempt proves, however, weapons were still readily available, and a small group of well-trained and armed martial artists could be a direct threat to the ruler's life. The technology to make steel, iron, or bronze weapons of all kinds was widespread throughout Chinese society after centuries of warfare. Knowledge of martial arts was similarly ubiquitous. Forbidding the practice of martial arts and the ownership of weapons was thus more a general attempt to disarm society as a whole and prevent armed insurrection than an effective policy to entirely expunge martial skills.

Indeed, the prevalence of martial arts in Chinese society was so widespread that some substitute had to be provided that would replace it without endangering the state. Regular military training was therefore abolished and replaced with wrestling competitions and displays. Wrestling was practiced inside and outside the army, and was known as a martial art among a good portion of the population. Zhang Chunren and Cui Lequan suggested that wrestling, since it was confined to techniques for throwing, was less likely to result in injury than boxing, but this is hard to prove.[8] Being thrown onto an unpadded surface could be quite dangerous. Wrestling contests were ordinary entertainments among the upper class, and probably among the commoners as well.[9]

The Qin dynasty did not last long. As Zhang Liang's assassination attempt demonstrated, there was widespread opposition to Qin rule among the elite. Qin Shihuang died peacefully, but the Qin government collapsed rapidly afterward. For all of the power of the Qin system, it failed to provide for a smooth imperial succession. Nearly paralyzed with internal struggles for power, the government could not suppress the rising tide of warlords fighting to destroy it. Two men emerged as the major contestants in this conflagration: Xiang Yu and Liu Bang.

XIANG YU AND LIU BANG

The struggle between Xiang Yu and Liu Bang to overthrow the emperor and then rule the Qin empire is replete with casual mentions of martial arts. This is not surprising in a colossal armed contest that involved more than just these two men and ranged over all of China. Both men were literate and trained in martial arts, a characteristic of their class. Although Xiang Yu's background was more elevated, they were virtually identical in every area of education and skills. The accounts of both men are heavily biased by the need of the historians living under the Han dynasty, the regime founded by Liu Bang, to legitimate Liu's victory, but a number of events in their lives and interactions with each other bear directly on the question of the place of martial arts in upper-class Chinese society. Liu is often described as having a peasant background, but it is clear from his access to education that he was of a higher class. Their biographies were written in such a way as to juxtapose Liu Bang's superior character with Xiang Yu's; this juxtaposition, of course, is effective because of their overall similarities.

Near the beginning of Xiang Yu's biography in the *Shiji*, it says:

When Xiang Ji (Yu) was young, he studied writing but failed to complete [his studies]. He quit to study fencing, but again failed to complete [his studies]. Xiang Liang was angry with him.

Xiang Ji said: "Writing is only good for recording people's names. Fencing is only for contending with one man. Neither is worth learning. I want to learn how to contend with ten thousand men."

Xiang Liang therefore taught him the art of war. Xiang Ji was greatly pleased. But when he had grasped the general idea of it, he again was unwilling to finish his study.[10]

While the main character point of this passage is to make it clear that Xiang Yu was not a man who ever did anything completely, a sign of underlying immaturity, his course of education is instructive. In all three areas – writing (literacy), fencing, and the art of war – it was possible to complete an area of study. This is to say that there was an established body of readings or skills in the respective areas that could be known and completed by a young man. Xiang Yu himself was described as very tall, and strong enough to "lift a tripod," inborn characteristics of a great martial artist. And despite Xiang Yu's truncated training in fencing, he was an extremely capable swordsman.

Xiang Yu followed his uncle, Xiang Liang, into rebellion against the Qin in 209 BCE. One of their first acts was to murder Yin Tong, the governor of Kuaiji. At Xiang Liang's order during an audience with Yin, Xiang Yu suddenly drew his sword and cut off the governor's head. He then killed "almost a hundred" of the governor's attendants.[11] Despite the likely exaggeration, Xiang Yu was an effective martial artist who, it seems, single-handedly slaughtered much of a government office full of people.

He demonstrated similar skill and ruthlessness on other occasions, for example, suddenly beheading his commanding general, Song Yi, at a morning meeting. Song Yi himself had earlier criticized Xiang Yu's military plans, saying: "In donning armor and handling weapons, I am not as good as you. But in sitting down and working out strategy, you are not as good as I." Song Yi had been following a less aggressive strategy against the Qin, and followed up his admonition to Xiang Yu by ordering the execution of all fierce and aggressive soldiers. Xiang Yu's solution was to murder Song Yi, and prosecute the more aggressive strategy he had been advocating.

Liu Bang, for his part, is portrayed as a much more convivial fellow in his youth, mostly interested in women, drinking, and money. On one occasion, while drunk and walking through a marsh, he was warned that a large snake blocked the way. He responded: "What is there to fear when a strong man walks along?" Proceeding ahead, he came upon the snake, drew his long sword, and cut it in two. He managed to walk a little further before falling into a drunken sleep.[12] The significance of the incident in the *History of the Former Han Dynasty* is portrayed in supernatural terms, with a mysterious old woman found lamenting that the son of the Red God (Liu Bang) had just killed her son, the son of the White God. For our purposes, it is more important that a man like Liu Bang would carry a long sword as part of his ordinary accoutrement, and be ready, willing, and able to use it.

Possibly the most famous display of martial arts in the interaction between Liu Bang and Xiang Yu occurred in 206 BCE, shortly after Liu had captured the Qin capital. Although Liu and Xiang Yu were both on the same side, their armies nearly clashed when Xiang Yu insisted upon taking possession of the territory Liu had recently conquered. Conflict was narrowly avoided, and Liu came to Xiang Yu's camp to apologize and take part in a feast. One of Xiang Yu's retainers tried to indicate to him that they should kill Liu while he was there, but Xiang Yu did not respond. The retainer thereupon directed Xiang Zhuang to perform a sword dance during the feasting, and take the opportunity to kill Liu. Xiang Zhuang followed these instructions, entered the feast, drank a toast to Liu, and said: "There is no [entertainment] in our camp, I beg permission to dance a sword-dance." He then drew his long sword and began the dance. Seeing its purpose, another man, Xiang Bo, drew his long sword and also danced, but he kept himself between Xiang Zhuang and Liu, preventing the assassination.[13]

It is not clear what the sword dance in question was in terms of a performance. Music is not noted in the account, nor is there mention of any greater spiritual or ceremonial value. It was an entertainment that a warrior could reasonably perform as an aesthetic practice, and that another warrior could also perform when needed. The form was also not set, in the sense of a strictly ordered series of movements, since Xiang Bo was able to place himself between Xiang Zhuang and Liu as needed. Xiang Bo elegantly and decisively frustrated the assassination without directly clashing with Xiang Zhuang. The matter did not degenerate into a duel, so a multiparticipant sword dance was quite possible, and the etiquette for the practice did not allow for physical contact between dancers. Xiang Zhuang could not simply push past Xiang Bo and maintain the fiction that he was innocently doing a sword dance.

The military contest between Liu Bang and Xiang Yu continued, and in 204 BCE, while their armies were camped nearby, they parleyed across a stream. Xiang Yu suggested settling the military contest with a personal duel. Here again we see Xiang Yu's self-identification as a fighter and martial artist overwhelming his role as general and contender for the throne. Liu Bang not only rejected the notion of a duel, something he probably would not expect to win, but also responded with a ten-point indictment of Xiang Yu's behavior. This indictment was not just a polished summation of Xiang Yu's faults and the reason he could not be a legitimate ruler, but was also a very carefully crafted excuse for why Liu would not fight the duel. He concludes the speech by saying, "I should send an ex-convict to strike you, sir. How could I trouble myself to duel with you, sir?"[14] Xiang Yu responded to this by pulling out a crossbow and shooting Liu Bang in the chest. Liu grabbed his foot and claimed aloud to have been hit in the toe. Although seriously wounded, Liu was then forced to pretend to be well in front of his troops after he returned (he later recovered).

The parley between Liu and Xiang Yu does not just reveal Xiang Yu's bad character. Liu had to present a very strong case for not accepting Xiang Yu's challenge. The substance of that case was that Xiang Yu had traduced the social mores of the upper class, not only undermining his legitimacy as a leader but also invalidating his status as an aristocrat. As such, he no longer had the right to fight a duel with another aristocrat. Liu could not simply reject the duel based on the likelihood that Xiang Yu would win. At root, these men were warriors and martial artists, and their

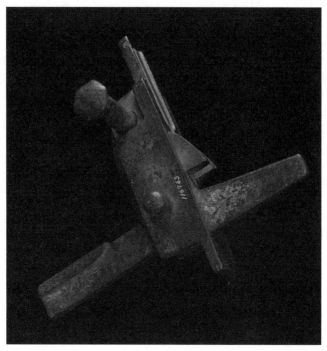

ILLUSTRATION 5. Bronze crossbow trigger mechanism, late Warring States to Han Dynasty, Laufer Collection. Courtesy of the Field Museum and Ernest Caldwell. Photo by Ernest Caldwell.

high social standing required a response of some kind to a challenge to personal combat. Xiang Yu's proposal of a duel was not something which was obviously ridiculous or beyond the realm of possibility. Having received the rejection he had probably expected, Xiang Yu then felt justified in trying to kill Liu Bang at long range with a crossbow. If Liu would not accept a challenge to close combat, then he became fair game for long-range crossbow archery. And, of course, Xiang Yu was a skilled crossbow archer.

At the end of his life, after military fortune had turned against him, Xiang Yu wanted to prove his personal invincibility before he was completely defeated. Down to a mere twenty-eight cavalrymen accompanying him he said:

It has been eight years now since I rose in arms. I have personally fought more than seventy battles, in which whomever I was matched with, I vanquished, whomever I set upon, I subdued. Never once defeated, I finally became the Hegemon and possessed the world. Yet in the end I have now been cornered here. It is Heaven that destroys me. It is not any fault of mine in battle. Today, I must surely resolve to die, but let me fight a joyful battle for you first. I vow to defeat them three times, break the siege for you, cut off the heads of their general, and cut down their banners, so that you will see it is Heaven that destroys me, not any fault of mine in battle.[15]

Xiang Yu then proceeded to do as he had promised, leading his small force into battle against the pursuing Han troops. Xiang Yu personally cut the head off the Han commander and killed "dozens of men, nearly one hundred." Having temporarily broken free of the Han encirclement, he then rejected the possibility of escape. His men were ordered to dismount, and they received their pursuers on foot with close combat weapons. Xiang Yu again "alone killed several hundred men of the Han army. He himself also suffered more than ten wounds." Rather than allow an enemy to kill him, Xiang Yu cut his own throat.

Xiang Yu and Liu Bang epitomized two frequently juxtaposed archetypes of the Chinese hero. Both, of course, were warriors and generals. Xiang Yu was the greater warrior and general, full of arrogant self-confidence, who believed that his unsurpassed capabilities as a fighter were enough to conquer the world. Yet his individual martial skills were not sufficient to rule the world that he conquered. His victories were fleeting because they were only on the battlefield. Liu Bang was the less-skilled fighter and general, sometimes displaying poor behavior that bordered on cowardice, or at the very least acting in a less than admirable way. What Liu understood was that conquest and ruling required a team of accomplished people, and that the leader of that group needed effectively to subordinate his own ego to the larger purpose. Only by humbling oneself before the goal of creating and ruling an empire could one achieve it. A supremely skilled martial artist like Xiang Yu risked mistaking his own immense power for the much greater power that could only come from leading others by praising them above oneself.

The formation of the Han dynasty was not revolutionary in any sense, however, particularly in martial arts. Many Qin reforms, particularly in the area of defeudalization, were rolled back, and the nature of Han dynasty society and culture began as an amalgam of pre-Qin and Qin practices. In the realm of martial arts, ordinary farmers were still required to render regular military service and so practiced martial arts as a part of ordinary rural life. Liu Bang did take steps to distinguish classes of people; in 199 BCE, for example, he prohibited merchants not only from wearing certain kinds of cloth but also from carrying weapons or riding a horse.[16] Interestingly, when Chen Xi (the Marquis of Yangxia and commander of a border army) rebelled in 197 BCE, Liu Bang discovered that all of Chen's generals were formerly merchants. Their background, at least from the historian Ban Gu's perspective, allowed Liu to bribe a number of them to surrender.[17] Who fought was still an important question for Liu Bang, as he, on the one hand, demobilized some of his former soldiers and exempted them from further military service, but on the other hand, spent the rest of his reign putting down rebellions across the Han empire.

Liu Bang himself provided an interesting coda to his life. The Han emperor was wounded by an arrow in 195 BCE while suppressing yet another rebellion. A doctor was called, and though he said he could heal him, Liu rejected the aid: "Wearing plain clothes and raising three feet [of steel (i.e., a sword)], I seized the empire. Was this not Heaven's Mandate? My fate is then with Heaven."[18] Liu chose to die in much the same way as Xiang Yu, wounded in battle and functionally by his own hand. And like Xiang Yu, it was very much a warrior's death, reflecting the ethos of a man who had taken a personal part in combat his entire adult life.

THE HAN DYNASTY HUNDRED EVENTS (百戲) AND MARTIAL ARTS

Subsequent emperors, of course, were not warriors by training, though they may have had some introduction to the martial arts as part of their basic education. Martial arts nevertheless remained popular in the realm of entertainment. The Hundred Events performances and competitions of the Han dynasty may have had their start in the wrestling competitions of the Qin, but they included a much wider range of entertainments and martial contests beyond just wrestling.[19] Wrestling nevertheless remained a very important component of the Hundred Events. The specific activities included in a Hundred Events performance might vary, and the term seems a general one for a kind of variety show. Hundred Events performances were often enacted for visiting guests from the various non-Han peoples.

In addition to the singing and dancing performances, the Hundred Events could also include archery and contests of strength. These latter martial practices had formerly been part of local and court ceremonies, or parts of military training. Visiting non-Han envoys could therefore view the Hundred Events performances staged in their honor in a number of ways. First, was simple entertainment value. The Hundred Events was popular even among ordinary Chinese. When Han emperor Wudi held a wrestling competition in the spring of 112 BCE at the capital, it was said that people came from a hundred miles around to watch it. Similarly, the population of the capital came to watch a wrestling competition three years later.[20] The party atmosphere for foreign envoys was no doubt helped by the "pools of wine and forests of meat" that accompanied the Hundred Events.[21] A visit to the Han court allowed the emperor to display the wealth, culture, and power of his empire and to provide an attractive reward for envoys who cooperated with his wishes.

The sheer wealth of the Han emperor was probably stunning, but it was also in keeping with more general rules of hospitality and etiquette. Foreign envoys could see the Hundred Events as a display of military power. All the martial arts displayed were familiar to them, forming a common cultural touchstone that could be appreciated across differences in language and custom. The very fact that the imperial court and the surrounding citizenry all enjoyed martial competitions demonstrated the martial orientation of the Han dynasty itself. These were not effete, sedentary littérateurs, but martial men, who knew and valued martial skills. A skilled martial artist could get noticed and rewarded at the Han imperial court and in Han society. The performance of the martial arts for foreign envoys thus served very directly to impress the martial vitality of the Han dynasty on its guests.

Wrestling was particularly associated with non-Han or non-Chinese men. A belt ornament unearthed from a Han tomb in 1955 showed a struggle between two wrestlers. The wrestlers have large noses and deep-set eyes, clear indicators that they are not Chinese. For visiting foreign envoys, then, the inclusion of wrestling may also have shown Chinese openness or appreciation of foreign culture. A markedly Central Eurasian martial art was one of the most avidly practiced and watched competitive events at the Han imperial court. The Han court may have inherited this interest from the Qin dynasty court, or perhaps wrestling had thoroughly permeated elite and popular Chinese culture by the third and second centuries BCE. Chinese culture and martial practice, we should keep in mind, was often quite open to foreign and Central Eurasian influence. Wrestling, like the use of chariots in warfare and cavalry, came from Central Eurasia and the steppe. A wrestling competition was therefore a sign of cosmopolitanism at the Han court and a marked lack of Chinese exclusion of foreign martial arts.

Wrestling was also useful outside the Hundred Events. Jin Midi, a Xiongnu who had formerly been Heir Apparent of the Xiongnu king Xiuchu and was subsequently forced into Han service as a teenager after his father's defeat, rendered his most important service to Han emperor Wudi by preventing Mu Heluo and his brother Mu Tong from assassinating the emperor. Jin encountered Mu Heluo, armed with a knife hidden in his sleeve, on his way to attack the emperor. Jin was able to seize Mang and to throw him down from the hall by "throwing his neck" (捽胡).[22] This is a reminder that the martial arts always maintained both a performance and a practical function. More people enjoyed watching martial arts performances than practiced martial arts as serious competitors, but given the prevalence of martial arts training in the early Han dynasty among both elite and commoner, this was a question of degree of training and practice rather than capability. It nevertheless took an extraordinary martial artist with great bravery to attack and subdue an armed man.

Several other kinds of martial arts were also regularly demonstrated in the Hundred Events and other public performances. These arts, particularly those involving weapons, were practical military skills that transferred well into the realm of sport or entertainment. The separate arts of using each different weapon were variously grouped together, reflecting different ideas of the martial arts themselves. Similarly, unarmed fighting skills were differentiated. Boxing, which also included kicking and all manner of unarmed striking, was clearly separated from wrestling. There were the "Five Weapons" 五兵: sword, spear, long sword, (*ji*) halberd, and staff[23] (though another text defines the Five Weapons as bow and crossbow, halberd, shield, sword and long sword, and armor).[24] Archery remained of paramount importance both in war and competition, as well as tripod lifting and the other pure strength exercises.

The level of distinction among the martial arts in the Han dynasty is remarkable, if for no other reason than it demonstrates an acute consciousness of separate skills with similar purposes. We have no mention of an individual who was capable in all of these martial arts, though it is likely that some professional fighters trained in several weapons as well as unarmed fighting. Soldiers, a category that encompassed most of the adult male population in the former Han dynasty, learned a set of martial arts so that they could serve in the army.

Boxing was practiced under an evolving set of names, as I discussed in the introduction. Various mentions of practitioners in the *Hanshu* (*History of the Former Han*) attest to its widespread practice as a form of fighting and competitive display. It also began to be written about, with the *Hanshu* listing a book, "*Boxing* 手搏 (*shoubo*)" in six chapters, in its bibliography section. This work is no longer extant, but it is the oldest known book on boxing. Boxing also entered the language with the expression "attacking naked blades empty handed 空手入白刀" or "attacking naked blades empty fisted 空拳入白刀." What may have initially been a description of the combination of skill and courage of an extraordinary boxer, or unarmed fighter (see Jin Midi introduced earlier), became an expression meaning simply extraordinary bravery.[25] There is some archaeological evidence showing images of men boxing in a variety of stances not entirely inconsistent with some modern practices.[26]

Trials of strength also continued as competitive performances and markers of martial prowess. The Hundred Events included stone turning and tripod lifting. Strength was directly connected to *qi* or physical power. Xiang Yu was not only described as "eight feet tall" but also strong enough to lift a tripod. He declared, "My strength uprooted mountains, my power covered the age." The close connection between strength, martial arts, and hunting is clearly expressed in a Han dynasty image on a stone portraying seven men in various activities. These men not only lift things like tripods, but also bear weapons, carry dead animals, and tie up tigers. This image seems to encompass a lifestyle or culture of powerful male activities.[27]

The long sword continued to be a popular weapon during the Han dynasty, giving rise to "Long sword guests" 劍客, or perhaps "Swordsmen," who made their living based on their fencing skills. Swordsmen like Qi Zhangzhong and Qu Chenghou established empire-wide reputations based on their fencing. Not surprisingly, many of these swordsmen could be found among the warriors camped on the border, where the major Han armies were posted to deal with incursions from the steppe. Li Lu reported that the extraordinarily talented swordsmen on the border were all from Jing and Chu (regions of south and central China).[28] Unfortunately, he does not explain why the best swordsmen came from these two regions. The widespread interest in long sword fencing led some scholars to write a fencing manual *The Way of the Long Sword* 劍道 in thirty-seven chapters, no longer extant.

Long sword fencing was both popular as an entertainment and extremely dangerous. The crown prince of the king of Huainan, for example, loved fencing and believed himself to be the best in the empire. When he heard that Lei Bei was an excellent fencer, he challenged him to a duel. Unfortunately for the crown prince, Lei proved the better fencer. The crown prince not only lost but was also wounded in the process. Fencing was a perfectly acceptable pursuit for a poet as well as an aristocrat. Of the famed *fu* poet Sima Xiangru, it was said, "In his youth, [he] loved to read books and study long sword fencing."[29]

A new form of the long sword appeared about this time. The Ring Pommel or Round Grip Sword 環柄刀, originally a cavalry weapon, came into widespread use during the early Han dynasty. This was a single-edged, straight sword, very similar in overall form to the long sword. There was no hilt to protect the hand or separate the grip from the blade. Archaeological finds of this form of weapon have lengths between 85 and 114 centimeters.[30] The advantage of the single-edged sword was that the back, or dull side, of the sword could be thickened to strengthen the weapon as a whole. It was a much sturdier weapon than the long sword, and much less prone to breaking. The sword retained its point but improved its ability to hack or cut. The heavier back also added weight to hacking swings. This form of sword spread to the rest of east and southeast Asia.

The sword began to displace the long sword on the battlefield, particularly when paired with a square or rectangular shield. Depictions of battles toward the end of the Han dynasty show bows and arrows, and swords and shields among the combatants. This is true of both the cavalry and infantry. The growing ubiquity of the sword within the military was a tribute to its greater durability – and probably its improved hacking ability as well. Most soldiers would not have been very skilled swordsmen and would have tended toward hacking at their opponents rather than using the sword point. Direct textual evidence for sword dances using the sword rather than the long sword does not appear until shortly after the Han dynasty, but the infiltration of the sword into the larger military sphere would have mandated some form of sword training, however rudimentary. Fencing with a sword was likely based, at least initially, on fencing with the long sword.

While short weapons like the long sword and sword held a critical place on the battlefield, in personal defense, and in entertainment, long weapons like the halberd and spear also maintained a place in these arenas. Military writers had long stressed the importance of combining long and short weapons, along with long-range missile weapons. Ordinary soldiers therefore learned to cooperate in interlocking formations that took advantage of the strengths of each weapon. Spears were vital for cavalry who needed the extra reach to strike men on foot. Conversely, spears were important for infantry to fend off cavalry. Spears and halberds, along with the less widely used wolf-tooth clubs and axes, became noteworthy weapons of individual warriors after the Han dynasty, though the arts of spear and halberd fighting had been around for centuries.

Finally, archery retained its place on the battlefield and in competitions. The bow was not the only weapon for missile fire, of course, as the crossbow had been around for several centuries in general use. The crossbow would never gain the symbolic or cultural cachet of the bow, and it remained a purely practical weapon for all of imperial Chinese history. The crossbow was much more closely tied to the battlefield and the army. With respect to archery practice, there were no changes during the Han

ILLUSTRATION 6. Mao spear head, Warring States period, Laufer Collection. Courtesy of the Field Museum and Ernest Caldwell. Photo by Ernest Caldwell.

dynasty. Arrows or quarrels for the crossbows increasingly shifted to steel heads, demonstrating greater production of steel and steel weapons. The trigger mechanism for the crossbow continued to be manufactured of bronze, with Han dynasty trigger mechanisms surrounded by a bronze box. Qin trigger mechanisms lacked the bronze box, and were simply slotted into the wooden stock.

The variety of weapons was matched by a variety of weapon dances and a better understanding of opposing weapon techniques. Weapon dances of all kinds presumably grew out of set training patterns, where an instructor would demonstrate how to use the weapon to a large number of soldiers or a smaller number of students. This, in turn, extended into the realm of performance as these same routines took on an aesthetic value. The necessity of learning how to oppose a variety of weapons was inherent in the military writers' discussion of the advantages of short and long weapons. There was a way, for example, that a halberd could best contend with a long sword. No weapon had an absolute advantage over another, of course, but each had a set of strengths and weaknesses that interacted dynamically with the opposing weapon's strengths and weaknesses. The deciding factor in any contest was the overall situation and the martial arts skill of the fighters.

CONCLUSION

The Qin and Han dynasties faced new problems with respect to the place of martial arts in Chinese society. Both were inheritors of Warring States period military systems that had wholly militarized both commoners and elites in the service of massive wars of conquest. The Qin unification did not immediately transform Chinese society into a peaceful, nonmartial state. Indeed, the repeated uprisings, wars, and conflicts of the following centuries would show that all efforts by the government to restrict access to martial arts training and weapons was never more than partially effective. Many elites would continue to maintain a harsh warrior ethos that sometimes belied their cultivated, literate personae. A proper aristocratic education included both literacy and martial arts.

Commoners also maintained considerable familiarity with the martial arts. Farmers were expected to render military service and practice the necessary skills for the first two centuries of the Han dynasty. It was only after the dynasty was reconstituted following the Wang Mang interregnum that military service for Han subjects was done away with. This was a change in politics and society, and the relationship of the ordinary subject to military service, but its actual effects are hard to gauge. There was certainly no lack of martial arts skills or even tactical military training in the second century CE when the first religiously inspired uprising irrupted.

The rebellion of the Yellow Turbans in 184 was tinged with Daoist ideas that spread throughout Han society. It presented a serious military threat to the dynasty for some time, defeating the imperial army repeatedly, before being put down in 185. It flared up again and again over the next few years, and was finally crushed in 205. The process of fighting the Yellow Turbans empowered a number of generals, setting up the closing act of the Han dynasty in 220, and opening act of the Three Kingdoms period (220–280) that immediately followed it. China once again entered a period of widespread warfare that divided the Han empire.

4

The Six Dynasties

The Six Dynasties period, running from the fall of the Han dynasty to rise of the Sui (589–618) and Tang dynasties (618–907), was marked by political division within the territory of the former Han empire. It has also been called the "Wei-Jin and Northern and Southern Dynasties period," in recognition of the separate governments in northern and southern China, or even simply the "Period of Disunion" or "Period of Division."[1] Both traditional and contemporary Chinese historians portray this period of division as an anomalous and unnatural detour from China's fundamental geopolitical unity rather than a centuries-long struggle to establish the Qin-Han political unity as a Chinese cultural norm. The Six Dynasties was particularly colored by the extensive involvement of non-Chinese forces from the northern steppes in the military, politics, and culture of the formerly Han empire's territories, mostly in north China. At various times during this period, non-Chinese ruled and immigrated into north China. Society and culture were the product of centuries of cultural inter-mixing between Chinese and various steppe practices. This was true of martial arts as well.

Steppe influence grew markedly in China in the later part of the Han dynasty. Tribal leaders and their cohorts of cavalrymen were regularly recruited as a group into Han armies to fight other steppe groups. Over time, steppe leaders and their forces were drawn into regional power struggles within the Han dynasty as well. Tribal leaders then shifted from working as mercenary commanders to having direct participation in the struggle for power. Steppe martial arts and fighting techniques responded to the preexisting Chinese martial arts, and Chinese martial arts responded to steppe martial arts as the respective sides interacted.[2]

This was not a simple matter of Chinese armies learning how to fight steppe armies, or steppe armies learning how to fight Chinese armies. In many battles, armies combined steppe cavalrymen with Chinese infantry, and they might fight similarly mixed opponents.

A new invention in the fourth century, the stirrup, shifted steppe and Chinese cavalry practice, though its effects off the battlefield were much less pronounced than in Europe. Heavily armored cavalry had appeared before the invention of the stirrup in Southwest Eurasia and Central Eurasia, but it appeared together with the stirrup in China.[3] Steppe cavalry used both charges of heavy cavalry, with men and horses completely armored, and mounted archery in battle. Heavy cavalry disappeared several centuries later, at the end of the sixth century and the beginning of the seventh. The reasons for this change, whether it was sudden or gradual, and when it actually took place, remain unclear. The available records are simply insufficient to answer these questions definitively. It might have been linked to the return of well-trained and armed infantry to the battlefield in the sixth century. As with the chariot, well-trained mass infantry could effectively neutralize heavy cavalry. Just as likely, cavalry practice changed as the regime controlling sedentary Chinese territory fought against steppe groups instead of groups within the Chinese ecumene fighting each other. Mobility was vital in coming to grips with steppe-based groups. Although the causes of this change are unclear, the change itself is not.

Martial arts were fundamental to distinguishing steppe people from the Chinese, in the eyes of both groups. The ability to ride a horse and shoot a bow while in motion, as well as dress and deportment, became an ethnographic marker of steppe cultural allegiance. Most steppe cavalrymen maintained these skills as part of their basic way of life, and then turned them into a military profession as their leaders increasingly involved themselves in Chinese politics. For the ordinary soldier, steppe martial practice could not be separated from their identity, and those men who shifted over to a sedentary lifestyle gave up both their skills and their identity. In north China, for most of the Six Dynasties, it was the various steppe groups that did all the serious fighting, while the Chinese attended to agriculture and other forms of production. Although the practice of martial arts on the battlefield was generally confined to steppe people in the north, in the south, northern Chinese émigrés brought martial skills with them and marked themselves out through those practices.

The steppe aristocracy often attempted to maintain both an imperial Chinese identity and a steppe identity. This required a very complex balancing of not only linguistic and behavioral displays but also accomplishment in the martial skills of both steppe and sedentary society. Intermarriage with Chinese elites created a hybrid martial culture that allowed for a spectrum of ethnically marked skills rather than widely separate categories. While most of the Chinese or steppe population functioned within only one culture, many elites even below the top level had to move between cultures regularly. Different groups understood the many necessary skills and behaviors differently, placing, for example, greater or lesser value on certain martial arts. Thus learning to practice particular martial arts directly shaped an individual's image and place in society at many separate and sometimes conflicting levels.

The main arc of martial arts development on the battlefield from the Six Dynasties to the early Tang dynasty was from steppe cavalry armies to conscripted infantry armies. Although steppe cavalry armies did most of the fighting, particularly in north China, in the Six Dynasties, local militias and security forces for local landlords, strongmen, and institutions were a regular part of Chinese society. Few governments were able to offer real protection for local communities from the depredations of bandits or other local security threats. Communities were forced to group together under some leader or other, train in fighting, and often build fortified positions where they could resist low-level military threats.[4] In a time of political and military turmoil anyone who had anything valuable had to be able to defend it to keep it safe.

THE NORTHERN AND SOUTHERN DYNASTIES

From the third to the sixth centuries the territory of what had been the Han dynasty was divided in a shifting pattern of kingdoms and dynasties. Non-Chinese rulers, officials, and families controlled most of the northern polities, though Chinese people did serve in government, intermarried with the ruling groups, and maintained considerable influence at the local level. A few states were even run by Chinese rulers. The designation "Six Dynasties" comes from the succession of regimes established in the south, with a capital at Jiankang (modern Nanjing), run by Chinese refugees from the north.[5] The northern émigrés controlled the army and court between 317 and 420, when a rebellion culminated in their displacement. From 420 until 589 southern politics was tumultuous with twenty-six rulers spread across four dynasties. Culture flowered in the south during this period despite, or perhaps because of, the political instability.

Northern China was similarly tumultuous, as the Xianbei pushed the Xiongnu, the group that had caused the Han dynasty so much trouble, south into Chinese territory. The Xiongnu settled along the frontier zone working for the Chinese regime as a bulwark against steppe aggression and for internal security. In 311, however, the Xiongnu sacked the capital city of Luoyang. Conditions had been deteriorating for some time in north China, with one official reporting in 307 that "the people had to wear armor to till the fields."[6] Across much of north China local elites fortified their estates and trained their dependents and family members in martial arts to defend themselves against bandits and raiders. Local elites were deeply involved in the martial arts and military matters. These measures did not challenge the powerful regimes controlling large armies, but they did limit the reach of those regimes into local society. A highly militarized and organized countryside could easily resist a government's ability to extract necessary resources. Under such conditions, the widespread practice of martial arts was a challenge and obstacle to the state.

The Tuoba, a part of the Xianbei confederation, emerged to unite the north in 439 under what is known as the Northern Wei dynasty (386–534), ultimately providing a century and half of stability. Chinese elites cooperated with Tuoba elites to maintain aristocratic privilege. Peace led to a number of changes in politics and society. The Northern Wei government became increasingly Chinese in its practices and customs, gradually alienating the Tuoba military garrisons guarding the state in the north. At the same time, the government began directly to apportion agricultural land to farmers in 477, drawing them away from local landlords. With generally more peaceful conditions, farmers no longer needed the protection of a local power holder, and fewer of them trained in martial arts. The Tuoba garrisons in the north were supplemented with Chinese criminals sentenced to serve on the frontier as a punishment.

The Northern Wei shattered after the Tuoba garrisons rebelled in the 520s. These soldiers found their martial skills devalued by a court that no longer practiced them. Martial arts had become a sign of low status, rather than of being a privileged member of the dominant ethnic group. The Northern Wei broke into an Eastern and a Western half in 534–5, with the Eastern Wei becoming the Northern Qi (550–77) and the Western Wei becoming the Northern Zhou (557–81). As we will see, it would be the Northern Zhou that would once again train and arm the Chinese farmers for war.

The period immediately following the end of the Han dynasty, known as the Three Kingdoms period – after the main contenders for power, the three states of Wei, Wu, and Shu – is one of the greatest mythological periods for martial arts in Chinese culture. This tri-lateral struggle was rendered into historical fiction during the Ming dynasty (1368–1644) in the *Romance of the Three Kingdoms* (*Sanguo Yanyi*). As in most cultures, the general understanding of a historical period derives from its fictional depiction rather than its historical records. While we will turn to the *Romance of the Three Kingdoms* as an example of Ming dynasty attitudes about the martial arts in Chapter 8, in this chapter our account will follow only the historical records.

The arch villain of the fictional account, Cao Cao (155–220), was a tremendously successful general and ruler. Cao and his sons were also

ILLUSTRATION 7. Zhuge Liang and Zhou Yu. From *Sanguozhi Tongsu Yanyi*, 1591.

accomplished martial artists and poets. But most of the sympathies of the fictional account lay with the state of Shu, where Liu Bei (161–223), its ruler, and his generals, Zhang Fei (167–221) and Guan Yu (160–219), were directed by the great strategist Zhuge Liang (181–234). Guan Yu's mythology would eventually elevate him to the officially recognized position of god of war a thousand years later, a place he still holds in Chinese culture. Zhuge Liang was transformed into the greatest strategist (as opposed to strategic writer, like Sunzi or Wuzi) in Chinese culture. Of course, most of the real contenders for power were warriors, and their martial arts practice was central to their survival or failure on the battlefield.

Battlefield weapon use was changing in the third century, continuing trends begun during the Han dynasty. Two particular trends are clearly visible in the Three Kingdoms period: the rise of the spear over the halberd, and the identification of horse archery with steppe martial practice. A third change, to the near exclusive use of the single-edged sword on the battlefield, occurred near the end or shortly after the Three Kingdoms period. These changes were incipient during the Three Kingdoms period, as the halberd was still in widespread use, and Chinese horse-archers had long been part of Chinese armies. The important distinction that needs to be made here is that these trends began before the introduction of the stirrup and heavily armored cavalry (contra Dien's argument cited above). Thus, martial practice was not driven by technology but by a set of choices of modes of combat that often were connected to the particular group most closely associated with that manner of fighting at that time.

Lin Boyuan explains the increasing use of the spear over the halberd as a product of steppe cavalry usage.[7] Cavalrymen used fairly long spears from horseback, "cavalry spears,"[8] to gain the reach to strike infantrymen. The infantry responded by also adopting long spears to increase their reach.

ILLUSTRATION 8. Bronze long sword, possibly Han Dynasty, Laufer Collection. Courtesy of the Field Museum and Ernest Caldwell. Photo by Ernest Caldwell.

Halberds in all shapes and sizes were still used by many famous warriors during the Three Kingdoms period, however, including one-handed halberds, and double-ended or paired halberds (both the term and context often leave this unclear). These idiosyncratic weapons appear primarily in the biographies of notable warriors, where their distinctiveness is a marker of the warrior's own outstanding martial arts, as well as a necessary literary device for physically or visually emphasizing the individual's prominence.

This wide range of variation reflects a later stage of the weapon development cycle. When a weapon is first produced, it comes in many forms as users search for a balance of form and practice. It then enters a mature stage where there is a fairly narrow range of form and practice, and the weapon's characteristics are well understood. We have seen this in earlier chapters with respect to swords in particular. After the uniform, mature stage, new variations sometimes develop as individuals seek customized forms that fit their own personal style of martial arts. A customized weapon may not only more closely match an individual's physical capabilities but it is also harder to defend against since it is not a standard weapon. The custom weapon emphasizes the user's separate martial arts capabilities by setting him or her apart from the general martial arts taught to all the soldiers. This is one of the reasons that later Chinese fiction regularly provided notable warriors with nonstandard weapons.

A Wei general, Zhang Liao, used a halberd while charging into the enemy ranks, killing "several tens of men and beheading two generals."[9] This appears to have been the standard form of the halberd. By contrast, one Zhang Rang, realizing he was being spied upon by his ruler in his own house, took up a one-handed halberd and began to perform a halberd dance. He then used the halberd to break a hole in the wall, and depart.[10] Presumably he did this suddenly rather than simply standing there hacking at a wall, and the action showed the power of his technique. The double halberd could be quite idiosyncratic: Dian Wei's double halberd reportedly weighed some eighty jin (somewhat over a hundred pounds).[11] It would have been made of solid steel and would have required immense strength and skill to be used effectively.

Yet the halberd was already disappearing from the battlefield in the third century as notable warriors as well as the rank-and-file soldiers turned to the spear. While Cao Cao was warned on one occasion of the difficulties of facing the strong soldiers of Guanxi who practiced with long spears,[12] an accomplished fighter and general, Gongsun Zan, could wield a two-bladed spear from horseback, and kill or wound several tens of the enemy when he and his horsemen charged their ranks.[13] Perhaps the most famous account of a skilled spearman, however, is the story of Zhang Fei single-handedly cowing a pursuing force at a broken bridge by standing there with his spear and challenging them: "I am Zhang Yide [Zhang Fei], you can come and together we'll fight to the death." Since no one had the courage to face him in individual combat, his army was able to escape.[14]

Some other notable warriors of the Three Kingdoms period demonstrated interesting combinations of weapon use that included the spear in individual combat, as one Chen An did: "[Chen] An held a seven foot great sword in his left hand, an eighteen foot snake spear in his right."[15] Chen was strong enough to use these two weapons in concert. An interesting comment on steppe women also shows the widespread use of the spear at that time; "The women bear halberds and wield spears, draw bows and carry arrows, how could they be so fierce?"[16] Here we see the attitude of the Chinese historian commenting on non-Chinese women who practiced martial arts. The steppe people were so fierce that their women bore the regular arms of the battlefield.

Archery grew in importance with the introduction of so many steppe warriors into north China. Both foot and horse archery were regularly practiced on training fields and archery platforms constructed for the purpose. The regular practice of archery became necessary as steppe warriors moved out of their steppe environment where archery was part of ordinary life. Emperors promoted the practice of archery by rewarding participants for hitting the target. Hunting was also a useful training activity in these martial arts. Archers were noted both for their strength (Liu Yao was said to be able to drive an arrow through an inch thick piece of iron)[17] and their accuracy (Murong Han shot an arrow through the ring of the pommel of a sword at one hundred paces).[18] Strength was also remarked upon with respect to the draw weight of an archer's bow. Another distinguishing accomplishment was to be able to shoot accurately to the left and right from horseback. Although the particular values of archery and horse archery were initially more characteristic of non-Chinese, over the course of the Six Dynasties they were absorbed into Chinese culture as well. Elite Chinese, of course, had to be taught these martial arts as a purely martial set of skills outside the daily need for them in the steppe.

Cao Pi, Cao Cao's son, noted that he began training in archery at the age of five *sui* (four or five years old) because times were tumultuous. By six *sui* he knew or understood archery and began to learn to ride a horse. When he was eight *sui* he was able to ride and shoot. As a consequence of this early training and his enjoyment of riding and shooting, he remained healthy and vigorous. He regularly shot at targets a hundred paces away while riding.[19] Cao Pi was an upper-class Chinese whose father had him trained in martial arts. To a great extent, his ability to perform those martial arts well required a certain acceptance of steppe values. Yet at the same time, Cao Pi, like his father and brother, was an accomplished Chinese poet. He was therefore one of those extraordinary individuals who excelled in both literary and martial pursuits.

Horse archery remained important during the period from the third to the seventh centuries and gradually became the dominant mode of steppe cavalry warfare over those centuries. This trajectory of development stands in stark contrast to that of cavalry in Europe. In China and the eastern part of the Eurasian steppe, the stirrup arrived with heavily armored cavalry. Although heavily armored cavalry charges predated the stirrup elsewhere, it greatly facilitated the practice. Archery from horseback also predated the arrival of the stirrup, though it similarly facilitated that practice. Yet, increasingly, mobile horse archery, rather than charges by heavily armored cavalry, became the preferred battlefield practice. Armored cavalrymen still charged into the ranks of infantry or other cavalry forces, but mobility, rather than weight, was valued.

The change in cavalry practice is particularly noteworthy for several reasons. First, it demonstrates a decision on the part of steppe and Chinese cavalrymen to change their mode of warfare. Second, the move away from charges of heavily armored cavalry was a permanent change in the mode of Chinese and steppe warfare. Third, the change in practice reflected a sharp change in the martial ethos of both steppe and Chinese cavalry. Cavalry would continue to play an important role on the Chinese battlefield until the nineteenth century. Indeed, some scholars have not only assumed that steppe cavalrymen had always been exclusively horse-archers but that this mode of cavalry warfare was a natural and inevitable extension of their society and culture. This was clearly not the case and provides another example of how martial arts has been used to distinguish, characterize, and ultimately generalize about a culture or society without taking due cognizance of the choices and changes in the martial arts over time.

The reasons that steppe cavalrymen moved away from heavy cavalry charges in the sixth and early seventh centuries are not clear. I speculated earlier that one reason may have been the rise of disciplined mass infantry forces. Even if this is true, the shift away from heavy cavalry is remarkable from a cultural rather than a military perspective. In Europe, for example, heavy cavalry remained on the battlefield even as new modes of warfare made it less and less effective. The attachment of the aristocratic class to heavy cavalry as a system of martial arts and warfare that distinguished it from lower-born people led to various innovations designed to maintain the military value of heavy cavalry on the battlefield. Vestigial forms of heavy cavalry in Europe, even when it was no longer made up of completely armored knights, continued in attenuated forms into the nineteenth century. Just as important, the ideal of the knight and his methods of fighting have continued over time even into popular culture today.

Another possibility, suggested by David Graff, is that in the Sui and Tang dynasties the chief concern of their respective armies was dealing with steppe groups where mobility was most important. A shift in military practice for purely military reasons is admirable, but the strong steppe cultural affinities of parts of the Sui and Tang ruling elites surely helped in this shift. The most effective response to fast-moving steppe cavalry forces was to create one's own fast-moving cavalry forces. Slow-moving infantry and extensive fortifications offered only passive defense of imperial territory and offered no possibility of offensive operations into the steppe.

Curiously, heavy cavalry not only ceased to be the decisive battlefield arm in China but it also disappeared entirely from warfare. Cavalry in the Chinese context came exclusively to mean horse-archers. These horse-archers were sometimes well armored, particularly those with access to manufacturing centers, and they were prepared to charge into an enemy formation after it had been softened up with missile fire. But the idea or even ideal of a direct force on force clash between heavy cavalrymen no longer existed. Cavalry forces strove for mobility, flexibility, and the development and exploitation of opportunities. Later Chinese writers sometimes complained that steppe cavalry forces refused to stand and fight, while Chinese infantry forces vainly sought to bring them to battle.

Another possibility is that the heavy cavalry of the Six Dynasties period was anomalous. Han dynasty armies frequently failed to force battle on steppe armies, who retreated before superior Han armies or otherwise outmaneuvered them. An ethos of heavy cavalry arose after the Han and operated for several centuries before disappearing completely. In its time it was effective, at least when opposing similar forces. The martial arts involved preexisted the use of heavy cavalry in battle and continued to exist after heavy cavalry were no longer used.

The third trend in weapons use that had begun during the Han and became fixed in Chinese martial arts soon after the Three Kingdoms period was the use of the single-edged sword as virtually the only close combat weapon. The sword could be used alone or, as it was most often

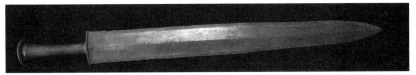

ILLUSTRATION 9. Bronze long sword, possibly Han Dynasty, Laufer Collection. Courtesy of the Field Museum and Ernest Caldwell. Photo by Ernest Caldwell.

used on the battlefield, paired with a shield. Straight, double-edged swords, or long swords (as I have designated them in this book), remained in limited use as personal weapons of self-defense or performance weapons. They were generally lighter weight and less durable than single-edged, curved swords. The long sword was a more elegant weapon, and the weapon of choice for female sword dance performers, officials, and some expert warriors.

Fencing with a long sword was still taught in the Three Kingdoms period, and occasionally had practical applications. Tian Chou was described as someone who "liked to read books, and good at long sword fencing."[20] Cui Yan "liked long sword fencing, and loved military affairs."[21] Xu Shu, as a young man, "liked [knight] errantry and long sword fencing."[22] "When All under heaven was in chaos, Lu Su studied long sword fencing and horse archery ... discussed martiality and practiced martial arts."[23] When mutinous soldiers attacked the first emperor of Wei in his tent, "[He] with a long sword in his hand killed several tens of men."[24]

A single-edged sword is a more durable weapon in general and much more effective in cutting or slashing attacks, something discussed in the previous chapter. By shifting to a cutting weapon for close fighting, the art of fencing for the vast majority of practitioners must also have changed. If we recall the difficulties that the first emperor of China, Qin Shihuangdi, had in drawing his long sword when attacked by the assassin Jing Ke, it is also clear that the very manner of unsheathing a curved sword in close quarters is different, and easier, than unsheathing a straight sword. This would have changed dress and deportment, as men who wore a sword established ways to sit, stand, and ride that allowed them ready access to their weapon.

Long swords were still worn as part of court dress by emperors, courtiers, and officials. Indeed, it was pointed out in the *Songshu* that the long sword was the weapon of the ruler and that "from the ruler [down] to the gentlemen (*shi*), all wear long swords. Since the Jin dynasty [they] began to use wooden long swords in place of long swords and swords."[25] The *Jinshu* account of the same issue is slightly more detailed: "In the Han regulations, from the Son of Heaven to the hundred officials, there were none who did not wear a long sword. Afterward, it was only in court that they brought long swords. In the generation of the Jin they began to substitute using wood, the aristocrats only used jade heads, the mean also used pearls, gold and silver, and tortoise-shell as engraved ornaments."[26] We see here a clear separation between the real warrior and the court in weaponry. Self-defense at court, at least, was no longer important. At the same time, however, the sword, even a wooden one, remained an important symbol of martial orientation. Court officials and the ruler should be armed, if only ritually. And the ritual weapon of choice was not only made of wood, it was a long sword, an already outdated weapon. This may have been an expression of persistent tradition or an effort to emphasize that the courtiers' weapons were not really for combat and they were not martial artists. Of course, a de-emphasis on martial deportment could also undermine army morale. Conversely, the victorious emperor Wu of the Northern Zhou wore military clothing even in his capital to enhance his martial demeanor. He also personally participated in the fighting that so improved the fortunes of his dynasty.[27]

The long sword also persisted in sword dances and gained a new use as an element of religious Daoist rituals. Several men were noted for being accomplished long sword dancers when young, as one characteristic among many admirable qualities. One man was credited as pursuing knight-errantry and liking to patronize or entertain long sword guests when he was young. At least in some sense, then, wandering martial artists were still around to entertain. As religious Daoism developed, religiously empowered long swords also appeared. This use of long swords continued in religious Daoism in both physical and graphic forms up through portrayals in twentieth-century movies.[28]

The sword, as opposed to the long sword, became so ubiquitous that it did not warrant particular notice. Unless otherwise noted, all soldiers were assumed to be armed with swords. Much more rarely seen are references to staffs or clubs. On one occasion General He Ji armed five thousand strong, well-trained soldiers with staffs when he needed to destroy a large number of mountain bandits. His tactic was so effective that his troops killed some ten thousand bandits (somewhat exaggerated).[29] A staff was understood to be a very effective weapon; as described by one text, "studying the seven foot staff techniques, one can face naked blades, or handle large halberds."[30]

While weaponry changed, unarmed fighting techniques remained important. Wrestling competitions were still held, in some parts of north China four times a year. A new kind of contest of strength appeared, a form of tug-of-war. This had its antecedents in individual contests of strength and in the group training of soldiers and militiamen. Wrestling grew in importance with the large numbers of steppe peoples now resident in north China. Steppe enthusiasm for wrestling met the preexisting and well-developed Chinese tradition of wrestling, leading to even more frequent public competitions.

Boxing received less attention in the Six Dynasties period, though it clearly remained in use. This was partly a cultural trend, with steppe warriors more concerned with wrestling, and partly because the period was one in which war on the battlefield dominated most fighting men's consciousness. Skill in boxing, as well as bravery and ferocity, was demonstrated by men like Ke Xiling, who, at the age of seventeen, encountered a tiger and subdued it bare-handed with boxing.[31] Several other warriors, like Yi Huan and Er Zhuzhao, are described, in addition to having skills in riding and shooting and extraordinary strength, as able to fight wild beasts bare-handed.[32] The idea of subduing a tiger bare-handed even led to an incident when soldiers who found a tiger on their drill field were ordered to capture it empty-handed. They succeeded, but at the cost of several lives.[33]

Men noted for their boxing skills were almost always also recognized for their great physical strength. There was a clear connection between boxing, strength, agility, and bravery. Xiu You was brave and powerful, and so skilled in striking that no one was able to get close to him.[34] Boxers were also capable of killing people with their strikes, a persistent description used to emphasize great skill and power. Particularly in a time and place when many men were armed, the ability to kill someone bare-handed was impressive. And while it was brave to charge into an enemy's ranks in full armor and carrying a weapon, it was another order of bravery entirely to fight animals or men unarmed.

WOMEN MARTIAL ARTISTS IN THE SIX DYNASTIES

Most soldiers, and hence most people practicing martial arts, were men. But in the Six Dynasties, as in earlier periods, many women also practiced martial arts. Lin Boyuan attributes the prevalence of martial women during the Six Dynasties to the influence of steppe culture. The maternal lines of descent were more important among steppe society, giving women greater political power. Just as significantly, steppe people had a culture wherein women practiced martial arts. Steppe women trained to ride and shoot were able to lead troops in battle, as some did, and to have considerable political influence.[35] Steppe women fought in the same manner that men did, with the same weapons.

Chinese women also practiced martial arts, though it is unclear whether this practice had anything to do with steppe influence. The ruler of Wu, Sun Quan, during the Three Kingdoms period, was always nervous when he visited his wife because she had over a hundred female attendants all armed with swords.[36] These weapons were not for show alone, and the fact that these women carried swords, not long swords, in the Three Kingdoms period alerts us to the martial atmosphere Sun Quan's wife established for her boudoir. The daughter of Xun Song, Xun Guan, at the age of thirteen led several tens of troops in breaking out of a surrounded city.[37] These were all women either of the upper class or living in the environment of the upper classes. Not surprisingly, we lack information on ordinary women. Chinese women did not regularly participate in war or fighting of any kind, but some were capable of it. Chinese influence on those steppe people who settled in China did gradually lead to a more gendered separation of women from martial and political practice.

The complexities of warfare and the place of martial arts in Six Dynasties' society are exemplified in the poetic account of Mulan, a name familiar to modern Westerners. The particularities of martial arts are not discussed in the poem for a number of reasons. First, of course, the audience for the poem would be well aware of the martial arts practiced by soldiers. These skills were all around them and were commonplace. Much of the power of the poem rests on the ordinary service of Mulan. Second, there was no poetic or literary tradition of describing such practices. The poem is elegant in its indirect discussion of what was required for war. Third, Mulan is not a notable martial artist. Like most people who practiced martial arts in the military, it is her service rather than any particular skill in fighting that is admirable. She served and performed martial arts as a duty, not for personal glory.

MULAN

The anonymous author of a poem about a young woman named Mulan, who took her father's place in the army, initiated an evolving mythological narrative that has continued to the present day. Here we are only concerned with its place in the culture and martial arts during the Northern and Southern dynasties period, but it is worth noting that Mulan's story was preserved, expanded, and elaborated upon into the twentieth century. It has also jumped cultures into popular modern Western entertainment, demonstrating both its flexibility as a tale and its enduring attraction.

The continued resonance of the character of Mulan cannot be separated from her mixture of filial regard for her father coupled with her martial service in the army. She becomes a veteran soldier who turns down an official post after ten years of campaigning. Her story assumes not only that an adult male was subject to military service but also that a woman was perfectly capable of performing that service. Women were not subject to military service because they were women, not because they were incapable of the martial arts required of a soldier. Also, it is clear that the Mulan of the original poem is not Chinese, based upon her purchase of a horse and horse accoutrement to go to war (serving in the cavalry being characteristic of steppe culture, or at least indicative of being part of a Chinese family who practiced steppe culture), and that the ruler she serves is not a Chinese ruler. Yet the poem was written in Literary Chinese and emphasizes the critical Chinese value of filial piety.

Mulan does not lay claim to particular martial arts skill, though she successfully performs her duties over a decade of service. Setting aside the conceit of her sex remaining disguised for so long and in such close quarters with men, we see an idea of army life that valorizes extended military service and martial service to the ruler. Yet her disguised sex and subsequent offer of a government post argue that she was not, in fact, a common soldier, but rather a higher-ranking member of a steppe community living in China. This would also explain her knowledge of martial arts, something unmentioned in the poem but virtually assumed by her ability to serve in her father's place. Among many steppe groups, women learned and practiced the skills of riding and shooting. The ballad was written in Chinese to satisfy an ethnically hybrid ruling class who functioned in both steppe and Chinese culture.

The ballad itself is worth recounting (in part):

> . . .
> Last night I saw the draft list –
> The Khan's mustering a great army;
> The armies' rosters ran many rolls,
> Roll after roll held my father's name!
> And Father has no grown-up son,
> And I've no elder brother!
> So I offered to buy a saddle and horse
> And campaign from now on for Father.

In the eastern market she bought a steed,
At the western a saddle and cloth;
In the southern market she bought a bridle,
At the northern a long whip;

. . .

Hastening thousands of miles to decisive battles,
Crossing mountains and passes as if flying!
The northern air carries the sentry's drum,
A wintry sun glints off her coat of mail.

After a hundred battles the generals are dead,
Ten years now, and the brave soldiers are returning!

The poem goes on to describe Mulan's rejection of an official post and her desire simply to return home. Once home, she removes her campaigning clothing, does her hair and makeup, and dresses in her female robes. It is only then that her comrades in arms realize that she is a woman.[38] Of course, the reference to makeup reinforces the notion that she was of the upper classes (who could afford such luxuries). The army she served in fought on the northern border, not within the settled agricultural lands of China. Like Fu Hao, the fictional Mulan fought northern enemies of the ruler without giving up her core femininity. Even so, Mulan, unlike Fu Hao, had to hide her sex and change her clothes (and roles) to resume her place as a female. Fu Hao openly performed all of her roles; by the Northern and Southern dynasties period, a woman, even in fiction, had to distinguish between a martial, or at least military, role in a masculine realm, and the role of a woman.

THE RETURN OF CHINESE INFANTRY

The ethnic split between those who fought and those who farmed was most clearly explained by Gao Huan in the sixth century:

To the Xianbei he would say, "The Han are your slaves. The men till for you; the women weave for you. They provide you with grain and silk so that you are warm and well-fed. For what reason do you bully them?" The Han Chinese were treated to a different speech. "The Xianbei are your retainers [*ke*]. For a single measure of your grain and single length of your silk they attack bandits so that you are safe. For what reason do you regard them as a scourge?"[39]

But while Gao Huan's regime, the Eastern Wei, was well supplied with cavalry, his opponents were not.

Gao Huan himself exemplified the fluidity of family and culture. Gao was descended from a Chinese family, grew up on the frontier where he was steeped in Xianbei culture, and married a Xianbei woman. His modes of warfare were Xianbei, not Chinese, but many of his subjects were Chinese. He fought over lands that were primarily Chinese: inhabited by Chinese people living a sedentary agricultural life. At the same time, he drew strength from his steppe culture and the frontiersmen who moved between the steppe and the sedentary worlds of north China. Martial arts formed part of this cultural matrix, though his choice of military methods was also based upon the availability of cavalrymen.

This is not to say that Gao Huan's army was entirely composed of steppe cavalrymen. Gao drew upon some local Chinese troops for his army, but he had strong reservations about their value on the battlefield.[40] Some of the Chinese troops were militiamen brought in from powerful Chinese families who supported Gao. Very few of these soldiers would have been trained to fight in mass formations against large numbers of well-trained steppe cavalrymen. Since most of Gao's troops were steppe cavalrymen, he would tend to choose battlefields and campaign strategies that played to those strengths. Another group of Chinese troops were men directly recruited by Gao's government in the 550s. These Chinese "braves" (*yongfu*) were brought into the army if their courage and martial arts met Gao's Xianbei standard. Some Chinese farmers were also inducted into the army to fulfill their state labor service. It was extremely difficult to integrate these Chinese troops with their very different martial skills and capabilities into the Eastern Wei army.

At a fundamental level, the split in martial arts practice and the inability of the Eastern Wei to integrate fully Chinese martial practice with steppe martial practice mirrored a cultural and political fracture line. This separation, as Gao Huan himself demonstrated, was cultural and grew out of ethnic identity. How one fought, the kind of martial arts one practiced, and the place of someone adept at martial arts in that person's own society was culturally determined. An individual could learn a different system of martial arts, along with deportment and dress, and, at least in North China, shift between cultures. Yet as shown by Gao's two-faced admonition cited earlier, the relative value of farming versus fighting was perceived quite differently by the two sides of the steppe-Chinese cultural divide. Some Chinese did fight, however, and presumably many steppe people were more inclined to tend their herds and avoid fighting.

Gao Huan had sufficient steppe cavalry to continue the preferred mode of warfare of the succession of regimes that had ruled north China for centuries; his opponent to the west had to find another source of military power. While it is clear that local Chinese power holders, and perhaps other landlords of non-Chinese culture, maintained some level of security forces or militias, the amount of participation of those forces in the Western Wei army is less certain. Local security forces or ordinary farmers were brought into the Western Wei army in the middle of the sixth century out of sheer necessity. Since the Western Wei–Northern Zhou army was the foundation of what would become the Sui and then Tang imperial army, the origin of these infantry forces has been the subject of considerable academic interest.

Yuwen Tai, Gao Huan's Western Wei opponent, found himself cut off from the steppe manpower that supplied the Eastern Wei. Where the Eastern Wei had used its Chinese subjects in the military in a very limited fashion, the Western Wei was forced to recruit its Chinese subjects in large numbers. Yuwen Tai, like Gao Huan, drew upon the preexisting local militias to bolster his forces. But the Western Wei could neither limit the number of Chinese troops it recruited nor accept that they would play a subordinate role in any fighting. The Western Wei government was forced to engage in the tricky process of drawing in local strongmen, who often differed very little from bandits, because they were accomplished martial artists and military leaders, giving them official sanction to fight and also somehow gaining control over them.

Initially, the main Western Wei method for incorporating bands of strongmen or local leaders was to invest them with official government titles or positions. This incorporated them within the regular hierarchical command structure, either civil or military, and gave them a direct stake in maintaining the power of the government. In some cases this was simply a matter of recognizing the existing local power structure; an individual or head of a powerful family who had established local control by force was made part of the government. Martial skill thus led directly to political power. A man who could recruit fighters was obviously someone worth employing.

A middle rank of men trusted by the Western Wei rulers on the one hand, and able to recruit and gain the trust of local strongmen on the other, were carefully selected to be in charge of these new forces. Perhaps just as important, this forged political ties between local Chinese society and the steppe rulers of the Western Wei. These initial forays into co-opting the martial power of the Chinese may or may not have contributed directly to the creation of the "territorial soldiery" or *fubing*, the military system that was so important to the Sui and early Tang dynasties. In 550, the Twenty-four Armies are first mentioned, with an initial strength of about 50,000 men, and over 100,000 by the 570s. Scholars do not agree on the source of manpower for these early armies, with some arguing for the incorporation of local troops into these formations and others for the direct recruitment of the Chinese farming population. Whichever is true, over the succeeding decades, the Twenty-four Armies came under the direct control of the emperor and became directly recruited from the Chinese population.

An exaggerated account of the 574 recruitment of Chinese commoners into the army, in return for freedom from tax and labor requirements, states: "after this half the Chinese became soldiers." At least some part of this army rotated fifteen days of guard duty with fifteen days of combat training. Some, however, seem to have remained at home part of the time actually farming. In any case, this represented a massive expansion of martial arts training among the Chinese populace. As the size of the army grew, so too did the number of adult males trained in martial arts. Just as important, the profession of arms was made into a respectable practice among the Chinese. Northern Chinese society became deeply infused with martial arts and military training; it was no longer the exclusive province of steppe cavalrymen or local thugs.

The multi-ethnic armies of the Western Wei, which was replaced by the Northern Zhou around 556, were now mostly disciplined infantry armies. Steppe cavalry was still important, but the backbone of the army was its infantry. Just as significantly, the active recruitment of the Chinese population into the now honorable profession of arms tied the population more closely to the government and allowed that government to exploit the inherent power of the Chinese population. Chinese infantry were now composed of some of the best elements of society, rather than the worst, and bypassed local strongmen to harness military power to central government purposes. Martial arts now served government, rather than local, goals.

CONCLUSION

Over the course of the Six Dynasties period the kinds of weapons used and martial arts practiced in China shifted markedly. Just as important, the men who practiced those martial arts, the conditions under which they practiced them, and the place in society of those men also changed considerably. The Han dynasty social order changed, as did the cultural background of the rulers of north China, and the social and political organization of south China. Over the course of the four centuries from the fall of the Han dynasty to the rise of the Sui and Tang dynasties, different peoples from the steppe and within the Chinese ecumene circulated in unprecedented numbers, generating great turmoil as well as great cultural flourishing. In short, it is a hard period to simplify.

The most important changes in martial arts would remain in place until fully modern military practice in the nineteenth century rendered them obsolete. The sword pushed out the long sword as the primary close combat weapon, the spear displaced the halberd as the main polearm, and, by the end of the period, heavy cavalry yielded precedence to horse archery aided by stirrups. There were some notable individual exceptions to the first two of these changes, and this would continue to be the case in the succeeding centuries. Individual martial artists sometimes chose idiosyncratic weapons, but the common soldier and the majority of martial artists relied upon swords and spears. Archery in general remained a critical martial skill, though the non-Chinese engagement with archery as a martial art had different cultural implications than had existed within the earlier Chinese cultural context. Archery for Confucius was different from archery for a steppe warrior.

Also important, the people who practiced martial arts went through a series of changes and regional variations with the influx of steppe warriors. Northern émigrés went south and temporarily formed a group marked by their military orientation. The remaining Chinese in the north sometimes separated themselves from the warrior class and sometimes joined it by learning steppe martial arts. Local strongmen all over China formed bands of men trained in martial arts that were effective below the battlefield level. Prolonged exposure to Chinese culture also changed steppe martial arts as it changed steppe culture. Some steppe aristocratic women, for example, gradually moved away from practicing martial arts. There was a dynamic intermixing of skills and cultures, and over time, individuals could learn parts of these formerly tightly connected suites. Chinese soldiers, for example, could learn to ride and shoot without adopting steppe culture.

The major political and military shift that was closely, if not conclusively causally, related to the unification of China in the sixth century, was the large-scale recruitment of Chinese commoners into the army. This new force of infantry connected Chinese farmers directly to the state through honorable military service. Battlefield martial arts became a widespread skill among ordinary Chinese men, reversing the Later Han dynasty shift away from universal military service. Steppe martial practice was still important on the battlefield, however, and not surprisingly, the ruling group that emerged to unify China was military and a cultural hybrid of Chinese and steppe.

5

The Sui and Tang Dynasties

The Sui Dynasty unified China in 589 under a Chinese emperor for the first time since the fall of the Han Dynasty. Yang Jian, the founding emperor, posthumously known as Sui Wendi, began his career as a high official under the Northern Zhou and was actually the father-in-law of the last Northern Zhou emperor. Yang had worked dutifully for the Yuwen imperial house, earning a Xianbei surname as a mark of favor, in addition to marrying his daughter to the emperor. Yang seized power soon after a six-year-old child succeeded to the throne, and he exterminated most of the Yuwen clan. He established the Sui dynasty on 4 March 581. Yang was remarkably successful in quickly consolidating his power and shifting over to the conquest of southern China. By 589, Sui navies and armies had defeated every polity in the Chinese ecumene.

Yang Jian himself, though a member of the northern Chinese aristocracy, was fully conversant with Xianbei culture. He was also a devout Buddhist, who hoped that his religion would help unite his empire, while at the same time promoting Confucianism to aid in governing society. Even Daoism was not wholly neglected. Yang reorganized the government institutions he had inherited in order to centralize power. His interest in controlling the reins of power extended even to the Buddhism he supported; he was careful to regulate the Buddhist clergy. He and his son, Yang Guang, posthumously known as Sui Yangdi, understood the need to rule by means other than force of arms alone. They also knew that they had to gain firm control over the soldiers and armies if they were to stay in power.

The Sui government instituted two policies after conquering southern China that had important consequences for martial arts as well as governing. In 590, Yang Jian ordered soldiers and their families to be settled on farmland and registered with the civilian population. This removed them from the immediate control of their military commanders and gave them a way to provide for their own upkeep. Local military authorities maintained a list of these soldiers who were now farming so that they could be called up as needed. Some of these units served in rotation at the capital. Thus soldiers and their martial arts were broadly dispersed into the rural countryside.

The second important policy of the Sui was instituted in 595. On 12 April of that year, the government gathered all the weapons in its territory and forbade the manufacture of any new arms (outside of its own arsenals, of course). The Guanzhong area, the original territorial core of the Sui, was exempted from the weapons prohibition. This was an attempt to demilitarize the populace in general and to prevent any organized, armed, large-scale uprisings. Given the centuries of warfare that had preceded this policy, it was unlikely to have been wholly successful, but it was a start. Weapons and the martial arts that made them effective were widespread in society. Blacksmiths all over China would have been similarly experienced in manufacturing weapons. The 595 edict attempted to maintain martial capabilities in the Sui core and remove them from the less politically reliable parts of the empire.

Yang Jian's 590 order was instrumental in transforming what had been the Twenty-four Armies of the Northern Zhou into what would become the *fubing* (territorial soldiery). Yang Guang took further steps in 605 to diminish the power of regional commanders by completely abolishing positions that combined civil and military authority in a locality. Henceforth, all troops were controlled by the central government directly. This military system was spread from the northwest to the south and east both to draw in the Chinese elites in those areas and to recruit men with military skills. The path of career advancement through military accomplishment removed a martial threat to the state and placed it in service to state power.

All of these organizational processes strengthened the Sui state but were not enough to preserve it when Yang Guang overreached in a massive attack on Koguryo (a state in what is now north and central Korea) from 611 to 612. Despite enormous losses and growing banditry in China, the emperor resolved to try again in 613. This time a rebellion in his rear cut short a campaign that was not progressing well. Yang Guang's fortunes continued to decline, and his own troops killed him in 618. Constant campaigning had weakened the Sui state in men and material. The collapse of Sui authority starting about 612 unleashed a familiar set of players in the struggle for power. David Graff describes these as "bandit-rebels whose activities were of a 'predatory' nature, local elites who organized forces to protect their communities from the depredations of the bandits, and local Sui officials, who now enjoyed unaccustomed freedom of maneuver as a result of the weakness of the center."[1]

Despite the brevity of the Sui Dynasty, and the intensity of the struggle for power that followed its disintegration, China did not fall back into divisions of the Six Dynasties period for very long. It only took about a decade for Li Yuan, posthumously known as Tang Gaozu (r. 618–626), a member of the northwestern aristocracy and former Sui official, to establish the Tang Dynasty and destroy all his rivals.[2] Violence and martial arts were everywhere, as vast numbers of men were recruited or drafted into armies and armed bands of all sizes. The contest was a massive military contest won by Li Yuan. One of his most important generals was his second son, Li Shimin, posthumously known as Tang Taizong (r. 626–649), who would exemplify the martial traditions of both the steppe and the Chinese.

Li Shimin had begun his career as a military commander as early as 617 when he was in his late teens. He was both literate and trained in the martial arts, as would be expected from someone of his aristocratic background. These were necessary skills for administration and leadership in battle. On the literary side, he was familiar with the Confucian Classics and some of the histories, could compose functional poetry, and could do reasonably good calligraphy (being particularly known for the "Flying White" style, a style characterized by speed and energy). On the martial arts side, he was quite capable in riding, shooting, and fencing. Moreover, he was an apparently enthusiastic participant in combat, "fighting until his sword was broken and his sleeves filled with blood."[3] Li Shimin later claimed that he had personally killed more than a thousand men over the course of his military career.[4] This may have been an exaggeration, though not necessarily a gross one, but it does make clear the sort of martial values an aristocrat and ruler thought valuable in legitimating his political power. The early Tang rulers were men who had directed battles and took part in them.

The Tang imperial family was itself partly non-Chinese, both culturally and through marriage. Tang culture was also the product of centuries of cultural intermixing between Chinese and various steppe practices. This was true of martial arts as well. The ruling house of the Tang dynasty initially exemplified this hybrid martial culture, and it is during this time that civil oriented elites began to formulate a clear split between civil and military values (a split that may also have had ethnic undertones). At the same time, the middle Tang saw the collapse of the *fubing* system as the

山西雁
徐良
白眉表
吳豪
俠性
藏膽大心
小過於
乃翁

ILLUSTRATION 10. Theatrical representation of the hero Xu Liang, wielding a single-edged curved sword. From *Xiaowuyi* (*Zhonglie Xiaowuyi Zhuan*), 1890.

basis for its armies, the concomitant distribution of martial skills among the populace it had required, and the rise of a professional class of soldiers.

As powerful as the Tang dynasty was militarily in its early years, the development of professional soldiers in the early eighth century and the return to prominence of steppe generals within the Tang army in the later part of the seventh century led to increasing tensions between the army and the imperial court. These tensions nearly shattered the Tang dynasty during the An Lushan Rebellion (755–63). Even after the rebellion was suppressed, the relative peace of the early Tang dynasty could not be fully restored. Power once again devolved onto regional strongmen, who balanced regional military and political power against the local forces beneath them and the central authorities of the imperial court above them. Military force was the direct measure of political influence. An ambitious young man skilled in the martial arts and capable of leading men in battle could rise to great heights of power from humble beginnings. The prospects for an educated man without aristocratic pedigree were far more limited, though considerably less risky. Tang imperial power essentially collapsed with the Huang Chao Rebellion (875–84). Generals, warlords, and local strongmen of all stripes arose in this environment to fight for power. Ultimately, the Tang dynasty degenerated into the same environment of armed chaos from which it had emerged.

THE TANG MILITARY

Most of the early Tang army was composed of infantrymen, drafted into service under the *fubing* system. *Fubing* units served in the capital, typically for a one-month tour, chosen on a rotating basis calculated by distance from the capital. A given unit might serve two tours in the capital each year. While a *fubing* unit could be sent to the frontier for up to three years, some units went decades without a frontier deployment. This system, like the one inherited by the Qin and Han, owed its development to the preceding centuries of warfare rather than being a distinctly Tang innovation. As we saw in the previous chapter, its emergence in the late sixth century was tied to the need to supplement the limited number of North Eurasian cavalry of the Western Wei, soon to become the Northern Zhou, regime in its struggle against the Eastern Wei. The shift away from armies composed exclusively of steppe cavalry, whether Xianbei, Gaoju Türk, or some other group, to armies of Chinese infantrymen was a sea change in martial enfranchisement. Soldiers in the *fubing* system farmed when not called up for duty and maintained their martial arts skills year-round. A *fubing* soldier was supposed to practice archery every day. In the field, he was armed with sword, spear, bow and arrows, and wore a suit of armor. During the winter, *fubing* units drilled and trained together to maintain battlefield skills and check on the martial arts of the soldiers as a whole.

Men were enrolled for *fubing* service at twenty-one and continued in this status to the age of sixty. The percentage of male population actually serving in this capacity varied across China, from zero, in areas that for a variety of reasons had no *fubing* units, to essentially 100 percent in areas on the northwest frontier. In the latter areas, martial arts practice would have been virtually universal among all adult males. Martial arts skills thus marked not only the different threat levels of a region but also cultural traditions that grew out of a locality's relationship to the central government. Because the martial arts of the *fubing* had to integrate with other *fubing* units on campaign or on duty in the capital, their martial arts would have necessarily been uniform across the empire. While the prevalence of those skills varied from place to place, the content of the skills was the same.

A minority of *fubing* units were cavalry, with most cavalry forces provided by steppe groups who served under their own leader. While members of the Tang imperial family and aristocrats like them, at least in the early part of the dynasty, spanned the Chinese-steppe/Türkic cultural and martial divide, in the army modes of fighting were closely linked to ethnic identity. The Chinese were infantry, and the Türks or other steppe groups were cavalry. After the initial establishment of Tang authority throughout the empire, the military problems shifted to the northern border. While *fubing* units were very effective on campaign, they were relatively slow-moving infantry designed to serve for short periods of time. On the border, however, problems with steppe groups could be endemic, far ranging, and fast moving. The best response for these problems was standing bodies of light cavalry.

Tang light cavalry marked the final shift over from the heavy cavalry of the Six Dynasties. Even in the Sui, heavy cavalry, with both horse and rider armored, remained in use within China to break through infantry formations. In the battles following the Sui collapse, however, Tang cavalry lightened its load by removing armor from the horses. Tang cavalry formations might still charge into infantry, but this was usually done on a vulnerable flank or rear, or when the infantry was weak or in disorder. Light cavalry was faster and offered a wider range of tactical and strategic uses than heavy cavalry. It was also able to engage and pursue light steppe cavalry forces.

Once the dynasty was established, however, the military problems facing it changed. The need to maintain garrisons on the borders clashed directly with the *fubing* system, since the *fubing* units could not stay in the field year-round and simultaneously farm their own lands. Consequently, a new class of professional soldiers arose to man these border defenses and the *fubing* system crumbled. By the late seventh century the *fubing* system was in full decline. This diminished the practice of martial arts among the general population in the interior of the empire, particularly among the wealthy and upper classes. While some poor farmers might have seen opportunities in the professional military, elites had no interest in giving up their local influence and comforts to travel to the border. Under the *fubing* system those elites had often held positions of command. Another draw for those local elites was the possibility of entering imperial government service by passing the civil service exams. Recruitment of lower elites through the exam system became increasingly possible during the seventh century, providing a less risky and more refined way of advancement. These civil elites did not, for the most part, practice martial arts, creating the foundation for a distinction between refined, upper-class men who earned their positions through education, and rough, vulgar, illiterate men who earned their positions through fighting. The full development of this division was still some way off, but there were certainly signs of its development during the Tang.

The professionalization of the military in the middle and late Tang not only made the martial arts a more specialized skill set but it also attached a social and ethnic component to their practice. Border defense was originally in the hands of Chinese officials, but in the eighth century it was argued that non-Chinese generals were better suited to such highly militarized positions. A number of non-Chinese generals were given increasing amounts of power, with large professional armies on the borders, while the capital and interior parts of the empire lacked armies or significant numbers of trained men.

MARTIAL ARTS TRAINING

At least in the early part of the Tang dynasty, a great deal of stress was put on maintaining martial arts practice. This was a sign of the increased presence of conscripted Chinese soldiers who had to be trained in martial arts (as opposed to the steppe cavalrymen who learned their martial skills as part of their lifestyle), and the continued problems maintaining the skills of steppe people living in the Chinese environment. Archery remained central to military practice and a key martial art. It was also an expected skill for court officials, as it had been in the Sui, when, for example, the Sui emperor went out to the archery hall and ordered his court officials to shoot.[5] A similar incident occurred in the early Tang, which included an explicit admonition regarding the need for constant training and the place of the trained warrior in society. Li Shimin addressed a gathering of generals after summoning them to practice archery in the courtyard of the Manifesting Virtue Hall on 17 October 626:

From ancient times there was flourishing and decline between the Türks and China. As the Yellow Emperor was skilled with the five weapons, he was able to north-wardly pursue the Xiongnu [Xunyu, Scythians according to Matthews, later called Xiongnu during the Qin and Han] . . .

  Coming to the rulers of the Han and Jin, up to the Sui, they did not make the soldiers and officers train regularly with the weapons of war (lit. shields and halberds). When the Türks invaded none were able to oppose them. Bringing about the sending away of Chinese people to great distress from invaders. I now do not let you dig ponds and construct parks, building these dissolute and wasteful things, the farmers will throw off restraint and give in to indolence and pleasure, the soldiers and officers only practice archery and riding, so that when you are sent to fight, then seeing you at the front there will not be unexpected enemies.[6]

Li was laying out a clear pact with his generals: if they and their troops worked hard at their skills, then the farmers would work hard and support them. After this, several hundred men were brought before the hall every day for instruction in archery. The emperor personally observed this train-ing, awarding bows and swords to the men who hit the target. Direct imperial supervision drove home the critical importance of archery and maintained a high level of training in general. The emperor made martial arts a matter of imperial interest and provided an opportunity for a skilled soldier to stand out in front of his ruler.

  Soldiers were usually armed with one bow and thirty arrows. There were four kinds of bows, with the two main ones being long bows for the infantry and "horn" bows for the cavalry. Assignment to infantry or cavalry was straightforward: "Generally the people become soldiers at 20 and retire at sixty. Those able to ride and shoot become cavalry, the remainder become infantry."[7] This separation at recruitment would have biased the cavalry toward upper-class and non-Chinese men; ordinary Chinese farmers would have been unlikely to have learned to ride, let alone ride and shoot. While it was policy and practice to train the men in archery and to maintain that skill through repetition, it does not seem that men unfamiliar with horses were recruited into the army and then trained to ride. In both the Sui and the Tang, many men were noted for their skill with archery, or archery and riding. Skill at archery was an important marker of martial prowess.

There was also a slight shift in archery in the Tang back to the use of the crossbow. The crossbow had been very important in the Han and before, but it seems to have been little noted in battle during the Six Dynasties period. Perhaps as a result of increased Chinese participation in warfare, the crossbow made a significant comeback. It also had a number of varieties, seven in fact, including one used from horseback. The standard infantry model fired at a practice range of 230 paces (377 yds), and the standard cavalry model at 200 paces (328 yds).[8] The crossbow was understood as a very long-range missile weapon, in contradistinction to the greater fire-power of the bow. Despite this return to the battlefield, the lower rate of fire and emphasis on the bow, particularly for the cavalry, kept the cross-bow a marginal weapon. This is to say that there were cultural, rather than strictly practical, reasons for the limited place of crossbows. Earlier and later dynasties placed much greater emphasis on its use, even against cavalry.

In close combat, infantry and cavalry both relied upon spears and swords. Cavalrymen used spears extremely effectively against infantry and each other, showing the importance, despite the lightening of the cavalry by dropping horse armor, of cavalry charges and direct hand-to-hand combat. All of our direct mentions of spear use by individual cavalry-men are of officers who earned reputations for their martial arts skill with the weapon, but this is likely due mostly to the bias of the sources. Lower-ranking soldiers would probably not have been noticed by anyone in a position to record their exploits or, if they were, they would probably have been promoted to the officer ranks. There was more range for individual display of spear skills for the cavalry than for the infantry since the infantry would have stood in tighter formations. Cavalry commanders were also able to individually charge enemy formations and display their skills. Displays of martial arts, bravery, and élan of this kind were, if not expected, then certainly a useful enhancement to a commander's reputation.

By one account there were four kinds of spears, with a shorter one for the cavalry, a longer one for the infantry, and the remaining two specialized weapons of the guards in the imperial palace.[9] A more idiosyncratic weapon was the double or paired spears. This was the particular armament of one Bai Xiaode but does not appear in general use. Spear techniques would have varied considerably between infantry and cavalry, though it is likely that many cavalrymen would have also learned to fight on foot with their spears. The cavalryman's advantage in stabbing down was amply compensated for by the infantryman's longer weapon and more stable position.

The sword was the other basic hand-to-hand weapon in the Sui and Tang Dynasties. In the Tang there were four kinds of sword, all single-edged: the

ILLUSTRATION II. Theatrical respresentation of the hero Zhi Hua, the Black Fox, wielding a single-edged curved sword. From *Xiaowuyi* (*Zhonglie Xiaowuyi Zhuan*), 1890.

Ceremonial Sword (*yidao* 儀刀), the Defense Sword (*zhangdao* 障刀), the Cross Sword (*Hengdao* 橫刀), and the Divided Sword (*modao* 陌刀).[10] The Ceremonial Sword was a court weapon that could be decorated with gold and silver; in the Six Dynasties period it was also referred to as an "Imperial Sword" (*yudao* 御刀). The Defense Sword was a weapon of personal defense. The latter two kinds of sword, the Cross Sword and the Divided Sword, were the weapons used in the military. The Cross Sword was called a Belt Sword (*peidao* 佩刀) before the Sui, when it started being called a Cross Sword. The Divided Sword was a new kind of sword that first saw use in the Tang dynasty.

The Divided Sword is described as having an overall length of seven feet, divided between a three-foot blade and a four-foot handle, with an iron butt point. It was believed to have developed out of the "Horse Beheading Long Sword" of the Han Dynasty. The weapon was so named because it was able to behead a horse. This same weapon in the Tang was also called a Long Blade (*Changdao* 長刀).[11] Unlike the double spear mentioned above, this was not the idiosyncratic weapon of an individual warrior, but something wielded by large units of men. One military encyclopedia states:

In one army, there are 12,500 officers and men. Ten thousand men in eight sections bearing Belt Swords; Two thousand five hundred men in two sections with Divided Swords.[12]

A number of other accounts bear witness to the use of the Divided Sword in large army formations, noting on one occasion a formation of 5,000 men armed with this weapon. The leverage of the long handle would have made it a devastating weapon at close range. It lacked the ability to fend off cavalry like a spear, which was a serious weakness, yet it saw action on a number of battlefields. Curiously, despite its popularity in the Tang, the Divided Sword seems to have disappeared from the battlefield afterward.

Some warriors continued to use the long sword even though it was no longer in general use on the battlefield. Apart from these individuals, the long sword was most likely to be seen as a weapon of self-defense for gentlemen, or in performances. As the long sword moved firmly, and permanently, away from general battlefield use, it came to be associated in a positive way as the elegant weapon of a cultivated, literate man. A good example of this was in the person of Li Bo (Bai), one of the greatest poets of the Tang. Not only did he "fence with the long sword" but he also "practiced knight errantry," in his younger days actually killing some people. Other educated men as well as a few generals were also noted for their practice of long sword fencing. Sword dances with the long sword were clearly associated with aesthetic pursuits as on one occasion when Li Bo was ordered by the emperor to sing his own poetry while Pei Min, a renowned martial artist and general, accompanied him with a long sword dance. Pei Min generally used a sword on the battlefield, but his skill with the long sword went beyond dancing to combat as well. He could also dance with a sword, in one instance cutting four arrows out of the air while on horseback.

While Pei Min fits the earlier pattern of a martial artist whose skill with a weapon was aesthetically pleasing when presented in a long sword dance, and Li Bo may be seen as an example of a still partly martial variant of this in a man of letters, during the Tang an entirely new form of long sword dance arose that was purely aesthetic. This new form was a long sword dance performed by a woman at court for entertainment. The performer was not presumed to be a warrior, or someone who expected to engage in combat, but simply a woman whose long sword dance was beautiful. Previously, weapon dances likely derived from actual patterns of techniques used in martial arts training and were performed by and for warriors in an explicitly martial context. The Hundred Events of the Han dynasty grew out of martial arts training, martial ceremonies, and competitions. In the Tang dynasty we first see mention of a martial display by a nonwarrior in a nonmartial context.

WOMEN IN MARTIAL ARTS ENTERTAINMENT

This clear separation between the demonstration of a combat skill abstracted from its violent context, and the purely aesthetic coupling of beautiful women and elegant martial arts was a new development. By the Tang dynasty, as we have seen, the martial arts had a long tradition of performance as entertainments, including the use of weapon dances. The reason for the shift to a nonmartial woman performing the sword dance is indicated obliquely by Du Fu, another great Tang poet, when he referred to the dance of the Gongsun family as "Long sword of Huntuo [Persia]." During the Tang, a new kind of dance connected for some reason to Persia began to be performed. This dance was apparently performed by naked, or possibly scantily clad, women. It may also have been simply regarded as lascivious because of the body movements involved. Indeed, one Tang emperor (Xuanzong) prohibited its performance as harmful to customs. His prohibition failed, it seems, and the dancing continued.

Persian dancing and long sword dancing combined into a form where a fully clothed woman performed a long sword dance. The woman most famously known for her performances was Lady Gongsun (ca. 700–56),

whose dancing was lavishly praised by Du Fu.[13] She was known throughout the Tang empire, and performed for the emperor, gaining a following
of female students. Lady Gongsun wore beautiful military garments for
her dances and used two long swords. It is impossible to say how close her
dances were to the patterns practiced by people learning fencing. Given
that most of her audience was aristocrats and elites who would have had
some familiarity with fencing, it seems unlikely that her movements were
too divergent.

Lady Gongsun's long sword dance should be seen not just as an isolated
but interesting phenomenon. While at the beginning of the Tang dynasty,
Li Shimin's sister could herself raise military forces and participate in
warfare, a marker of the imperial family's hybrid cultural background,
by the eighth century a woman's martial performance could be completely
abstracted from fighting. An audience of elite men and women in the eighth
century could watch a long sword dance as a purely aesthetic event, itself
a hybrid form that drew upon foreign dance to make it interesting. The
imperial court was becoming more disassociated from military affairs,
leaving war to the professional soldiers, Chinese and steppe, on the border,
and their non-Chinese generals.

In terms of performance, however, while long sword dancing under-
went a radical change in practice, wrestling remained the most popular
martial art in the Sui and Tang dynasties. Wrestling was practiced extensively across China, for military purposes within the army, and for entertainment at festivals and other events. Striking skills were still a separate
category of martial art, though at least one notable wrestler was also
known for his boxing. Wrestling was performed in the imperial palace
and in street performances, attracting spectators from every level of society. Regional variations remained in practice and nomenclature, but overall, wrestling was ubiquitous.

MONKS AND BANDITS

The first Buddhist monasteries were established in China in the first
century CE. Over the succeeding centuries, this form of religious life
became a familiar and accepted part of Chinese society. Some Daoist
religious professionals later adopted a similar form of religious life.
Buddhism nevertheless always retained a certain taint of foreignness for
some Chinese, even while it enjoyed widespread popularity among both
elites and commoners. The monastic life itself was similarly problematic in
its insistence on separation from the family and abstention from sex.

Family cohesion and the filial requirement to produce heirs were bedrock values in Chinese society from very early times and were best articulated under the rubric of Confucian thought.

More problematic still was the itinerant practice of many monks, wandering from place to place and monastery to monastery, sometimes begging for alms along the way. Like most sedentary agricultural cultures, Chinese society was based upon people living in fixed locations among familiar neighbors. The government's bureaucratic control apparatus reinforced the importance of home place, registering the population in family units in specific locations. Even government officials, who were prohibited from serving in their home districts, retained their associations with their family's home as they traveled about. Buddhist monks therefore stood outside of mainstream Chinese society in a very fundamental, and disturbing, way. Traveling could also be extremely dangerous as one left the direct supervision of government or close-knit community. The roads and uninhabited areas between communities were the realm of bandits.

Cut off from family and hometown, with no productive economic activity, monks developed an association with banditry and the thuggish and violent society of the road. Many people, it seemed, might shave their heads, don monastic robes, and claim to be monks if for no other reason than to avoid government control. The government responded to this by requiring monks to obtain official ordination certificates. This practice brought in revenue to the government and allowed some measure of control over the monastic ranks. Sometimes a Chinese government might even impose tests on prospective monks, to ensure that they were actual religious professionals rather than mere tax dodgers. These tests were never more than occasionally successful, and in any case the majority of men and women claiming to be Buddhist monks or nuns greatly exceeded the number of ordination certificates.

While there was always some question about the extent of religious training, not to say devotion, of someone claiming to be a monk, there also seemed to be a fairly consistent skepticism about monastic commitments to celibacy and vegetarianism. When combined with the tinge of banditry that the monastic tonsure and dress retained, it often seems that lecherous monks were a commonplace. It is difficult to separate the criminal behavior of the bandit, who might be dressed as a monk, from the hypocritical conduct of a given religious professional.

This association is clearly demonstrated in a story from the ninth-century *Youyang Zazu*, compiled by Duan Chengshi. Duan relates an anecdote from the early eighth century concerning an imperial prince, the Prince of

Ning, who came upon a wardrobe sitting in the grass while out hunting. When his attendants opened the wardrobe, they discovered a beautiful young woman whose father had been a government official. Bandits had accosted her the previous night, two of whom were monks. The monks stole her from the others and locked her in the wardrobe. The prince had a bear captured and placed in the wardrobe while he brought the young woman to the palace and presented her to his younger brother, the emperor. A report arrived three days later about two monks who had taken a wardrobe to an inn one night, claiming that their activities were religious. At night, there were the sounds of struggle, and in the morning, the monks did not emerge. When the innkeeper checked on them, a bear rushed out, having already killed the monks.[14]

While wandering monks were strongly associated with bandits, a connection we will see again and again, the monastic authorities at large institutions represented the opposite end of the social hierarchy. Monasteries were large institutional landowners that often amassed enormous tracts of land and industrial production facilities, like water mills.[15] Such powerful institutions controlled their tenants just like powerful local families, often treating them in the same domineering and exploitative manner. And also like local lineages and landlords, they organized their tenants into defense forces and employed martial artists to train and lead those forces. The leaders of major monasteries were often themselves members of the social elite.

The early forms of Buddhism that reached China were heavily dependent upon literacy, and many of the monks described in Huijiao's (d. 554) *Biographies of Eminent Monks* (*Gaoseng zhuan*), Daoxuan's (d. 667) *Further Biographies of Eminent Monks* (*Xu Gaoseng zhuan*), and Zanning's (d. 1001) *Song Biographies of Eminent Monks* (*Song Gaoseng zhuan*) were scholar-monks.[16] Literacy and education were markers of high status in Chinese society, indicating beyond all protests of poverty in a biography that a monk came from the elite. A new form of Buddhism, Chan (Zen in Japanese), developed in China some time in the fifth century. Its introduction was connected to a legendary figure, Bodhidharma, who took up residence at the Shaolin Monastery. The Northern Wei emperor Xiaowendi (r. 471–99) established Shaolin for the monk Batuo.[17] Chan Buddhism argued strongly against any preoccupation with text, something that Daoxuan and some later Buddhist biographers had some difficulty accommodating in their histories. It must be pointed out, however, that Bodhidharma was usually described as a member of the Bramin class from India, and his early disciples were themselves well educated. The choice to turn away from textual erudition is only a significant act for the educated; the uneducated have no choice.

Heinrich Dumoulin points out that the legendary Bodhidharma cannot be distilled into a historical figure with a fixed background and biography.[18] According to Bernard Faure:

> The legend connecting Bodhidharma to Shaolin took shape after the first Chan monks, Faru (638–89) and Huian (d. 709), moved from the East Mountain community of Daoxin (580–651) and Hongren (601–74) to Song Shan. Thus, it is during the last decades of the seventh century that the legends of Bodhidharma's nine years of "wall contemplation" in a cave near Shaolin and of his disciple Huike (487–593) standing all night in the snow and eventually cutting off his arm to show his religious zeal seem to have taken shape.[19]

Sectarian divisions within Buddhism, not to mention conflicts with Daoists and Confucians, bounded and shaped the biographies of monks.[20] Yet in all of this, Bodhidharma and his "wall contemplation" had no connection whatsoever with martial arts. These disparate strands – Chan, meditation, martial arts, and Shaolin – were twisted together into a single thread nearly a millennium later, transforming Bodhidharma into a foundational martial artist.

The signal event that provided the historical kernel of this mythological narrative was the participation of a group of Shaolin monks in the wars that took place after the Sui dynasty fell. When a warlord seized some of the Shaolin lands in 621, the monks raised a force and struck back, directly contributing to the efforts of Li Shimin, the future emperor Tang Taizong, in his efforts to secure the city of Luoyang. The monastery was rewarded with confirmation of its rights to the land and water mill in question and later with a certain measure of imperial protection from official harassment. The monks involved were rewarded with military titles.[21]

No further mention of combat or martial arts at Shaolin Monastery appears for nearly nine hundred years following this event, though the monastery was frequently visited and written about. Shaolin's prominence was the result of its importance as a center of Chan Buddhism. The spurious connection of a distinct tradition of martial arts at Shaolin to these monks was created in the Ming dynasty. The real connection between the monks and their military activities was land. As an institution whose wealth was based upon the lands and water mill granted to it by an earlier emperor, Shaolin had to defend its property from seizure. There was no religious connection to the martial arts.

In addition to the need for a large landowning institution to defend itself in a period of upheaval, there is also the possibility that the monastic leaders had themselves held military positions before becoming Buddhist monks. As we have seen, martial arts skills were common throughout Chinese society at this time. Most men whether commoner or elite would have had some skill with weapons, particularly in the frequently fought over area around Luoyang. The Shaolin leadership was fortunate to have helped out the winning side in the struggle for empire. Li Shimin's endorsement protected the monastery's lands and the monastery itself from future Tang governmental seizure; the monastery was keen to demonstrate its imperial connection, and so the document and ultimately stelae inscription were prominently displayed.

MILITARY EXAMS

A final innovation of the Tang period was the introduction of military exams. The formal and recognizable system of military exams was instituted in 702 during the reign of Wu Zetian. Technically, this occurred during Wu Zetian's reign as emperor of the Zhou dynasty, rather than the Tang Dynasty. Wu had been empress with Tang emperor Gaozong (r. 649–83), and then regent and empress dowager for Tang Zhongzong and then Tang Ruizong, before overthrowing the Tang dynasty to form her own Zhou Dynasty, with herself as emperor. She was the only woman to rule as emperor in Chinese history. She was herself overthrown in 705, and the Tang house restored.

There was a Sui precedent for the military exam, but up until 702 most officers achieved their positions either from battlefield exploits or because they came from a family of officers. A few men were recommended to the throne directly by officials for their military talents, but this was a limited route to command positions. Although several subsequent dynasties used military exam systems for varying amounts of time, military families remained the most important source of officers. Nevertheless, the exam system offered Wu Zetian an important recruiting avenue. Her position as usurper left her politically vulnerable and in desperate need of loyal military commanders. The exam system offered the possibility of bringing in men who would owe her their positions. Some of those men would be local strongmen who lacked connections at court. Not only did it allow her to recruit such men but it also removed them from recruitment by her enemies. Wu Zetian herself explained the reasons for the exam as she was "afraid of people's forgetting war."[22]

There was an earlier military test from 638, which required a man to be six feet tall and able to carry five bushels of rice thirty paces, in addition to

襄
陽
王

ILLUSTRATION 12. Theatrical representation of the hero Xiangyang Wang (The Prince of Xiangyang). From *Qixia Wuyi*, 1889. He wears a sheathed long sword with his court dress and is dramatically posed grasping one of the feathers from his headgear.

riding and shooting. Wu Zetian's formal exam had five aspects: firing an arrow for distance, mounted archery, mounted spear fighting, foot archery, and verbal responses. Some of these areas were important for ranking, and there were a number of other areas, like height and strength tests, which were also used. Once again, we see the centrality of archery as a military skill, as well as riding and mounted spear fighting. The men being recruited through this system were to serve as officers, not common soldiers, and would have been expected to be able to ride. Of course relatively few Chinese men outside the elites would have been horsemen, so this exam was aimed squarely at elites and possibly non-Chinese men. The verbal response was not only a test of intelligence but also of basic language skills. It is likely that this required the applicant to speak the Chinese court dialect. Any non-Chinese attempting to use the exam system, or even provincial Chinese, would have had to have had enough education to at least speak to the elites. Thus, the exams were really about recruiting Chinese, or culturally hybrid Chinese-Türkic elites.

CONCLUSION

Warfare and martial arts practice continued to change during the Sui and Tang dynasties, though perhaps not as radically as during the Six Dynasties period. Some of the changes that began during the late sixth century reached maturity during the Tang and then receded. The armed forces moved between more and less professional soldiers, and between more and less culturally Chinese commanders. While in many senses these shifts were caused by politics, they cannot be fully separated from cultural and social changes, or from the effects shifts in one area had on the others. War and martial arts were, as always, intimately tied to society, culture, and politics.

The ethnic divide in martial arts was straddled by many elites, the most prominent of these being the Tang imperial family itself. It was not easy to maintain two sets of fully developed cultural and martial skills so that one could choose among these identities when desired. Most individuals were naturally better at one or the other set, either through inclination or upbringing. In the fluid and chaotic times of the Six Dynasties, Sui and early Tang dynasties, it was particularly useful for even culturally Chinese elites to develop some non-Chinese military and political capabilities, and for steppe elites to develop Chinese military and political capabilities. Once the Tang Dynasty was established and the wars within China settled down, the need to work in both environments diminished. It became easier to live in one world, and martial arts and the military began to separate from the world of civil elites. This divide was ethnic as well, with a Chinese civil elite ruling at court and employing a non-Chinese military elite to run the army. While it is an oversimplification to say that the army was run by non-Chinese elites before the An Lushan Rebellion, there were great numbers of non-Chinese in the upper ranks of the Tang army, and a large number of the strongest military units, particularly on the border or in the cavalry, were predominantly non-Chinese.[23] The connections between the civil elite at court and the military leadership on the border broke down with the An Lushan Rebellion.

The Tang empire was less unified even after An Lushan had been put down, and imperial authority reached less far than before outside the capital. Once again, regional armies and local forces built themselves up to maintain local order and to struggle for power with others. Martial arts had diminished in importance among the Chinese population before the An Lushan Rebellion, particularly as the *fubing* system collapsed and was replaced by full-time military professionals. The necessity for self-protection and for regional strongmen to recruit large armies brought the martial arts back to the Chinese population. At the same time, steppe forces were quite active in north China, once again offering their services for pay or sometimes carving out their own areas of control. The need for self-defense was further exacerbated by the Huang Chao Rebellion, which diminished central authority even more. When the dynasty was officially ended in 907, the Chinese ecumene was once again split north and south.

6

The Five Dynasties and Ten Kingdoms
and the Song Dynasty

Very little changed immediately after the official end of the Tang Dynasty in 907. Tang central authority had evaporated well before the Later Liang Dynasty was established putatively on the ruins of the Tang Dynasty. In reality, the government of the Liang Dynasty controlled only a large part of north China, with powerful enemies on its northern border; it had no authority in south China. A new steppe empire, the Kitan, was also established in 907, and it would play an active role in Chinese politics until the beginning of the eleventh century. Southern China and Sichuan were governed by a number of different states, with rulers claiming a wide variety of titles from emperor on down. Just as the north would see a succession of imperial houses, so too would those states in the south and Sichuan see a succession of rulers and imperial houses.

At first, this multistate environment seemed likely to replay the centuries of struggle for dominance of the Six Dynasties period. Many of the same forces and divisions were in place. Türkic elites with extensive involvement in north China were locked in a struggle with other Türkic, steppe, and Chinese elites to control the government, and southern elites largely governed their own states. But this time the period of division lasted only fifty years, a lifetime for many, yet otherwise a relatively brief interregnum over the course of Chinese history. The new dynasty that emerged in 960, the Song Dynasty, was, like so many things in Chinese history, both very familiar and very different from the dynasties that had preceded it. Most notably, in sharp contrast to the Tang, there was no Türkic influence within the imperial families or the elites, and a new bureaucratic elite emerged in the late tenth century who earned their positions not from aristocratic pedigree, but from passing civil service exams alone.

Also unlike the Tang Dynasty, the Song would confront a large, power-ful, and coherent steppe empire to its northeast, the Kitan Liao Dynasty, and a smaller, but still potent kingdom to its northwest, the Tanguts, or Xixia (as the Song called them). These polities presented a number of challenges to the Song and limited its northward influence. Beginning in the early twelfth century a new steppe power developed to the north of the Liao. The Jurchen, formerly a people subject to the Liao, began what would prove to be an inexorable process of destroying their overlords. The Song government, implacably, if irrationally, hostile to the Liao even after a century of peace, allied themselves with the Jurchen to destroy the Liao. This move was successful in some respects – the Liao Dynasty was destroyed in 1125 – but it ultimately turned out poorly for the Song as well. The Jurchen, like the Kitan Liao before them, adopted a Chinese style dynastic name, the Jin, and a hybrid steppe-Chinese government system; they quarreled with the Song over the spoils of the war against the Liao. In the conflict that followed, the Jurchen Jin army captured the Song capital at Kaifeng, along with the emperor, retired emperor, and most of the imperial family in 1127.

One of the imperial princes who escaped this disaster reformed the Song government in south China. The Jurchen, who had not expected to capture the Song capital, quickly shifted their efforts to destroying completely the remnants of the Song imperial house. One of the great patriotic heroes of Chinese history, a general named Yue Fei (1103–42), emerged in the ultimately successful struggle for Song survival. But the Song did not recover the north and remained deadlocked with the Jurchen at the line of the Huai River. Repeated major wars with the Jin did little to change things until, as happened before, a new power arose to the north of the Jin. Once again the Song court allied itself with the new power, the Mongols, and once again the object of their mutual hostility was duly destroyed. History continued to replay itself, though this time it took half a century for the Mongols to conquer the Song. While the Song held out for fifty years, the Mongols conquered enormous swathes of Eurasia, establishing the largest land empire in human history.

The period between the Tang and the Song dynasties was first called the Five Dynasties and Ten Kingdoms period in the eleventh century. Ever since then Chinese historians have generally neglected the period, summa-rily dismissing it as an aberrant time of disunion between great dynasties. Perhaps just as important, at least for modern historians, the period lacked a unifying political focus and is therefore extremely difficult to study. In terms of martial arts, apart from the extensive amount of fighting and many impressive warriors, the only innovation seems to be the appearance of the iron spear, a metal-hafted spear of considerable weight. Yet the social and cultural changes that took place during this period were significant. In the first half of the tenth century, Türkic power in north China was destroyed and any other significant steppe elites were killed, driven off, or otherwise removed. For the first time since the late Han Dynasty, non-Chinese people and their leaders either served the military on the borders without significant political power, or were outside of China.

A main reason that these steppe groups lost power was simple attrition. Right after the Tang ended, Türkic strongmen were still extremely powerful in the military and wielded commensurate political authority. The second and fourth of the Five Dynasties were Türkic, and the third, a client of the Kitan. But Kitan and Chinese power was rising and Türkic power was falling; the constant campaigning killed so many Türkic leaders that the old families, whose feuds had begun before the Tang ended, simply succumbed. The long tenure of these steppe people, however, left a lasting impression on the martial culture of the Chinese. The founding emperor of the Song, Zhao Kuangyin (927–76), posthumously known as Song Taizu, was born in a military camp near Luoyang. He and his comrades began their careers serving in the bodyguard troops of leaders and emperors. They were all accomplished martial artists.

The power of these various states during the Five Dynasties and Ten Kingdoms period was built on the control of armies. With so many states contending, much of China was highly militarized. At the same time, however, the particular modes of warfare of the different parts of China were more pronounced. Whereas the Song military had to be capable of fighting across a wide range of environments, from the plains of north China to the rivers of south China, the more regional powers of the first half of the tenth century mostly fought in one area alone. Local power also developed in this period, with local strongmen and powerful lineages organizing for self-defense. These self-defense forces were essentially sub-military units useful only for local fighting, but their formation required the broad teaching of at least rudimentary martial arts skills throughout the countryside. North China remained militarized throughout the Song Dynasty, with the manorial lords maintaining well-developed local forces.

A related group of martial artists existed alongside these self-defense forces. These were the trainers and thugs brought in by the locally powerful to bolster their own authority and to teach their tenants, retainers, and clan members how to fight. Many of these martial artists were local men with family traditions of fighting who were hired by individuals or families interested in using force to maintain or advance their local authority, be it economic, social, or political. Some of them were simply violent men without formal martial arts training, inclined to use force for gain. Others had spent time in the military and had formally learned not only martial arts skills but also the organizational, tactical, and possibly even strategic skills of established military units. This combination of men of violence, from the mere criminal to the military officer, had always existed in Chinese society, but in the Song we begin to find direct evidence for their activities.

Yue Fei (1103–42), to use a prominent example, reportedly had a martial arts teacher as a young man. Although we are not explicitly told this for other generals or martial figures, the same must have been true. The Song military was a professional force, with the occasional addition of some militia forces in emergencies. Officers, for their part, mostly came from families of officers, though a few did rise from the ranks. The sons of officers and generals grew up in the military and learned their martial arts there. It is likely, though we have no evidence of this, that many of the common soldiers were men who followed their fathers into the ranks. Later fictional accounts of the Song, like *The Water Margin* (*Shuihuzhuan*), include characters like Panther Head Lin Chong, a martial arts instructor for the Song army. While the account is fiction, there were numerous actual instructors in the army.[1]

On the criminal side, it seems as if the Chinese countryside was always well populated with bandits. These were not Robin Hood–like men, though they were portrayed as such in fiction, but usually predatory criminals robbing passersby or shaking down ordinary farmers and merchants. Most were not well trained in the martial arts, though some, particularly former soldiers, would have been. As long as their activities were strictly local and did not rise to the level of a major disturbance of order, the government might leave them alone. If they spread their influence or became a major problem, then the army would be forced to destroy them. Yet at the same time, these bandits formed a possible pool of recruits for the army. One of the government's reactions to more organized bandits was to offer them amnesty and recruitment into the army. Their violent behavior demonstrated their qualifications for military service. Some bandits, notably the Shandong bandit Li Quan, discussed in the following chapter, took advantage of chaotic times and rose to the level of a regional warlord.

The flip side of the power of bandits was the need for protection from bandits. In addition to the local self-defense forces already discussed, merchants needed armed guards to protect the transport and storage of their goods. While bulk goods like grains were unlikely to be robbed by ordinary bandits unless they were hungry, light, high-value goods, like tea,

病夫蔣平字澤長

其身不長其貌不揚能言

剎口俠義肝腸

ILLUSTRATION 13. Theatrical representation of the hero Jiang Ping, the River Rat, wielding paired cudgels. From Xiaowuyi (*Zhonglie Xiaowuyi Zhuan*), 1890.

were a rich target for bandits. Thus on one occasion the Song government was able in an emergency to draft the tea merchants' protection force into a Tea Merchants Army. These guards would have had a high level of martial arts skills because merchants would have stressed, and paid for, quality over quantity.

Society and martial arts were rather different in the Liao, Xixia, and Jin states. Steppe society in these states remained relatively stable in terms of martial arts practice. Riding and shooting were still both the everyday and military campaign skills of most of the adult populace, male and female. Where in Song society the army was a quite separate entity, a professional force of paid martial artists, in steppe society most of the army was simply drawn from the ordinary populace. Steppe leaders needed to prove their legitimacy by going on military campaigns and demonstrating an interest in warfare. Archery contests were held at steppe courts as basic to culture. Such contests fell out of favor at the Song court by the early eleventh century, if not earlier. They were revived only briefly when the dynasty's military fortunes declined and it was hoped that a return to more martial pursuits at court might somehow improve things. In the steppe, martial arts was nearly universal and skills in war highly valued.

Song society and culture was far more reticulated and specialized than steppe society. The rise of a professional bureaucratic class of highly educated civil service exam graduates who did not, with very few exceptions, practice martial arts or lead in war brought about a concomitant subordination of warriors in government and in overall status. With the exception of the highest-ranking military families, national-level Song elites did not practice martial arts. Physical skills were, by definition, markers of low status. The shift away from the martial arts required of the founding emperor and generals of the Song was extremely rapid. By the reign of the second emperor, the younger brother of the first emperor, posthumously known as Song Taizong, poetry competitions were more valued in court than martial demonstrations. When Cao Han, a general, asked to take part in a poetry competition since he had had some formal education as a youth, he was laughed at and told he could use the rhyme "sword."

Local society in north China was dominated by elites who often practiced martial arts themselves and maintained well-armed retainers and tenants. The countryside in most of Song China was controlled by manors, large areas of land owned and dominated by powerful landlords with immense authority over the population. The north's constant exposure to steppe raids required a general familiarity with the martial arts. This often created problems for public order as the highly militarized population could just as easily resort to crime and banditry. The court was concerned on several occasions about martial arts groups who called themselves not just "Staff Societies" but also "No Orders Societies 沒命社," "Hegemons and Kings Society 霸王社," and "Forgetting Orders Societies 亡命社."[2] In 1041, the court outlawed private martial arts teachers in the vain hope of restoring order.[3]

Although martial arts held a lower social status in Song China, we are fortunate in the sorts of written records for martial practice existing for this period – much more so than for earlier periods. In part, this is simply because more material survived than from earlier times, and in part it resulted from an effort to compile knowledge of military affairs. The *Complete Essentials from the Military Classics* (*Wujing Zongyao*) was completed in 1044 and catalogued the entirety of military information available to the Song government.[4] The *Complete Essentials* was illustrated as well, though it is unclear whether the current illustrations are original, later copies, or later replacements, and for the first time we have descriptions of weapons with matching images. Because the compilers were trying to be comprehensive, most of the weapons listed are archaic or marginal. The regular weapons of war remained bows, crossbows, swords, and spears.

The *Complete Essentials* was also remarkable for providing the first published formula for gunpowder in history. Although gunpowder weapons were rudimentary in the eleventh century, during the twelfth and thirteenth centuries true guns were developed in China. These were truly a new kind of weapon, something chemically powered rather than mechanically powered. Guns were in widespread use by at least the thirteenth century, being manufactured by the thousands in government arsenals. Early guns were not technically difficult to manufacture once the basic design was understood, and these weapons were in fact cheaper and faster to produce than the steppe composite bows. No real "art" of shooting emerged at this time, and it would take many more centuries before we find precise descriptions of shooting practice. Indeed, the most careful descriptions of shooting with a firearm would emerge after different weapons from outside China became available. It was then necessary to formally record the foreign methods of shooting. From the thirteenth if not the twelfth century onward, guns, both handheld and larger cannon, became a regular and critical weapon of war. As we will see in a later chapter, guns were so central to military practice that they were included in the martial arts stories of *The Water Margin*.

The presence of guns in twelfth- and thirteenth-century China should make it clear that any attempt to separate our understanding of Chinese

南侠御貓展昭

ILLUSTRATION 14. Theatrical representation of the hero Zhan Zhao, the Southern Hero, wielding a long sword. From *Qixia Wuyi*, 1889.

martial arts into a pre- and post-firearms world is problematic. Guns do not appear to have had any noticeable impact on the martial arts beyond simply adding a new weapon to the means of violence. Guns did not make swords, spears, or even bows and crossbows immediately obsolete. Indeed, as we shall see in Chapter 10, Chinese and Japanese soldiers fought hand-to-hand battles with swords in the middle decades of the twentieth century. The notion, often promoted in Chinese martial arts films, that guns were foreign or unknown to the Chinese before the arrival of the West, is baseless nonsense. The Chinese martial arts have flourished as effective fighting skills in the presence of guns for over seven centuries.

There were some changes in the martial arts during the Song Dynasty. The importance of archery remained paramount, but its practice meant very different things to the new literati elite. The staff also gained in importance during the Song, though the spear and the sword were the main weapons for close fighting. Perhaps most important for our modern understanding of the martial arts, the use of martial arts for entertainment grew during the Song, leading some to argue that the previously purely functional skills were made more flowery to please audiences. Military exams were also promoted, leading to the same sorts of questions about physical versus mental skills. Use of such exams was one of several attempts to improve the Song Dynasty's military strength.

Another policy for strengthening the military, the *baojia* system, tried to reverse the split between soldiers and farmers and bring back the soldier-farmer of the *fubing* system and before. The idea was to militarize the farmers through training in the martial arts and to create a vast pool of armed men. This would have offset the advantage of highly militarized steppe people and produced overwhelming power when multiplied by the Chinese population. It was a complete failure, but it did promote martial arts skills throughout the rural population.

ARCHERY

Hua Yue wrote, "There are thirty-six military weapons and the bow is called the head. There are eighteen martial arts (*wuyi*) and archery is the first."[5] As we have seen and will continue to see, until perhaps the nineteenth century, archery was the most fundamental battlefield and martial skill; however, the emphasis in archery did change during the Song. There were two main areas of change: an increased emphasis on crossbow archery, and the almost total absence of archery practice among the ruling class. Both of these changes were driven by cultural, political, and social factors rather than questions of effectiveness. And, at least in the case of the ruling class, a vaguely martial substitute was found that provided some connection to past archery practice among Confucian gentlemen.

With respect to crossbow archery, Hua Yue further wrote: "The barbarians have long had the horse, the Han (Chinese) have long had the crossbow."[6] Hua's point, written in the later part of the Song Dynasty, was to reassert for the reader the fundamental differences in martial practice between steppe and sedentary Chinese society. He was not attempting to change what he saw as long-standing cultural orientations but to proceed from these realities. Since things had always been this way, one should work within these parameters. Yet at the same time, he just as clearly understood that steppe people and Chinese people shared the bow in their respective cultures. The differences were in the steppe use of the horse in everyday life and then in warfare, and the Chinese use of the crossbow. The crossbow was, and always had been, a distinctly Chinese weapon, and its use was almost unheard of in the steppe.

These differences became more pronounced after the Song lost control of north China to the Jurchen Jin. In the eleventh century the Song government had struggled to provide enough horses for the army, but this became even more difficult when the Song controlled none of the territory north of the Huai River.[7] As hard as it was to get horses in southern China, it was even harder to keep them healthy. The Song military's offensive power was severely curtailed by the lack of horses; its great defensive strength came from naval forces and fortifications along the Huai River. Crossbows were extremely effective in naval and siege warfare, and first the Jurchen and then the Mongols found it very difficult to breach the Song defenses. The emphasis on naval and siege warfare also boosted the use of early firearms.

The main advantages of the crossbow were greater range and penetrating power. It could also be spanned (the string pulled back to firing position) using one's legs and back strength, rather than arm strength, and the string held in place until the trigger was pulled. Song soldiers were tested on the draw weight of the crossbow they could span. They were also tested on the draw weight of the bow they could pull. As in earlier times, basic tests of strength were used as a measure of martial capability. Crossbow firing was tested mostly on the basis of range rather than accuracy. This may well have been because it would have been nearly impossible to pick out a target at long crossbow range with the naked eye.

The weakness of the crossbow was its slow rate of fire. Xu Dong, writing in the early eleventh century, figured that a crossbow could only fire once or twice before enemy cavalry reached the shooter.[8] Crossbows were therefore a specialty weapon on the battlefield that could only be used in conjunction with bows and solid infantry formations, or from fortifications and ships. They were probably similar to early firearms in rate of fire,

ILLUSTRATION 15. Theatrical representation of the female heroes Sha Fengxian (Phoenix Sprite) and Qiu Kui (Autumn Sunflower), one wearing a sheathed, single-edged curved sword and the other carrying a bow (but no arrows). From *Qixia Wuyi*, 1889.

if not a bit faster, and had much greater range and accuracy than early guns. Guns had much greater penetration and lethality, but in the early forms were both inaccurate and short-ranged.

It was the Song Dynasty's Chinese identification and cultural orientation that brought the crossbow back to the battlefield in significant numbers. At times, at least among the Song elite, the Chinese expressed deeply racist and negative views of steppe people. This was not a new intellectual position, but what was curious in the Song was that the literati elite were so divorced from the martial arts that they did not learn to use the most identifiably Chinese weapon they had available. The Divine Elbow crossbow became a symbol of Song interest in recapturing north China, but by then the literati had come to distinguish themselves as a group as men who did not practice martial arts. Were they to practice martial arts, only bow archery had an impeccably Confucian pedigree.

Very few Song literati practiced martial arts of any kind. Occasional mentions of a literatus foreseeing coming bad times and having his sons trained in fencing emphasize how extraordinary this came to be. At the same time, any highly educated man was acutely aware that men like Confucius practiced archery and strongly argued for the importance of properly performed archery ceremonies. While no Song literati contravened Confucius directly on the importance of archery, they simply did not practice it. Archery had come to be a strictly martial skill, the practice of which implied that one was a martial person. It was not acceptable for a literary man to practice martial skills. The closest most literati came to an archery-like contest was the game of *tuohu* which involved throwing weighted arrows into a narrow-necked pot.

A good example of the place and problems of practicing archery for a literatus is an early Song official by the name of Chen Yaozi (970–?). Chen came from a family of distinguished civil officials, with both his father and two brothers holding positions. Chen himself had also passed the civil service exams – coming in first, in fact – and held a position in the civil administration. He was also, quite strangely, an excellent archer and indeed is best known for a number of anecdotes related to that skill. Here we must also keep in mind that Chen lived in the early Song, when the split between civil and military careers had not yet become as absolute as it would later.

The third Song emperor, posthumously known as Song Zhenzong (r. 997–1022) wanted to appoint Chen as an envoy to the Kitan Liao court because he was handsome and a skilled archer.[9] It was important for an envoy to acquit himself well in a steppe court where archery was still practiced as a regular pastime. In order to fill the position, however, Chen would have had to transfer from his civil position and be given a military posting. The emperor offered him a high position if he would accept the transfer. Chen had to check with his mother before accepting. His mother responded by beating him with a staff and berating him for considering degrading the family, whose position had been established through literary merit, just for a bigger salary. From a later Confucian perspective, for a civil official to take a military position was simply unacceptable.

Having not received a response from Chen, Zhenzong sent a short message to the intermediary in the matter that read: "Did the archer's arrow go through the leather?" This was a direct reference, keeping on the theme of archery, to the passage in Confucius: "In archery, one does not emphasize piercing the hide of the target, because people's strengths differ. Such is the ancient Way."[10] The message was misdirected, causing considerable confusion. The opposition of Chen's mother, however, prevented him from taking the position.

On another occasion, when Chen had returned from a tour of duty, his mother asked him if he had accomplished anything.[11] He replied that the area he had served in was strategically important, and he therefore had had many meetings with army officers. He always demonstrated his skill as an archer, for which they all praised him. This spurred his mother to berate and beat him again. Her argument was that he had been trained to do important government work and chose instead to pride himself on a mere physical skill.

Finally, the most important story demonstrating the Song Confucian perspective on martial arts also involves Chen Yaozi's skill as an archer. This apocryphal anecdote was recorded by the statesman and Confucian moralist Ouyang Xiu (1007–72).[12] While Chen was practicing archery in his garden one day, an oil peddler stopped to watch him. When Chen asked whether he knew something about archery, the peddler discounted Chen's skill as merely the product of practice. Chen was incensed that the peddler scorned his accuracy. The peddler thereupon put a coin (Chinese coins had a square hole in the middle) over the opening of a gourd and ladled oil into it without touching the sides. This was easy, the peddler related, because he practiced this task all the time. Physical skills, in this perspective, might seem impressive, but in reality are quite banal.

Ouyang Xiu used Chen Yaozi as a perfect foil to denigrate archery and all things physical in comparison to the intellectual and moral attainments of the literati. Skill with archery was no different from oil pouring. This particular story is well known to all Taiwanese school children, and many in China as well. It makes a fundamental value judgment in favor of studying over physical pursuits. Ouyang's position is in stark contrast to the story recounted in Chapter 2 of Liezi being challenged concerning his skill with archery. It is worth repeating here. Liezi's friend took him up to the edge of a cliff and challenged him to shoot from there. Liezi was paralyzed with fear, and his friend admonished him:

> The master archer can fire an arrow under any condition. Whether he sees the clear sky or faces the yawning abyss, he can still shoot with the same state of mind. He is not affected by conditions of life and death, for nothing can move the stillness of his mind. Look at yourself now. You are so scared that you can't stand up or look straight. How can you even begin to demonstrate the art of archery?[13]

Confucius, for his part, separated archery as a military or hunting skill from its value in ceremonial performance. He emphasized the proper form and mental state required for archery and devalued penetrating the target. Of course, for the warrior, strength was just as important as accuracy, since merely striking a target with insufficient force to damage it was useless. This is one of the reasons that military competitions, displays, and tests always included some kind of strength test, both in general and with respect to the draw weight of a bow. Mencius followed Confucius along these lines and used archery as an analogy for virtue. The archery of the gentleman was, for Confucius, an opportunity to distinguish him from the more usual values of a contest, as gentlemen did not compete against each other in terms of accuracy; archery was a means to display cultivation and to seek inner development within oneself.

While Ouyang Xiu certainly identified himself very strongly with Confucius and Mencius, and believed himself also to be a member of the knightly (士) class – understood in the Song as the literati class – he could not understand archery in the same way. This was a major intellectual step for the literati away from the martial arts, one that would be given even fuller expression in the twelfth century by Zhu Xi (1130–1200), the founder of what is usually known in the West as Neo-Confucianism. Zhu took pains to explain the Confucius comment about not concerning oneself with penetrating the target. Archery had ideally been practiced to observe a man's virtue. Virtue was displayed by deportment and behavior, not "success" in the contest. For Zhu, of course, this was an apposite analogy for moral behavior in general, particularly for the literati. By as early as the eleventh century, many literati who studied to pass the civil service exams and become government officials were unable to achieve those goals because there were more applicants than positions available.

What then was the value of learning, absent the nominal goal of government service? For the Neo-Confucians, learning and self-cultivation were the real goal, regardless of achieving government office.

Yet Zhu Xi went on to contrast the moral values produced in the peaceful environment after the Zhou overthrew the Shang (no more target piercing), with the collapse of those values when the Zhou disintegrated (a return to target piercing). Zhu in a certain sense rejects Ouyang Xiu's dismissal of the value of Chen Yaozi's archery skill. Chen, after all, was only demonstrating his accuracy, not his penetration. For Confucius, Chen Yaozi's fault would have been his pride in his skills rather than the skills themselves. Ouyang Xiu, by contrast, found the idea of Chen – a *zhuang-yuan*, the man who placed first in the civil service exams for that round – practicing archery deeply disturbing. The two stories of Chen told by other authors relate a similar distaste for a distinguished literatus practicing martial arts with any seriousness, or investing any value in it.

Zhu Xi and Ouyang Xiu lived in very different times, however, and their approaches to the martial arts were not simply the product of abstract intellectual considerations. The Song Dynasty lost control of north China just before Zhu was born, and it continued to struggle militarily and politically with the Jurchen Jin. Zhu's father resigned his official post over a peace deal with the Jin. And Zhu himself was zealous in repairing and maintaining defensive structures when he was a magistrate, in addition to pursuing his puritanical Confucian values. Ouyang Xiu, in contrast, lived in a generally peaceful time, with the only exception being a minor war with the Tanguts. In Ouyang Xiu's time the literati were fully defining themselves as purely civil officials who earned their position through the civil service exams. This was in contrast to Tang officials, particularly in the early part of the dynasty, who achieved their positions because they were members of a hereditary elite. The eleventh century saw the expanding bureaucratic elite take over both the civil and military sides of the Song government and fully subordinate the military to civil control. The disadvantage of this civil dominance, some argued, was a concomitant diminished military strength.

Song officials looked back to the Tang *fubing* system, and the farmer-soldier ideal of early times, with great nostalgia. The professional Song military was extremely expensive to maintain and was not capable of defeating either the Kitan or the Tanguts. This was a misleading simplification of the situation, but it led to the revival of a militia system as part of a major governmental reform program in the later eleventh century under Wang Anshi. Wang's *baojia* system was built on the preexisting practice in some communities of Archery Societies 弓箭社 or Loyal and Upright Societies 忠義社.[14] While Song elites were rejecting martial arts practice as antithetical to their group identity, local communities, particularly those in the path of steppe raiders or those afflicted by banditry, banded together to train in martial arts for self-protection. This was a practical necessity given the limited ability of the central government to provide local security.

Archery Societies and Loyal and Upright Societies appear to have arisen in many cases without the participation of the literati elite. The equipment of some of the participants was quite simple: "one bow, thirty arrows, one sword."[15] They practiced on the third, sixth, and ninth days of the traditional Chinese ten-day week, though presumably there was considerable variety of practice across the empire. As one observer pointed out concerning these northern Chinese archers: "[They] are no different than the barbarians."[16] Northern Chinese, at least in martial arts practice, and probably in other cultural aspects as well, were quite similar to the steppe people farther north. Indeed, there was considerable intermarriage in the area, as there had been for centuries. Archery practice also had a strong cultural origin in north China.

In order to practice archery, an archer or group of archers needed an open space. When the Song government was promoting archery practice, particularly around the capital, it constructed those practice fields. This was unnecessary in rural north China, of course, where there was plenty of flat, open space. Urban archery societies did not always have the direct support of the government for these activities and often met on temple grounds. After the fall of north China, Song archery societies were confined to the less open areas of southern China and to its more crowded cities. Of course, even in rural areas, most of the cleared ground would be occupied with crops. Apart from military practice fields, temples provided the only consistently available open space for martial arts training.

Wang Anshi's *baojia* system attempted to formalize and expand upon the preexisting Archery and Loyal and Upright Societies and the militarized northern society, in order to create a large pool of cheap military manpower. The *baojia*'s other functions, as an internal security and tax system, were equally important – and ultimately more effective. Under the system, families were grouped together into units that were mutually responsible for each other and had to contribute a certain number of men for martial arts training. In effect, vast swathes of Song society would be militarized under the control of the government. The need to train these units in martial arts provided the impetus for much greater control of the population, a control more similar to that of the military. For a classicist like Wang Anshi, the possibility of bringing back the farmer-soldier of antiquity was compelling in and of itself; as the prime minister, of course, even more attractive was gaining the services of enormous numbers of cheap soldiers.

The *baojia* system did not, however, return literati to their dual role of official in peacetime and military officer in wartime. Leadership would have fallen to the locally prominent, or at least wealthier, farmers and landlords. For most involved in this system, practicing martial arts was now a burden imposed by the state that reinforced the local power structure. In terms of martial arts practice, however, it may have changed things very little. Under the *baojia* system, archery was still the primary skill tested and practiced. State intervention strengthened state power over these martial artists without improving the military situation. Local self-defense forces remained extremely limited in their ability to serve on the battlefield. Moreover, they tended not to have, or at least to the same extent as regular units, the armor and small and large unit training to function as tactical units on a battlefield.

Archery Societies were of similarly limited use on battlefields in southern China. There were other, better established and trained local militia forces in southern China that had developed to combat local banditry rather than northern cavalry raiders. These militia forces were often very effective against bandits, who were endemic in Fujian and other parts of south China. After the loss of north China, however, the reconstituted Song state drafted many of these militia forces into fighting against the Jurchen Jin. The militias could not truly fill the same role the decimated regular imperial army had performed; they did not have the training, equipment, or leadership to do so. Removing those units from their local area allowed banditry to flourish again. Local archers and militia forces were critical for local security but limited in function.

MARTIAL ARTS PERFORMANCES

Displays of martial arts were widespread in China during the Song Dynasty, as they had been in earlier times. These exhibitions were done in the court and in more public venues as before, and also as more regular urban entertainments. Court performances were used for political and entertainment purposes, just as the Han Hundred Events and wrestling exhibitions were in the past. Archery was not a regular pastime of the Song court, as it was in the steppe courts, and with the possible exception of some attending generals, most of the viewers of these exhibitions were not versed in the martial arts. The army itself did some public displays as part of their training, though it is unclear who was able to watch these. The military displays were in addition to military parades where some part of the army was arrayed for the emperor to review. The new performance venue for martial arts in the urban entertainment precincts had an important influence on the development of martial arts. This was where the entertainment aspect of the martial arts was emphasized over the combat aspect, leading to an aesthetic elaboration of previously simple forms.

The first Song emperor was an accomplished warrior and general with enough personal experience of hand-to-hand combat to guarantee him the respect of the military. Like anyone of his background, he had personally killed men in battle, though he did not boast of it as Tang Taizong had. Partly this was personality and partly political and cultural orientation. Tang Taizong had usurped his father's rule and retrospectively justified this based upon his centrality in the campaigns that founded the Tang. He also functioned in a partly Türkic martial culture that valued and expected a leader to have direct experience of combat. Song Taizu lived in a Chinese martial culture that had fully subsumed and adapted those Türkic martial values during the Tang. The Song founder needed to portray himself as less battle oriented and more interested in administration and government. His younger brother, Song Taizong, was in a much different position and used martial arts in a much more direct way to bolster his position.

The second Song emperor was strongly suspected of poisoning his elder brother and usurping the throne from his nephews. Song Taizong was also not the warrior and successful general his brother had been. Lacking the martial aura of his elder brother, and worried about the loyalty of the Song military, Song Taizong made an ostentatious display of a special troop of soldiers he had trained to do long sword dances:

He selected several hundred brave soldiers from the various armies and taught them to do long sword dances. All of them were able to catch swords from out of the air, jumping their bodies left and right to receive them. Of those who saw this, there were none who were not frightened. When the Kitan sent an envoy to discuss tribute, the emperor held a banquet at the temporary hall [the emperor was besieging Taiyuan at the time] and the soldiers entered with drawn long swords to perform. Several hundred men in a great clamor with bare arms entered holding blades, leaping, catching and throwing, the performance complete in its wonder. The Kitan envoy did not dare look at it directly.

And when he [the emperor] inspected the city he certainly ordered the dancing long sword soldiers to lead before him. Each time they displayed their skills the Northern Han people ascended the walls and watching it broke their spirit.[17]

Song Taizong used martial arts performances to intimidate his opponents – in this case, the Kitan and their clients the Northern Han – and to cloak himself in an aura of martial arts prowess. The long sword troop of several hundred soldiers also acted as a personal guard, something he felt he needed. It is noteworthy that they did their performance with long swords rather than swords, and that they were intentionally acrobatic and showy. The long sword was the weapon of martial arts performance and the specialized martial artist. It was distinct from the regular military close combat weapon of the ordinary soldier.

The distinction of the long sword as a specialized weapon not used on the battlefield appears to carry over into the regular martial arts performances of the Song army. The Office of Military Commanders (軍頭司) held bouts every ten days of wrestlers (*xiangpushou*) as well as long sword and staff fighters.[18] This was clearly understood to be a performance of martial arts rather than a demonstration of battlefield combat techniques. These regular events were designed to improve the participants' skills so that they would be in good form when they were called upon to perform at imperial banquets.[19] Martial arts demonstrations were part of the basic entertainment appropriate to formal government events. Wrestling had a very, very long history as a Chinese court entertainment, of course, as a generally nonlethal martial art. It is interesting that in the Song, long sword and staff were added to this category. Given Lady Gongsun's long sword dances in the Tang Dynasty and the second Song emperor's use of long sword dances, it is perhaps not surprising that long swords held this position at the Song court.

While the army maintained a specialized martial arts performance troupe, it also held demonstrations of unit formation and mock combat, at least in the northern capital, Kaifeng. Some mock combat took place with wooden swords, fighting with spears against shields, and even long swords against shields. Sword dances were also done during these demonstrations, as well as exhibitions showing a wide variety of other weapon skills. Lin Boyuan believes that military martial arts were directly influenced by the civilian practice of martial arts on a scale greater than in previous dynasties.[20] This is hard to prove, but it seems to be a reasonable assumption. The regularity with which the Song army apparently demonstrated its martial arts was new, possibly influenced by the presence in the capital of half the imperial army at any given time. Song soldiers were supposed to practice unit tactics daily, or every other day, depending upon their position and pay grade.[21]

Outside of the army, a new martial arts performance development in the Song capital was the creation of the "entertainment quarters 瓦肆," a special section of the city that developed out of a flourishing merchant culture and the usual entertainment mainstay of brothels. Thus the capital supported restaurants, brothels, and martial arts performances for the increasingly wealthy and well-traveled population centered there. Even after north China was lost to the Jurchen and the capital reestablished at Hangzhou in south China, a similar section was established in the new capital. In this area of the city, a wide variety of martial arts was performed purely to entertain an audience: boxing, wrestling, archery (with bow and crossbow), fencing, sword dances, and so on. The men and women who performed there were professional martial artists expert in particular fighting skills. These martial arts would have grown out of both the fighting techniques of the military and the arts practiced locally all over the empire.

Unlike the Hundred Events, official martial arts performances, government-sponsored wrestling and fighting competitions, or military exams, performances in the entertainment quarters were entirely in the private sphere. They were much more akin to local wrestling or martial arts competitions held on festival days, often in the village market or at a temple. The vast concentration of people in the Song capital – well over a million residents lived in Kaifeng in the eleventh century – created a large and permanent audience for these performances. This was part and parcel of the articulation of urban culture in the Song stimulated by the breakdown of the government-controlled market system. Under that system, markets were carefully regulated, fixed in both time and space and supervised by the government. The government's purpose in this was to tax goods and ensure accurate weights and measures. For a number of reasons, Kaifeng, though heavily patrolled and supervised by the army because it was the capital, did not restrict its marketplaces. This contributed to a vast increase in mercantile activity and enormous economic development. The martial arts flourished in this environment along with many other aspects of Chinese society.

These performers were originally mobile – one of the terms used for the troopes was "mobile tents 遊棚" – and they would set up wherever they had enough of an audience. The scale of these performance spaces varied considerably, with some seating somewhat more than fifty and the largest reportedly holding several thousand onlookers. At least in the capital, they were in constant operation: "Not considering wind, rain, cold, or heat, the audience for the various tents is day after day like this."[22] Some traveling medicine sellers tried to exploit the interest in martial arts performances to increase business. They would set up in a market with a sword or spear near them, though, as one text noted of these men, they were only trying to sell medicine and could not use the spear or sword.[23] Martial arts performances were thus a common and popular entertainment in marketplaces throughout China.

An indication of the variety of martial arts performed is contained in an account that lists the numbers and kinds of performers at one time: forty-four wrestlers (*jiaodi* 角抵), nine "grand" wrestlers 喬相撲, seven "female wind" 女颭 (the exact meaning of this term is unclear, but it appears to refer to female combatants of some kind), two staff men, two hard strikers 打碥, six weight lifters, and a number of other martial arts performers including those in bow and crossbow archery. It is hard to tell what some of these martial arts performances looked like or consisted of, but clearly variety was important. Not surprisingly, some of the categories closely followed the Hundred Events of earlier times, and current military practice. The inclusion of crossbow archery is a marker of the changing cultural environment of the Song, as opposed to the preceding Tang, Dynasty. The presence of the crossbow was not purely a matter of cultural identification, however; it was a reflection of changing battlefield weapon use. Performance martial arts were abstractions or representations of actual combat skills. Even in modified form, these martial arts drew from what the audience knew and expected. Expertise could be fully appreciated only if the viewer understood what he or she was seeing.

The performances were presented in a series of bouts within some sort of a ring 套子, probably with a roof or tent over it. One description says: "First there were several bouts of female winds causing people to watch. Afterward strongmen wrestled."[24] These contests and performances within a ring spread out of the capital to other parts of the empire, though it is impossible to determine what form they took. The circulation of martial artists was promoted by these performances, as the artists could now travel and perform as a regular entertainment, just like other services. This actually emphasized regional variation since different ways of fighting was an attraction. Whereas the martial arts in the army were constantly regularized and made uniform throughout all the units to the greatest extent possible (except in some special units), performance martial arts required differences to be maintained and promoted.

Female martial artists performed regularly in these venues, though it is unclear exactly what they did. We know from one memorial by the statesman and official Sima Guang that the emperor watched female wrestlers in the palace at least once. Sima actually wrote to chastise the emperor for watching this performance because the female wrestlers were naked.[25] It seems likely from one representation of female wrestlers on a wall painting that they wore some kind of g-string-like loincloth and shoes but were otherwise exposed. Male wrestlers were often bare-chested as well though without, it seems, the same unseemly connotations.

Lin Boyuan argues that the roots of the idea of different martial arts schools lies in the Song development of the entertainment quarters.[26] This seems circumstantially to be the case, though there is no hard evidence for it. Specifically, Lin believes that the articulation of separate schools happened in the later Song, after the fall of the north to the Jurchen. In the first part of the Song, the martial arts of the military were widely taught and spread into the farming population. These martial arts then evolved in the entertainment quarters. The requirements of providing an entertaining show forced performers to dramatize their arts and make them more elaborate. Where earlier martial arts dances were direct extensions of fighting techniques, performed on occasion for their aesthetic interest, the martial arts of the entertainment quarters were primarily concerned with aesthetics. The elaboration of the martial arts differentiated the practices of different performers much more clearly.

Prior to this emphasis on aesthetics, a martial arts instructor was only interested in teaching a student the basic use of infantry or cavalry weapons. For practical purposes, both armed and unarmed combat uses a very limited set of techniques. This simplicity is further emphasized by the need to teach large numbers of students simultaneously, and, in the military, for those students to fight as a unit rather than as individuals. A unit of spearmen, for example, has a small range of techniques for using their weapons en masse. Effective fighting is more the product of learning to perform a simple set of techniques with power, speed, and accuracy, and doing this correctly against an opponent, than of learning a large number of elaborate techniques. From an entertainment point of view, this may be acceptable in a genuine contest, but it is less so in a more staged event. Thus wrestling was probably not elaborated on since wrestling contests could and had always been used for entertainment in a nonlethal way. But sword and weapon bouts could not be real. Something had to be done to make the performances interesting over repeated viewings.

As these practices spread and were repeated, different troupes of performers would have developed their own particular systems of performance martial arts. Over time they would have taught new performers in the group their established repertoire. There were certainly regional differences in nomenclature with respect to the martial arts. Boxing went under an enormous variety of names, all of which, as far as we can tell, included kicking and sometimes throwing. Wrestling continued to maintain a similarly bewildering variety of names as well. At the very least, then, there were likely differences of practice in some respect among these differently designated martial arts. Particular elaborations handed down from a known or imagined person or place would have taken on the structure of a "school" named for its origin.

WEAPONS AND MILITARY TESTS

Although the *Complete Essentials from the Military Classics* presents an astonishing variety of weapons, most martial arts were confined to the usual battlefield choices. Swords (sometimes with a shield) and spears for contact weapons, and bows and crossbows for distance weapons. The astonishing array of weapons in the *Complete Essentials*, real and imagined, only came into use in the realm of literature as a means to distinguish characters from one another. Formulations like the "eighteen weapons" created an impossibly broad and impractical standard of martial arts skills. The only weapon that seems to have had any real use outside of the four mentioned above is the staff. There were some variations of use among these weapons, though it is difficult to pinpoint how widespread these practices were. Other differences were possibly simply the quality of the martial artist using the weapon. This mainstream of weapons use was reflected in the military exams used intermittently during the Song Dynasty.

Staffs had always been used as weapons, but in the Song they began to take on a more prominent role. There were, for example, "Staff Societies" in several northern regions that maintained family traditions of practice. A biographical entry on Wang Huan shows a family tradition of staff use: "At that time, Wang Huan's father was called 'Iron Staff Wang'. When Huan was young he struck a rock with a staff; the rock shattered and was completely smashed."[27] Skill with a staff was a particularly useful martial art because wooden poles would have been cheap and readily available to most rural people. Farmers would always have had some sort of pole around, requiring no investment in a specialized metal weapon. Staffs would also have been widely used in martial arts performances because they could be used with less likelihood of serious injury. In later descriptions of weapons instructors, staff and spear were frequently mentioned together, and these weapons had a somewhat intertwined relationship. Many of the movements would have been the same, with the spear the much more lethal weapon. Particularly in peacetime, staffs would have been useful for civilians who wanted to defend themselves with less likelihood of killing their opponent. Killing, even in self-defense, would be a serious crime.

Matters were quite different in the military, of course. There the question for the government was how to recruit or train effective soldiers and officers. Soldiers were less of a serious concern, since they were mostly required to perform a limited set of physical tasks under heavy discipline. The biggest concerns with respect to the common soldiers was developing effective tactics, keeping them obedient, and keeping costs down. Officers, on the other hand, were a serious problem. The men who commanded troops had to have strong martial arts skills, the ability to lead men, and tactical and strategic acumen. It was the mental skills that proved most elusive, and a number of ineffective measures were tried to address the problem. Our concern here, however, is the physical skills of combat. At a minimum, an officer needed to demonstrate strong combat skills, and this demonstration formed the bulk of the Song military exams.

Despite, or perhaps because of, the ubiquity of swords as a common close combat weapon, fencing was not emphasized in military exams. It was again archery, on foot and on horseback, using a bow and using a crossbow, which was tested first. The strength of bow a man was able to draw, or in the case of a crossbow, span, was also tested. Only after a man demonstrated a minimum strength and capability with archery could he go on to the oral part of the exam, which was just for placement. Officers were not expected to be expert martial artists, but facility with archery, particularly horse archery, was probably a good litmus test for overall martial arts training. The Song military exam system did not produce any generals or officers of note. Most officers achieved their initial positions either through family connections (they were born into an officer family) or through working their way up by success on the battlefield. Given the requirements of horse archery, it was highly unlikely that a man without access to military equipment and formal training could develop these skills. Of course, most men who already had access to this equipment and training did not need an exam to join the ranks of the officer class.

CONCLUSION

Martial arts permeated much of Song Chinese society, fully developing over the course of the dynasty into a regular, mainstream entertainment. The martial arts never left north China, maintaining a steady presence among a population that was under regular threat of steppe raiding. Local elites trained in the martial arts and required that their dependents also learn these skills. Weapons and martial arts were widely available at all levels of society. At the same time, however, an elite of civil service degree holders dominated the imperial government at every level. Even the military side of the government was controlled by these highly educated civil servants. This new bureaucratic elite did not practice martial arts as previous national elites had, going so far as to separate themselves from the time-honored Confucian practice of archery.

The bureaucratic elite actively defined itself against the martial ideals, insisting that generals and the military be subordinate to civil control. With the exception of the founding emperor and his immediate successor, Song emperors were educated in the civil and literary arts and did not practice martial arts. These rulers and their closest officials ran a bureaucratic institution without any personal experience of combat or war. Even so, they did watch martial arts performances as part of military reviews, and probably as entertainment as well. They were also concerned with the preparedness of the military, and the problems of social order, both issues that directly related to training in martial arts. The constant goal was to develop martial artists who would use their abilities in the service of state policy. Unfortunately, it was often difficult to convince men versed in the means of violence to wait humbly for the government to provide for their needs.

The social organization of martial arts in local Song society would persist until well into the Ming Dynasty. This was a reflection of the persistence of the particular pattern of local power that developed in the eleventh century and continued into the sixteenth century. The particular ups and downs of imperial houses were less pertinent at these lower levels than the economic system and land tenure. While an imperial government could always send its army to enforce its authority in any one place, it could not, or at least did not, try to do so everywhere. Local society was left to mostly local strongmen or elites to police, and these men used trained martial artists to carry out their will.

Purely with respect to martial arts history, the rise of the entertainment quarters, the performance spaces for martial arts, was the most important change in the Song. The requirements of performing for entertainment led to elaboration and differentiation that were tied to lineages of practice. This coincided with the rise of theater and intertwined with oral storytelling traditions. While most martial arts was still used as a means of violence by the imperial army, or by local strongmen, it now expanded permanently into the world of entertainment. Martial artists would therefore come to be romanticized for their ability to defy authority in an unjust world. Martial arts empowered the individual against the larger structures of power, at least in fiction. Some articulation of this emerged in the early stories of the bandit Song Jiang first written down about 1300, probably from oral tales already in circulation.

The Song imperial house itself was completely stamped out by the Mongols in 1279. Once again a steppe group came into China, bringing a new culture to imperial government. Much of their culture and martial arts were familiar to the Chinese, and many of the trends in the martial arts would simply continue the path begun under the Song.

7

The Yuan Dynasty

The rise of the Mongols under Chinggis Khan in the thirteenth century was a signal event in world history. Following the pattern of the preceding Kitans and Jurchens, the Mongols began by overthrowing the preexisting steppe political order, and then advanced south into China. Of course, in the case of the Mongols, they also reached across Eurasia and founded the largest land empire in history. In China the Mongols founded a Chinese-style dynastic government to administer and rule the Chinese population. This dynasty, the Yuan (1272–1368), like the preceding steppe dynasties, used a hybrid Chinese-steppe government system. The privileges and power of the ruling Mongols were paramount, though some Chinese did achieve a measure of authority. For the most part, the Mongol emperors did not attempt to change Chinese culture or society, preferring to leave local society alone.

The Yuan government was most concerned with extracting taxes and labor from the Chinese population. Part of the labor was military forces. The Mongol army was made up of different components formed by combining specific groups with specific military skills. Mongols themselves served exclusively as horse-archers. Infantry, naval, or siege units were drafted from subject populations with these skills. When the Yuan invaded Japan, for example, the navy was Chinese and Korean, and many of the troops were Jurchen. Very few Mongols took part. As a category, Yuan Dynasty martial arts include both Chinese and various steppe practices. Whereas in the Six Dynasties and Tang Dynasty the meaning and practice of these martial arts was more combined, in the Yuan Dynasty, Chinese and steppe martial arts were quite distinct.

MONGOL MARTIAL ARTS

Mongol martial arts were similar to those of other steppe groups, with the greatest emphasis on horse archery. As Marco Polo described them: "Their weapons are bows and swords and clubs; but they rely mainly on their bows, for they are excellent archers. On their backs they wear an armour of buffalo hide or some other leather which is very tough."[1] The other steppe groups were able to integrate into the Mongol forces easily as horse-archers because they fought and were armed in the same way. Accomplished steppe warriors and generals could work their way up in the Mongol military in ways that Chinese could not. Chinese soldiers and officers served in separate units, and most did not share a common language with their Mongol overlords. Most Mongols, including Yuan emperors, did not read Chinese, and the language of war and government was Mongolian.

The Mongolian and steppe mode of warfare was extremely fluid, with large bodies of horsemen moving in coordinated units while firing at the enemy. Unlike Chinese infantry, who prized standing firm in the face of enemy attack, the Mongols

are never ashamed to have recourse to flight. They manoeuvre freely, shooting at the enemy, now from this quarter, now from that. They have trained their horses so well that they wheel this way or that as quickly as a dog would do. When they are pursued and take to flight, they fight as well and as effectively as when they are face to face with the enemy. When they are fleeing at top speed, they twist around with their bows and let fly their arrows to such good purpose that they kill the horses of the enemy and riders too.[2]

This firing while retreating, the "Parthian shot," was a well-known practice among steppe people, but extremely difficult to execute en masse.

Mongolian martial arts do not appear to have gone much beyond horse archery. With the exception of a few noted individuals, most Mongols and their steppe allies or subjects used close combat weapons without much specific martial arts training. The absence of any data on the contact weapon skills of the Mongols may be an artifact of the sources, however, since close combat weapons were used extensively in battle. It may well be that in Mongolian culture only horse archery was really valued. Skills with other weapons were simply not prized in the same way.

Martial arts practice among the Chinese subject population was carefully watched for signs of rebellion. As long as Chinese martial arts remained submilitary, that is to say, without large numbers of heavily armed and armored men training as units, it was ignored. Weapons were restricted, though given the limitations of the Yuan government's control of local society, this was probably only partially effective. Moreover, Chinese crafts-men would have been quite capable of producing large numbers of weap-ons. At the same time, Chinese troops were drafted into Mongol armies at various times and used the same sorts of martial arts they had used during the Song Dynasty, including shooting with firearms. As was always the case, it was not so much martial arts and weapons that concerned a government as the subordination of those skills and tools to government authority.

North China remained a highly militarized society, even among the Chinese. Many local or regional Chinese strongmen accommodated them-selves to Mongol rule and received, in turn, fiefs under the Yuan Dynasty. These men, perhaps the most notable of whom was Li Quan, controlled vast swathes of territory and commanded tens of thousands of armed men. They were allowed to pass their territories on to their descendants in return for contributing military manpower to the Yuan emperor's campaigns and accepting his rule. Many northern Chinese had been under steppe rule for almost two centuries by the time the Song house was completely wiped out in 1279, first with the Jurchen Jin and then the Mongol Yuan. Those in the area around modern Beijing had been under Kitan Liao rule since the middle of the tenth century before that. Yet those Chinese retained their sense of ethnic identity for the most part, and indeed were not pressured by their steppe overlords to adopt steppe culture.

Southern China had not been nearly as militarized and did not fall under steppe rule until the Yuan defeat of the Song in the late thirteenth century. Horse archery was not a well-practiced or widespread martial art in the south, even among the elites. There was all manner of local violence in the south, however, as endemic banditry induced local leaders to create self-defense forces. These units fought in the mountainous or riverine terrain of the south, mostly on foot or in boats. Southern Chinese were also the last group to come under Yuan authority, and therefore were the most suspect in the eyes of the government. They were officially classed last, in descend-ing order, for status in the Yuan.

The place of Chinese people under the Yuan was thus split: northerners were held in higher regard than southerners. Some northerners gained great power and operated in many respects like their Mongol overlords. Yet they understood themselves to be Chinese, not Mongol, and the government classed them as such. Southern Chinese also regarded themselves as Chinese, but they made few concessions, or at least as few as they could manage, to the Yuan government. Mongol garrisons were scattered across China to ensure order and prevent any uprisings. The Song had tried with very limited success to appeal to the ethnic identity of the northern Chinese, inciting them to rise up against the Mongols in aid of Song military efforts. Similarly, Li Quan's son, Li Tan, would attempt to form an alliance of Chinese strongmen when he rebelled against his Yuan masters. Ethnicity was not the overwhelming interest of the forces contending for power. Men like the older and younger Li straddled the Mongol and Chinese worlds in politics as well as martial arts.

The Yuan Dynasty crumbled rather than being destroyed by an outside power. It was the inherent instability of Mongolian politics that distracted and diminished Yuan authority. These internal leadership struggles allowed rebellions to develop and expand, and in the end they prevented even effective government officials from defeating them. The Yuan empire broke up; some Mongols retreated and others were pushed north as a new dynasty, the Ming, emerged from decades of warfare. The destruction across China was deep and widespread. Vast armed groups, some professing a version of Buddhism, pillaged and fought for territory. The Shaolin Temple, like so many other places, was burned to the ground in 1351 by the Red Turbans, a rebel group that arose in the fourteenth century to oppose the Mongols, just as it had been destroyed in the seventh century. As then, the temple was a repository of wealth, with gold-covered statues and other valuables. The same destruction was repeated in countless homes and temples. War once again brought weapons and martial arts back after a few generations of peace.

ARCHERY

Archery for the Mongols and other steppe peoples, as well as Tibetans, was more than just a martial art. As it was among the Chinese far in the past, archery had religious and spiritual implications. Shooting arrows could be both religious and apotropaic, that is, archery was done as part of religious ceremonies and was used to drive away bad spirits. Shooting had power, over both life and death, but also over the spirit world. Archery was basic to steppe life through hunting and fighting, and a key part of steppe identity. Given its ubiquity in the steppe among both sexes, but particularly for men, skill with archery would not require mention in a biography of a warrior or general. On the contrary, however, virtually every great warrior or general is noted in the Chinese sources as being a skilled archer. Archery was a definitive marker of steppe character.

There are far fewer non-Chinese historical sources available for the Mongols or any of the other steppe groups. Those few sources are less routine in their mention of horse archery skills, assuming that a steppe audience would understand that every Mongol could perform this martial art with basic competence. The Chinese historiographical tradition and historians writing in Chinese even for steppe rulers still required the inclusion of a note in the biography of a warrior or general that he or she was skilled in horse archery. It was an important distinction to make about someone's childhood or particular characteristics, something that set the individual apart from any number of other people who did not practice that particular martial art. Chinese literati were not horse-archers, even if many northern Chinese elites were. Probably by the Song Dynasty, but definitely by the Yuan Dynasty, the clearest indication that a man or woman was part of the martial (*wu*) rather than civil (*wen*) world was proficiency with horse archery. This emphasis no doubt grew during the Song Dynasty as the limited number of horses available to the Chinese even before the loss of north China increasingly made horse riding itself a military skill. During the second half of the Song, very few people who were not in the military would have been able to ride horses.

Hunting and the itinerant lifestyle of the steppe was a critical component of the Mongol identity that Yuan emperors cultivated for their Mongol subjects. Unlike Song emperors who, with the exception of the founding emperor, did not hunt, Yuan emperors all hunted. Yurts, the portable felt tents of the Mongols, were pitched on the grounds of the imperial palace. Imperial hunts were held that included Mongol and other steppe aristocrats. These hunts functioned as military exercises in coordinating groups of men as well as providing the opportunity to demonstrate archery skills. After the hunt there would be a large feast centered around eating enormous amounts of recently killed game accompanied by drinking (mostly of *koumiss*, fermented mare's milk). In Chinese stories of martial artists like *The Water Margin*, heroic fighters were frequently marked by their massive consumption of meat and alcohol. It is unclear when martial vigor became connected with ingesting large amounts of meat and wine, but it was so important that it carried through even to Buddhist figures who were, ostensibly, teetotaling vegetarians.

Under the Kitan rulers, military campaigns began with a ceremony called "Shooting Ghost Arrows." The practice originated with the ritualized execution of a prisoner by archery, but by the tenth and eleventh centuries it had also developed a somewhat abstracted form as well. In the original practice of shooting ghost arrows, the warriors, when going out on campaign, would tie to a post a prisoner already condemned to death and shoot him full of arrows. Upon returning from campaign, they would do the same thing to a spy. In the later version, a campaign would begin and after the first successful encounter with the enemy, the commanding general, or even the emperor, would shoot ghost arrows in four directions. Sometimes the shooting of ghost arrows was accompanied by the sacrifice of an animal like a white horse. This martial arts ceremony drove away misfortune through the power of archery.

Archery also had the power to summon rains, demonstrating again that this martial art had a meaning within some steppe cultures all out of proportion to its simple physical practice. During droughts, the Liao emperor would "shoot the willow" in an attempt to bring rain. In one version of this ceremony, a willow branch would be planted in the ground and the emperor and the rest of the court would take turns shooting at it. In another version, a willow branch was planted, consecrated with a libation of wine, offered crops and fodder, and then prayed to. Following this, members of the royal family would try to shoot the branch. If rain fell within three days, the officials were rewarded.

The Jurchen had a similar ceremony in which a double line of willow branches was set into the ground, and each participant marked one with a piece of cloth. Each man then galloped toward the branches and attempted to sever his designated branch with an arrow, and then grab the cut top as he rode by. This required considerable skill but shows what was possible for a steppe archer. In these very public displays in front of the emperor, a man could distinguish himself and win favor. The spiritual and ceremonial context connected with these archery displays directly tied martial arts skill to spiritual power. Bows and arrows and archery were spiritually powerful, and a highly skilled archer was someone who possessed and directed that power.

These ceremonial practices were also used among the Tanguts and Mongols. The Tanguts would take captured men and shoot them, calling it "killing the ghost, targeting the ghost."[3] Alternatively, they would make a straw man, plant it in the ground, and then have everyone shoot it. Particularly in the situation described for the Tanguts related to this specific instance, it seems as if the point was to embody a military defeat in a straw man or captive, and to expiate that failure by a ritualized killing. Perhaps the ghost in question was the spirit responsible for the defeat. This would make sense of the Kitan practice of shooting ghost arrows at the inception of a campaign as a way to drive away threatening spirits.

The Yuan emperors employed much the same ceremony in the last ten-day week of the twelfth month of the year. Straw effigies of a man and a dog, complete with inner organs rendered from cloth, were shot to pieces by aristocratic members of the court. This was all part of a religious process blessed by a shaman. The Yuan imperial court retained its Mongolian and steppe practices even within a nominally Chinese context. This was in sharp contrast to the disappearance of archery from the Song court. Archery for Mongols still had meaning beyond the prosaic ability to kill men or beasts.

Even so, the very real value of bows and arrows in warfare led to repeated edicts by the Yuan emperor forbidding Chinese people (*Hanren* 漢人), sometimes more specifically southern Chinese (*Nanren* 南人, or *Jiangnanren* 江南人), from owning or manufacturing bows and arrows.[4] These prohibitions often extended to the possession, storage, or manufacture of any kind of weapon, and to the practice of martial arts. Bows and weapons were supposed to be collected by government officials, with specific provisions, in at least one edict, for what should be done with them based upon their quality:

Divide the bows, arrows and weapons seized from the Han territory and Jiangnan into three groups. The lower group, destroy them; the middle group, bestow them on Mongols living nearby; the upper group, store them in the arsenal.[5]

The private production of weapons was prohibited as the corollary to government production of weapons:

The various circuits shall establish bureaus to manufacture military equipment. Private manufacture is a capital offense. [If] there are those among the people who have [military equipment] and do not report it to the officials, it is the same [offense] as private manufacturing.[6]

Sometimes these edicts were directed at *Hanren* or northern Chinese rather than the southern Chinese from Jiangnan (the area south of the Yangzi River). One edict was even directed at foreign Buddhist monks: "It is forbidden for Western foreign monks to possess weapons."[7] Of course, that there were so many edicts repeating the prohibition on weapon manufacture and ownership is proof that weapons were being widely produced and used. This was clearly a problem as far as the government saw it, though it never prohibited Mongols from making or owning weapons.

One of the punishments for someone from Jiangnan having a bow and arrows was registration as a soldier.[8] Service in the Yuan military was clearly not something that a southern Chinese wanted to enter into. Although *Hanren* were repeatedly prohibited from possessing weapons, and even from practicing martial arts (*wuyi*),[9] they could be subject to military service. One edict specified that *Hanren* were strictly forbidden to possess weapons; those who were on the military registers were to be issued weapons when they went on campaign, and on returning were required to hand them back to the government.[10] These edicts reflect a serious problem of recruitment and training for the Yuan army among the northern Chinese population. If even men registered for military service received weapons only when they went on campaign, then they would not have the martial arts skills to use them well. Yet again, for the government to insist on these practices shows that, in fact, the northern Chinese population was already armed. Yuan policy with respect to arms and martial arts reflects a conqueror's anxieties when ruling a restive and highly militarized population.

Control of archery through restricting access to bows and arrows was a critical aspect of Mongol rulership. Without bows and arrows the Chinese population could not practice archery and would be handicapped in resisting Mongol authority. In that sense, every edict prohibiting Chinese archery was a sign of Mongol anxiety and perhaps real weakness. Even if the prohibitions could not be completely enforced, they would still reduce the number and quality of skilled Chinese archers. From the Chinese perspective, of course, particularly the non-archery-practicing literati, archery was now tightly connected to barbarians and military men.

WEAPONS

The Mongols were also concerned about other weapons and martial arts practice among the Chinese. As with archery, the problem was how to keep people opposed to the Yuan Dynasty and Mongol power from learning how to fight and obtaining the means to do so. The Mongols themselves did use close combat weapons in addition to their bows, and there were some modifications and shifts in martial arts practice during the Yuan. Mongols often used a set of close combat weapons different from those of the Chinese, though they were heavily influenced by Chinese practice. Chinese manufacturing prowess more than anything else amplified the effects of Chinese choices about martial arts and weapon preferences.

The phrase "The Eighteen Martial Arts 十八般武藝" first appeared during the later part of the Song Dynasty referring to a vague set of eighteen weapon skills. It was not until the Yuan Dynasty that someone delineated what those eighteen martial arts were. The phrase was popularized in Yuan period theater, where it was used as a standard shorthand for complete martial arts knowledge. Over time a specific list of weapons was developed in the realm of fiction, first in the theater and then in oral tales. An anonymous play presents a list of twelve weapons in its discussion of the eighteen martial arts: "Bow, crossbow, spear, shield, ge-halberd, spear, long sword, ji-halberd, whip, chain, truncheon 檛, and mallet 槌."

The remaining six weapons of the eighteen are not named. Not until a Yuan version of *The Water Margin* does a full list of eighteen martial arts appear: "Spear, 鍾 (?), bow, crossbow, gun, whip, metal tablet,[11] long sword, chain, truncheon, fu-axe, yue-axe, ge-halberd, ji-halberd, shield, staff and spear, and toothless rake.

The literary origin of this delineation of the eighteen weapons is clear from the omission of the most basic close combat weapon, the sword, from the list, as well as the inclusion of weapons like the whip or the toothless rake. While many of these weapons presumably did appear on stage, most never made it to the battlefield or into the hands of most martial artists. Also, note the shift of the bow and the crossbow from their earlier positions at the head of the list, to third and fourth, respectively, and the entry of firearms into the formal description of martial arts skills. The resulting list is an inventive compilation of performative requirements and some actual changes in warfare, rather than being pure fiction or pure reality. As a whole, the mastery of the eighteen martial arts demonstrates that the warrior in question is a complete fighter.

Of course, the eighteen martial arts do not include unarmed combat or the ubiquitous sword. Unarmed combat skills are known under a variety of terms for boxing and wrestling and were likely assumed for someone mastering so many weapon skills. Unarmed combat was of less value in a real fight than armed combat, since most melees outside of stage performances would have been between armed fighters. A martial artist had the realistic expectation that he or she would need to be armed and know how to use weapons in a genuine fight. Weapons were also useful in the theatrical and storytelling realms as markers of individual warriors. A broad panoply of weapons allowed performers to distinguish between otherwise similarly described or made-up characters.

The absence of the sword in favor of the long sword is more problematic. It is possible that the long sword was understood to mean fencing in general and thus included the sword. Alternatively, the long sword was seen as the weapon of the highly skilled martial artist rather than the ordinary sword used by soldiers. While long swords were more widely used among the Mongols than the Chinese, the setting and Chinese identity of most of the martial arts heroes in Chinese fiction argue against the imposition of a chronologic bias on the material. Moreover, the stories began to form under the Song, were possibly first made into theatrical productions in the Yuan, but reached their most mature versions during the Ming. Some versions of *The Water Margin* only emerged in the Qing Dynasty. Ultimately then, the formulation of a specific eighteen martial arts was neither a direct reflection

of reality nor entirely separate from it. The requirements of fiction – poetic
license, if you will – took precedence over realism, subordinating real-world
martial arts to the visual and narrative needs of a good story.

Outside of the realm of fiction, there were some differences in weapon
use during the Yuan Dynasty. We first see mention of double swords being
used in battle in north China in the thirteenth century. One of the earliest
recorded fighters to use paired swords was Yang Miaozhen, the wife of the
Shandong bandit and warlord Li Quan. In addition to her skill at riding
and shooting, she also used paired swords and was proficient with the
"peach blossom spear."[12] Several other notable fighters are mentioned
using paired swords in battle. It appears that warriors using these swords
were particularly effective in confined terrain, where they were able to break
through deadlocked troops. At least in the case of Yang Miaozhen, of
course, the fighter in question was Chinese, not Mongol. Our last mention
of someone using double swords – in that case, double long swords – was
the female long sword dancers in the Tang Dynasty. Reports of this particular set of weapons on the battlefield in more than one instance attest to
its real-world use, however, rather than purely a performance martial art.

Mongol weapon use had two distinct aspects. The primary martial art
of the Mongols was horse archery, but they did have recourse to close
combat weapons as well. They were distinct in their use of the long sword
and the employment of the double-headed spear. Unlike the Chinese, or
indeed most of eastern Eurasia, the Mongols still made extensive use of
long swords. The reason for this is unclear. Where Chinese armies were
professional forces armed by the state with uniform weapons, Mongol
soldiers were essentially militia men who brought their own weapons to
the battlefield. At the same time, the Mongols did not themselves have a
very strong manufacturing base, and many of their iron combat weapons
would have been obtained from trading and raiding. Under these circumstances, it is possible that large numbers of long swords had found their
way into the steppe and continued to circulate there long after Chinese
armies stopped using them.

The second somewhat distinctively Mongol weapon was the double-
headed spear. Mongols appear to have preferred spears with metal spear
points at either end. Chinese spears, with a few exceptions, generally had
only a single head to them. Some Chinese double-headed polearms had
blades at either end as cavalry weapons for slashing rather than thrusting.
In the case of the Mongols, it may have had something to do with the short
ponies they rode into battle (though most Asian horses were small by
modern standards). Not only did they need to thrust at standing targets

but they may also have wanted to spike already prone opponents as they rode over them. This would have given them an efficient tool for finishing off broken enemy formations as they rode through, without having to turn their spears over. Indeed, it is possible that their short mounts also contributed to their continued use of the long sword, which was a much better thrusting weapon than the sword.

Some other weapons did find their way onto the battlefield in Mongol hands, but none proved especially effective. Mongols brought whatever weapons were available into battle, and this could sometimes be as simple as a club. The power of the Mongol army was not in the individual prowess of particular warriors. It was the coordinated actions of large groups of Mongol cavalry that proved so devastating. They did not close with an enemy before the opposing formation had already been shattered by missile fire. Close-range missile fire was preferable to hand-to-hand combat. It was simply more effective for Mongol cavalry to use accurate, close-range archery with heavier arrows than to come to grips with an enemy.

WRESTLING AND BOXING

Not surprisingly, given the long steppe association with wrestling, the Mongols were enthusiastic supporters of wrestling contests. Wrestling no longer had a strong association with prowess on the battlefield, making it a "safe" martial art from the perspective of the authorities. Nonetheless, Yuan government prohibitions on weapon ownership and practice had a limited effect on the martial arts. It was clear that unarmed martial arts were hard to separate from armed martial arts. Traveling merchants who of necessity knew martial arts or employed men who did contributed to a floating population of martial artists. These wandering martial artists practiced wrestling, boxing, staff fighting, and spear fighting, and they could attract many disciples. This appears to be consistent with what was happening during the Song Dynasty, particularly the later part of it, when martial arts teachers traveled around for a variety of reasons. A skilled martial artist could find work and students, and, as one text noted, "For long it has been like this without stop, customs are licentious and violent."[13]

If it was clear that there was a well-established population of martial artists who practiced and taught staff, spear, and wrestling (and sometimes boxing), it is less apparent why these skills were related. Staff and spear fighting are mentioned in accounts of the period and also in literary representations of martial artists. Many of the techniques of staff and spear were similar, but we simply have no information on how they related to unarmed combat. In Yuan period plays, some characters represent themselves as skilled with spear and staff, and having studied boxing and wrestling.

At least with respect to the martial arts, the terms used for "study" (學) or "practice" (習), among others, are used interchangeably in both the historical records and in fiction. This makes it impossible to determine based on the verb used whether the martial art referred to is concerned with armed or unarmed combat. A Yuan edict of 23 January 1322 states: "Han people are prohibited from holding [or having] weapons, going out to hunt and practicing martial arts 禁漢人執兵器出獵及習武藝."[14] The eighteen martial arts, as we have seen, do not include unarmed fighting skills, presenting us with the possibility that "martial arts" may only refer to armed fighting skills. In other texts, boxing and wrestling are listed in addition to skill with staff or spear. Thus, while the government was well aware that unarmed martial arts skills were strongly connected to armed martial arts skills, it was really only concerned about armed fighting and the ownership of weapons. Unarmed martial artists, no matter how skilled, were not a threat to the regime.

A number of men and women were noted for wrestling and boxing skills. Particular skill in boxing or wrestling was sometimes noted for men otherwise known for their performance on the battlefield. Following the usual description of them as being good at horse archery, it seemed noteworthy to point out that the person in question was also a skilled boxer and wrestler. Sometimes a martial artist is described as skilled at one of these skills, but several accounts group boxing and wrestling together. This is the equivalent of stating that the person is highly skilled in unarmed combat. Obviously, not everyone was so skilled or it would not require mention, but it is not clear how skilled in unarmed combat most warriors were. Were soldiers, Mongol, Chinese, or others, trained in unarmed combat? In this period we do not know for certain. There were traveling Chinese martial arts teachers who gave instruction in unarmed combat (boxing and wrestling), and in staff and spear.

Formal martial arts training in wrestling and boxing was available outside the military. Within the standing military, soldiers were formally trained to use weapons. Mongol soldiers were not, to our knowledge, instructed in weapon use as part of military training. They were expected to come to the battlefield armed with weapons they knew how to use, and riding on horses capable of bearing them in battle. Some group training was done so that units of cavalry could act in a coordinated fashion. Outside of the military on campaign, wrestling, but not boxing, was popular in the steppe. Boxing in particular then may have been more distinctly

ILLUSTRATIONS 16 AND 17. Detail from Yan Geng, *The Demon Queller Zhong Kui Giving his Sister Away in Marriage*, thirteenth-century source: Purchase, the Dillon Fund Gift and Rogers Fund, 1990 © Metropolitan Museum of Art.

Chinese, and something usually practiced outside of the formal military. There were no large standing formations of Chinese troops serving the Yuan government, but rather more ad hoc units recruited as needed. Thus, at least during the Yuan dynasty, boxing was more of a civilian than military art.

Men were not the only skilled wrestlers, nor were these skills confined to the lower classes, at least among the Mongols. Marco Polo recounts the story of a princess named Aiyaruk:

This damsel was so strong that in all the kingdom there was no squire or gallant who could vanquish her. . . .

The king her father wished to give her a husband. But she steadfastly refused, declaring that she would never take a husband till she found some nobleman who could get the better of her in a trial of strength. And the king her father had given her the privilege of marrying whom she would. ...

She made it known in many parts of the world that any youth of gentle birth might come and try his strength with her and if he could vanquish her she would take him as her husband. ...

This was the bargain: if the youth could so far vanquish her as to force her to the ground, he should have her to wife; if she vanquished him, he must forfeit a hundred horses to her. In this way she had gained more than 10,000 horses.

Aiyaruk later defeated another visiting prince, who forfeited a thousand horses to her. At least as far as Marco Polo's account goes, she was never defeated and did not get married, though she did accompany her father into battle where she acquitted herself very well.[15]

Elite Chinese women did not, to our knowledge, practice martial arts of any kind. The growing influence of Neo-Confucianism in the late thirteenth century severely circumscribed the activities of women, though this would have impacted the lives of elite Chinese women far more than poor women. Just as literati men had given up archery and martial arts practice in the Song, literati women also lost much of their freedom of movement outside the house. At the same time, however, female martial artists performed in shows, and steppe women of all ranks maintained varying degrees of martial arts skill.

Boxing and wrestling appear to have had a more tenuous relationship to the standing military during the Yuan period, if for no other reason than the more limited formal training of the Yuan army and navy. Where Song soldiers had been recruited and then trained, Yuan soldiers, drawn from many groups, were drafted into the army because of the skills they already had. Unarmed combat was of no particular battlefield use, and the Yuan government would not have seen much value in drafting men skilled in boxing and wrestling for a military campaign. At the same time, boxing and wrestling were widely represented in fiction, both storytelling and theater. Some government officials were even concerned enough about martial arts practice among the populace to advocate establishing formal military study and exams to recruit those with military talents into the army.[16]

Wrestling was popular for performances and was imperially patronized. Some merchants seem to have taken to it as a self-defense skill, though not, it seems, boxing. If anything, boxing appears to have been the more esoteric skill. On two separate occasions, Yuan emperors were so curious about men they heard of as skilled boxers that they ordered them to court. On both occasions, the emperors selected strong men to try to defeat them but the visitors proved able to beat multiple opponents. While wrestling had regular matches, boxing did not, and it seems that some Yuan emperors did not get much opportunity to see men skilled in the striking arts.

LI QUAN

Many of the issues discussed in this chapter played out in the lives of Li Quan, his wife, Yang Miaozhen, and their son, Li Tan.[17] Li Quan was an extremely important figure at the end of the Song and Jin Dynasties, and the beginning of the Yuan Dynasty. He has the longest individual biography in the official Song history, and there is an extensive secondary scholarship on him as well. He and his wife even appear as comic figures in a famous dramatic play. Some have speculated that Yang Miaozhen was the model for the character in *The Water Margin*, Ten Feet of Steel, a female fighter who used double swords.

From the Song perspective, Li Quan was an evil official who betrayed them; from the Jurchen perspective he was a rebellious bandit; and from the Mongol perspective he was a loyal hereditary lord who died fighting for their cause. He was all these things because his main goal was to establish himself as overlord of Shandong by playing off the three main powers against each other. When it became clear that the Mongols would destroy the Jurchen Jin and that loyalty to the Song was less valuable than loyalty to the Mongols, Li submitted to the Mongols. After Li's death, his wife temporarily held his position before she passed it to his son. In 1262, his son, Tan, rebelled against the Mongols in conjunction with a number of other Chinese warlords who held hereditary regional or local power under the Yuan Dynasty. When Tan was eventually defeated and captured, he was executed in the manner of a Mongol aristocrat, wrapped in a rug and trampled to death by horses.

Li Quan began his life as a farmer and worked for a time as a horse trader, merchant, and smuggler. He was "nimble and active with bow and horse, and capable of wielding an iron spear. At the time he was called: 'Iron Spear Li.'"[18] The iron spear was a formidable weapon requiring great strength and skill, not the standard military weapon of a soldier. Li's skills as a horseman and archer were basic martial arts for a northern Chinese strongman. He took up banditry in the chaos caused by Mongol raids into Jin-controlled north China, eventually taking the leadership of another bandit army controlled by Yang Miaozhen. Yang is described as "crafty and ruthless, good at horse archery."[19] She became leader of the bandit army when her brother was killed and no competent male heir was available. There appears to have been no difficulty with her becoming leader, though she did marry Li Quan and hand over control soon afterward.

Yang Miaozhen nevertheless remained important in the control and advancement of this force, though it was her husband who led in the field. The Song government both needed and distrusted Li Quan as they tried to run a clandestine war against the Jin by supplying Li with supplies and official titles. As he was Chinese, some seemed to think that he should by definition be loyal to the Song, and he used that to convince them of his reliability. The Jin saw Li as a disloyal subject and a bandit manipulated by the Song. In all of this, Li and his wife demonstrated the martial culture and skills of local northern Chinese power holders. Shandong had been under Jurchen rule since the early twelfth century, and the Chinese living there had no particular reason to be loyal to the Song. Their martial arts resembled those of the steppe more than those of the Song, yet they were unequivocally Chinese in self-identification.

The Mongols had no difficulty in incorporating Li Quan and his power base in Shandong into their system of government. Nor did they have any problem accommodating his wife's control over that same territory after his death. These northern Chinese warriors, husband and wife, built up their power base through their martial arts skills and political acumen. Even the rebellion of their son fit within Mongol norms. Mongol aristocrats constantly fought with each other over power, usually with contending armies. Of course, Li and his wife would be discussed and represented in the world of Chinese history and fiction. In that realm, they were bandits, or rough figures of low comedy.

CONCLUSION

Later Chinese rejected the Mongol Yuan Dynasty's separation of Chinese people into northerners and southerners, insisting that the division was perverse and inaccurate. Although regional identities were deeply imbedded in the Chinese consciousness, so was some sense of a shared larger culture. Some modern Chinese, fueled by late twentieth-century political concerns, go further still and insist that the Mongols, Jurchen, Tanguts, Kitan, and other steppe and minority groups are and *were* all part of a unified "Chinese" political body.[20] From the late twentieth- and early twenty-first-century Chinese perspective, a unified, nominally Chinese (in whatever sense) polity in the thirteenth century is an important proto-national entity with which to establish an enduring Chinese hegemony over territory that includes part of the steppe. Mongol rule thus becomes "Chinese" rule, or at least foreign control over an institutionally Chinese government administering an eternal, natural Chinese territory. The Jurchen were the progenitors of the Manchus, who would conquer and rule China under the Qing Dynasty (1644–1911). Certainly with respect to martial arts one might reasonably argue that many northern Chinese fought in ways similar to the Mongols or other steppe people.

The Yuan separation of Chinese into two groups principally reflected administrative concerns rather than ethnicity.[21] Northern Chinese had lived under steppe rule for longer and would have been easier to govern than southerners. The Yuan government was sensitive to the differences between many groups and tried to deal appropriately with its subjects. This was not an enlightened position but a pragmatic one. The Yuan state needed to be efficient in governing an extremely diverse population. Different groups had different military capabilities and could serve or oppose the Mongols in diverse ways. Northern Chinese might serve in the military when needed, but southern Chinese (and sometimes northern Chinese too) should be prohibited from practicing martial arts or owning weapons. The Yuan government was very interested in establishing who legitimately could maintain the means of violence. These attempts at control had only limited success.

Mongol martial arts were mostly unaffected by Yuan control of China. Most Mongols fought, and continued to fight, in the same manner, as horse-archers. The Yuan government expected this would always be the case, and because the dynasty was so short-lived, it did not have the chance to find out whether Mongols living in China would continue to practice those martial arts after long stretches of peace. The Yuan Dynasty fell relatively quickly, crumbling entirely by 1368. Its remnants fell back to the steppe, where its basic martial arts continued uninterrupted.

The Chinese practice of martial arts continued on much the same trajectory as it had under the Song Dynasty. Song Dynasty sources are the first to record family styles of martial arts and lineages of martial arts in the entertainment quarters. The Song military also employed martial arts instructors in its military. The only thing that changed under Mongol rule was that martial arts instruction in the military was much more limited. For the Mongols, particular martial arts skills were associated with a particular group. Mongols fought in a certain manner, Chinese fought in a different manner. Northern Chinese fought in many ways like Mongols, but, as in the case of a warlord like Li Quan, they also had skills peculiar to the Chinese. The martial arts were widely practiced in the villages and towns despite Yuan prohibitions, maintaining traditions of fighting arts begun much earlier. Banditry and crime were still a threat to ordinary Chinese, and the only effective response was to create or continue self-defense forces.

As Yuan authority began to break down, local and regional strongmen became increasingly powerful. When they began directly to challenge the Yuan government they shifted from being mere bandits to actual rebels and incurred a military response. Although the Yuan army was still capable of defeating these rebels, internal political concerns undermined the suppression efforts. Rebel forces were able to survive, expand, and improve their military capabilities, building on a foundation of widespread martial arts skill among the population. The contest was not between one rebel group and the Yuan government, but among a shifting constellation of rebels, bandits, and strongmen, who fought with each other for power, and also with the Yuan government until it finally collapsed entirely. In this chaotic struggle for dominance, continual fighting once again militarized Chinese society and brought martial arts into the lives of a significant part of the population.

8

The Ming Dynasty

Zhu Yuanzhang (1328–98), the man who founded the Ming Dynasty, began his life in abject poverty and spent much of his youth as a Buddhist disciple. He began his rise to power as a rebel leader, joining a Buddhist-inspired group known as the Red Turbans. He eventually gained control over a part of this group and built a military and political force able to conquer China as the Yuan Dynasty broke down. This connection to Buddhism did nothing to mitigate the violence necessary to defeat the other contenders for power in the fourteenth century, and Zhu would prove to be one of the most violent, paranoid, and murderous rulers in Chinese history. He did not learn his martial arts in the temple to which he was apprenticed (he did learn to read and write there) but in the chaotic and highly militarized world of mid-fourteenth-century China. As Yuan authority crumbled, groups rose all over China fighting for local power, with some going on to struggle for regional and eventually empire-wide control.

These struggles also took place within military and political groups, as individual warriors and advisors sought to improve their own fortunes at the expense of their putative comrades. The challenge was to reach the top of a winning group without undermining its success through infighting. Successful warriors were highly valued in this environment; those who could also lead and possessed organizational and strategic ability could aspire to reach the highest ranks of power. Zhu Yuanzhang, like all founding emperors, was a successful warrior and general, and he attracted and surrounded himself with other successful warriors and generals. At the same time, he needed bureaucrats and advisors who were neither fighters nor generals to build and run the institutional structures of his government. He sought to fix permanently the correct balance between the martial and civil in his dynasty, at least as he conceived it.

Officers and soldiers were registered as military families and given land on which to support themselves. In return, they would supply officers and soldiers to the imperial army in perpetuity. Zhu Yuanzhang imagined that this would create a self-sustaining military and limit the need for a large and expensive army dependent upon the imperial treasury. Zhu's sons were enfeoffed along the border in military commands to protect the empire from the steppe. His utopian vision went further, conceiving of an empire of satisfied farmers happily dwelling in their individual hamlets and villages without even venturing to a neighboring settlement. This static society would maintain its martial edge through those tasked to maintain military skills while most of its subjects were engaged in productive and peaceful farming.

Zhu's vision was impractical at its inception, and parts of it collapsed entirely after his death. His original heir, his eldest son, predeceased him, leaving a precarious political situation. Zhu Yuanzhang decided that his eldest son's son should then succeed him. His own highly militarized sons were ambitious and little inclined to accept their nephew's succession to the throne. A brutal civil war followed soon after the first emperor's death. His fourth son, the Prince of Yan, based at what became Beijing, defeated his nephew with the aid of Mongol cavalry and took the throne. The new Ming ruler, the Yongle emperor (1360–1424), moved the capital to Beijing and had the short reign of his nephew deleted from the records.

In spite of the founding emperor's vision, Ming society changed in many dynamic ways over nearly three centuries of the dynasty's rule. Commerce and trade expanded rapidly, for example, directly undercutting the notion of a static empire of disconnected farmers living in their villages. Trade with the outside world also increased, and Christian missionaries made their first attempts to enter China. The ranks of the educated elite increased as well, though the size of government did not, leaving larger and larger numbers of qualified men unable to pass the civil service exams and serve as officials. Even those who passed the exams had difficulty getting posts. This was a problem that had begun to appear as early as the eleventh century, leading Confucian thinkers, originally wedded to the idea that men studied in order to serve in government, to rethink the purpose of education. The Neo-Confucians argued that self-cultivation was the primary goal of study, offering some consolation to the tens of thousands of men whose family means and position in society required that they study, but recognized how slim their odds were of passing the exams. An increasing number of men competed for a more or less fixed number of slots, thus lowering everyone's chances of passing almost to the level of random chance.

The presence of this educated, elite audience of readers created a demand for books on every subject and in every genre, from fiction to history. Far more books on military affairs, for example, were written during the Ming Dynasty than in any earlier period. New and sometimes recycled ideas were introduced, explained, and expanded upon. Some argued that Confucianism, Daoism, and Buddhism were three aspects of the same underlying ideas. Others, like the great Confucian thinker Wang Yangming (1472–1529), argued for a new direction in Confucianism, rejecting the orthodox, Ming government–sanctioned Cheng-Zhu Neo-Confucianism. Wang was also interested in the practice of "quiet sitting 靜坐," a meditation practice similar to Chan Buddhist practice, as a way to focus the mind. This was particularly important for Wang, who argued for the unity of thought and action. Wang himself passed the civil service exams, held high office, and successfully suppressed rebellions. He was a man of literary, military, and political accomplishments, demonstrating the immense range of ideas and practices that a notable man might achieve during the Ming Dynasty.

Several of our contemporary legends about the martial arts were also formed in the Ming Dynasty, in part because we have more information on the Ming than earlier periods as the printing and publication of texts increased dramatically from the eleventh century onward. Prior to this period, the few texts that discussed the martial arts were mostly military texts, and those were usually devoted to very specific questions of training and practice. In the middle of the Ming Dynasty, however, more authors began writing about martial arts. This new development coincided with the publication of two great novels in the sixteenth century, *The Romance of the Three Kingdoms* and *The Water Margin*.

Both of these novels developed out of earlier history and storytelling traditions, and both, particularly *The Water Margin*, went through a number of editions and changes starting with Yuan theatrical versions and continuing, in the case of *The Water Margin*, until the middle of the seventeenth century. The performative traditions of martial arts and theater had ramified into what might fairly be considered martial arts novels by the middle of the Ming Dynasty. This shift from performance to text is a key marker in the development of individual, private literati writing about martial arts and the interest of the literati in these arts. Whereas theater could play to the illiterate commoners, a novel written in literary Chinese

霹靂震天錦鬼韓天

熱膽血心天

主撲魯儀表常力能敢當

ILLUSTRATION 18. Theatrical representation of the hero Han Tianjin, holding a staff in a dramatic pose. From *Xiaowuyi* (*Zhonglie Xiaowuyi Zhuan*), 1890.

was something composed for the educated elite. Some historians have read Ming literati writing on the martial arts transparently as simple descriptions of practice and the martial arts environment during the Ming Dynasty. Of course, these texts were written for other literati, often as a means to justify the author's peculiar interest in the martial arts. The act of writing about martial arts was itself a statement of the author's relationship to the balance of civil and martial culture, and his perceived or constructed place within that milieu.

Certainly the highly refined literati of the Ming, while for the most part not themselves participating in the martial arts, were quite interested in many aspects of the martial arts and martial culture. Sword collecting, for example, became extremely popular in the Ming, with literati, like scholars in any time or place, developing quite discerning opinions about the merits of swords and long swords from different periods.[1] Swords were collected and traded, and given as gifts to demonstrate one's own knowledge, to cement relationships, and even for purposes of self-defense. It is less clear whether the recipients of such gifts were expected to have any knowledge of fencing or if it was assumed that being armed in some way was preferable to being unarmed if one were attacked. Of particular interest to some collectors were Japanese swords captured from pirates after the *wokou* pirate raids of the sixteenth century that included many Japanese fighters.

Sword collecting was its own world, of course, quite divorced from questions of hand-to-hand combat. As objets d'art, swords could be appraised and discussed by gentlemen at some remove from either the military or the martial arts world. At the same time, however, a number of literati maintained direct relationships with generals. A sword was still a weapon, even if it were traded for a painting. At court, the military still held an important place – less so during times of peace, and more so during wars. Generals were well aware that their status and the importance of their skills were directly related to the government's need for their services. Some emperors were more interested in war than others, though some had war thrust upon them. After the first two emperors, as so often was the case, Ming emperors had no real military experience. War and the martial arts were intellectual rather than physical matters.

The involvement of Ming literati in martial culture was extremely varied, with some directly engaged with generals on a personal level, some dabbling in the martial arts or in writing fiction portraying martial arts, and others keeping everything martial at a distance. Literati attitudes reflected a strong undercurrent of the sharp civil-military split that developed during the Song

Dynasty, tempered by the practical need for armed forces and local security, and the widespread, popular performance of martial arts in contests and theater. When an educated man chose to pursue martial arts with any rigor, he had to explain why he was not pursuing more acceptable intellectual activities. Those literati who did write descriptions of their involvement in the martial arts world not only justified them in pragmatic terms but also brought to bear their considerable knowledge of literary and historical devices to legitimize those skills. Thus certain lineages of martial arts knowledge began to appear in writing – knowledge that had often before been left to unreliable or imaginative oral tradition. Local traditions were transformed into national martial arts history.

Several scholars date significant changes in the martial arts to the middle and late Ming Dynasty. While the hereditary Ming military system worked adequately for some time after the dynasty's founding, by the middle of the dynasty it had begun to fail badly. Military families were not producing a large pool of skilled soldiers available for army service or campaigns but rather a large pool of farmers exploited by the officer class. Despite efforts to maintain military training within the army itself, the long stretch of peace degraded fighting capabilities. Overall Ming strategy also changed. Whereas at the beginning of the dynasty a forward defense of military bases directly engaged the steppe, this was withdrawn due to expense, and strategy shifted toward static defense. Ming troops took fewer chances and fought less, ceding the initiative to the Mongols. The Ming court was unwilling to treat diplomatically with the Mongols or trade with them from a position of weakness. In response, the Mongols raided more frequently and in greater depth, at one point in 1550 reaching the suburbs of the capital, Beijing. Unwilling either to pull the border back to more defensible positions or to mount an expensive offensive campaign into the steppe, the court left it to local commanders to deal with the raiders. The result was a line of long walls that would eventually grow into what we now know as the Great Wall.[2]

Ming troops stood on the defensive behind the Great Wall armed with thousands of guns. The wall itself was never a complete solution, and, indeed, a Mongol force managed to capture one emperor in 1449 on the Chinese side of the wall. The importance of guns to the Ming military is also significant. Guns were critical military equipment but remained slow enough in operation to keep bows and crossbows in use. Guns were used extensively in the Ming conquest and were a basic part of the imperial military's armament. As with other weapons, however, soldiers needed training to use them properly and warriors armed with guns needed skillful deployment to function effectively in battle. The dynasty's original military system did not just fail to produce trained men but it also lost a substantial amount of its knowledge of how to train soldiers, use weapons, and fight battles. One of the reasons so many military and martial arts manuals were produced during the mid to late Ming Dynasty was the urgent need to recover lost military knowledge. Quite intriguingly, this was also when many martial arts novels emerged, though like the military writings, they were also built upon earlier traditions and stories.

Even while the Ming military as a whole declined, pockets of military knowledge and martial arts skills remained. Army units on the border or in the capital were the best maintained since they were on active service, however limited. The Ming government, like so many governments in premodern times, was unable to maintain a high level of readiness across its entire military apparatus. Given time, and under the pressure of a crisis, it could reinvigorate its army at least temporarily. Alternatively, it could rely solely on the limited number of functional units to deal with a problem. During the Wanli emperor's reign the paucity of good generals and troops forced delays in addressing nearly simultaneous problems. These problems were eventually solved, but only after several generals and their troops marched from one end of China to the other, and on into Korea.[3] In other cases, like Qi Jiguang's suppression of the *wokou* pirates, new units had to be raised and trained. When a problem was too large or time was too short, the military could simply be overwhelmed before it could rise to the task. This was largely what happened at the end of the dynasty.

More generally, knowledge of the martial arts was widespread in society. The traditions of martial arts were broadly maintained by individual families and in towns and villages for self-protection and as a legacy of the past. Theater troupes had their own traditions of martial arts, and they continued to travel around the empire performing. Increased commerce meant a concomitant increase in travel by merchants, their guards, and itinerant sellers of services. This floating population was joined by other travelers in the Ming: literati sightseeing or pursuing education, monks moving from monastery to monastery, and ambitious people seeking better lives or a way off the farm. This wide variety of people collected in towns and cities as they traveled, spreading and mixing their skills, meeting and performing their services at marketplaces. Many marketplaces were set up at temples, which offered both open space and sometimes accommodations for travelers.

There was also a darker side to the practice of martial arts, a similarly widespread "economy of violence" that operated in Ming China at every level of society.[4] Even confining our consideration to the use of martial arts in this economy (and excluding areas like domestic violence, penal violence, etc.), a vast and complex field remains. Rebellions, banditry, clan feuds, and ordinary criminal activity all used the martial arts as the basic skills of violence. All of these violent activities were endemic, regular parts of Ming Dynasty society, with extensive variations of practice and expression in the different regions of China and at different levels of society. It is possible – perhaps even likely – that a similar level and extent of violence was also present in earlier dynasties and that we simply lack the documentary evidence to describe it. While this remains a real but unprovable possibility, we are certain of the prevalence of violence during the Ming Dynasty.

Clan feuding was endemic in southeast China, with ongoing violent struggles persisting for years on end. Martial artists were hired from the outside to train and stiffen the ordinary clan fighters. These professional men of violence had a vested interest in prolonging rather than resolving any conflict. And while James Tong argued that group violence was "rampant in peripheral and mountainous regions, during the reigns of wanton and decrepit emperors, and in periods when government troops were preoccupied with defending the empire against foreign invasions,"[5] violence by individuals and groups was much more prevalent than that, and in more than just peripheral regions. David Robinson has argued convincingly that "violence was fully integrated into Ming life, during good times and bad."[6] Violence was not an aberration caused by a failure in some part of the Ming system but a regular and understood component of ordinary life.

Where bandits might prey upon travelers in the countryside, or attack towns and villages, criminal gangs operated within cities. Major cities like Hangzhou or Suzhou had "Fighters Guilds" (*dahang*) who could be paid to beat up or kill people, even doing so in broad daylight. These thugs were martial artists with some level of skill. Some were reputed to have a clearly fictional technique – the ability to strike a target's pressure points, leaving no mark but causing the victim to die weeks or months later.[7] While the "death touch" technique is nonsense, the very fact that it could be suggested argues that some of these thugs were serious martial artists with highly refined techniques.

The Ming government was more concerned with banditry that escalated to the level of rebellion. While it might tolerate a certain degree of crime in the cities and countryside, the court responded forcefully to groups directly and openly defying its authority. There was clearly a continuum of violent activity that involved men of similar inclinations in fighting, whether as urban thugs, bandits, rebels, soldiers, or traveling martial artists. Several officials recognized a unifying thread for men in these positions and recommended, following two Song Dynasty officials' writings in particular, that bandits, thugs and "heroes" be recruited into government service both to gain their services and to deny them to any rebels.[8] Martial arts and martial artists of many kinds abounded in the Ming Dynasty at every level of society and in every region.

The Ming army was, of course, deeply involved in training and practicing martial arts. This involvement extended from the military families to the military exams and on to efforts of generals like Qi Jiguang to raise new units to fight the *wokou* pirates. The Ming also saw the sudden elevation of the Shaolin Temple to a prominent place in some writers' conception of the martial arts world in the middle of the Ming Dynasty. Several aspects of martial arts either developed significantly during the Ming or were written down in currently extant manuals. Terminology continued to change, as did the list of the eighteen martial arts. Boxing, fencing with both the sword and long sword, spear fighting, and staff fighting all advanced or were written about in detail. The shifts in writing about the martial arts in the Ming, both in fiction and descriptively, present us with a clearer image of the place and form of martial arts in Ming society than for earlier periods.

THE MING MILITARY

The Ming military went through several stages of development over the course of the dynasty. Its original form, that of a hereditary military system, declined by the beginning of the sixteenth century, leaving the state with a partly functional military. It faced two problems, both of them structural. First, the army of conquest was not well suited to defending the Ming empire's territory. Like most dynastic armies of conquest, it succeeded because it was able to attack and defeat opposing concentrations of troops. Once the empire was established, however, it had to defend against internal and external disturbances. Most of these problems, at least until the early seventeenth century, were not threats to the existence of the dynasty but rather challenges to its authority along the border or in local areas. Even the most serious Mongol incursions were not directed at destroying the dynasty. This was even more true of the pirate raids on the southeastern coast. The Ming military struggled to re-create itself as a defense force against low-level threats. It was mostly successful in this effort, but then failed in the seventeenth century to adapt to the new Manchu threat.

神手大聖鄧車

ILLUSTRATION 19. Theatrical representation of the hero Deng Che, drawing a bow without an arrow. From *Qixia Wuyi*, 1889.

The second structural problem of the Ming military was its system of recruitment and training. Troops were recruited from designated military households, which were required to send one soldier to a designated unit, and one supernumerary soldier to assist him. Alongside the hereditary military families was a military exam system designed to supply soldiers and officers for the army. Unlike the Song Dynasty examination system, the Ming military exams produced some outstanding graduates, like Qi Jiguang and Yu Dayou. While the exam system had some value, it did not impose a baseline of quality for the entire officer corps. Training for the ordinary soldiers was supposed to be taken in rotation by all units in northern China at the capital, Beijing, to ensure high standards. As the registers of military households became increasingly outdated and inaccurate, however, and the regular training rotation of troops also declined, overall numbers and quality of the military collapsed. A smaller core of effective troops remained within the emptied rosters of established formations.

Local security, while theoretically within the purview of the regular army, was functionally and more usually the responsibility of local militias. Some of these militias were government-organized police forces, and others were created by local elites. In either case, they drew upon the same pool of violent local men from which sprang bandits and rebels. Martial arts was a common currency within this group, whether it was employed for or against the state, or simply used to prey upon or protect local people. These men of violence were everywhere, with many congregating at temples or markets. Militias were better suited to the low-level warfare of banditry or pirate attacks than the cumbersome and poorly maintained regular military. Just as happened during the Song Dynasty, when the imperial army failed, the government was forced to use various militia forces.

Regular training and the military exams stressed archery, with officers also being tested in riding and in shooting from horseback. Even though guns, both handguns and cannon, were extremely important to the Ming military, archery with bow and crossbow was still a central skill. And, as was true through so much of Chinese history, steppe cavalry were recruited into the Ming military. This was a pragmatic decision that brought large numbers of Mongols into north China and registered them as military households, to bolster the army and weaken the Mongols in the steppe. Horse-archers remained the most important striking force in north China, while infantry and naval forces were the dominant forces in south China. There was thus a wide divergence in military and martial practice in China's different regions. The Ming military was really a collection of separate forces: northern, southern, and naval.

These differences would be played out in several conflicts. In response to the *wokou* pirates, General Qi Jiguang was required to raise new military units from the pool of local militias. Qi stressed training and went to great lengths to improve and regularize the overall armament of his troops. His training manual, the *New Manual on Military Efficiency*, is one of the key sources for our knowledge of the martial arts in the sixteenth century. Qi needed to find a way to fight Japanese swordsmen in hand-to-hand combat and to create units that were fast enough to intercept the pirates. Training swordsmen was a usual sort of martial arts problem: formulating an effective response to a particular system of fighting. Battling pirates was a military problem: preventing enemy units from achieving their objectives.

The martial arts problem was easily solved through proper martial arts training. Rather than attempt to meet Japanese swordsmen at sword range or individually, Qi's men used spears and other polearms to negate Japanese fencing. The same shift in martial arts practice was actually going on in Japan at that time, as commoners armed with spears, and increasingly handguns, would overcome samurai with swords and mounted cavalry. Qi insisted on good physical conditioning for his men and a solid regimen of martial arts training (though without stress on missile weapons). He sought to condition the men to aggressively close with the enemy and beat them in hand-to-hand combat. In a later edition of his manual he actually removed the chapters on unarmed fighting while, of course, retaining the sections on weapons use.

Qi's naval units made extensive use of guns and gunpowder weapons, usually on light boats, to overwhelm the pirates with firepower. Although he catalogued a wide range of martial arts in his manual, noting which were the best, it is likely that his own background in military training formed the basis of most of his method. His goal was to use the simplest and most effective techniques. General Qi's force of three thousand men (later growing to 6,000 and then 10,000) was effective, as were those of Yu Dayou, but they were not decisive by themselves in defeating the pirates. The *wokou* were defeated by a combination of changing military policies, infighting among the pirates themselves, and more open commercial policies on the coast. The Ming court managed to formulate an effective response to the pirates after many false starts and its own political infighting. Despite this larger context, Qi Jiguang's success drove many martial arts practitioners to claim credit for the fighting abilities of his troops and to try and sort out which techniques came from which styles.

By the 1570s a paid army had replaced the hereditary military system. This new army would perform impressively in the last two decades of the sixteenth

北俠歐陽春

碧目虬鬚七寶刀霜鋒利刃等吹毛懶
他不共天長在殺盡人間惡主豪

ILLUSTRATION 20. Theatrical representation of the hero Ouyang Chun, the Northern Hero, in a highly stylized pose with the heavy, single-edged, curved sword. From *Qixia Wuyi*, 1889.

century, defeating or fighting to a standstill a mutiny, a rebellion, and the
Japanese army in Korea. These three campaigns, the Wanli emperor's Three
Great Campaigns, forced the Ming army to fight in its far northwest against a
rebellion of Mongol troops, then in Korea against the Japanese invasion of
Korea, and finally in the far southwest against a "Miao" rebellion. Guns,
particularly cannon, were critical in all of these fights, but the modes of
warfare all differed. The Mongol mutiny required cavalry and then siege
warfare, Korea required southern Chinese infantry trained to fight Japanese
and supported with cannon, and the Miao was a strict infantry and cannon
slog to root out rebels in mountainous jungle. Many of the generals and some
of the troops took part in more than one campaign.

The success of Wanli's campaigns obscured the limitations of the Ming
military. Although it had tens of thousands of effective troops, capable of
fighting under vastly different conditions with a variety of weapons, it did
not have *hundreds* of thousands of effective troops, nor did it have enough
competent generals. The underlying weakness in the Ming military was
caused by political failures within the government itself. Large pools of
violent men were not recruited into the military, leaving them to become
bandits and then rebels. At the same time, the court failed to develop an
effective military policy to deal with the rising power of the Manchus in the
steppe. Unable to control growing rebellions, a demonstration of an excess
of men skilled in the martial arts, the Ming was unprepared for the new
steppe threat.

SHAOLIN TEMPLE

The Shaolin Temple near Luoyang is currently one of the best-known
brand names in martial arts. Martial arts movies have created and elaborated upon the erroneous notion that the Chinese martial arts originated
there or that Shaolin monks possess secret techniques that give them
superhuman powers. Even some scholars in the West have confused the
practice of martial arts at Buddhist temples with a direct association
between Buddhism and the martial arts. This has led to further confusion
as some have looked for an Indian root to Chinese martial arts, assuming
that the martial arts arrived along with Buddhism. It has also tied the
contemplation and self-cultivation of Buddhism to the martial arts. The
close association of Chan (Zen) Buddhism, which began at Shaolin, with
the samurai class in Japan reinforces this false connection. The prevalent
modern notion, inside and outside China, that Chinese martial arts are

solely concerned with self-cultivation and self-defense makes a Buddhist origin for the martial arts logical – but erroneous.

Fortunately, a significant first step in sorting out this history in the West has recently been taken with the publication of Meir Shahar's *The Shaolin Monastery*.[9] Chinese martial arts historians, for their part, have been reasonably clear about the place of Shaolin, with the possible exception of those closely associated with the temple itself. Shahar's historical work presents a fairly straightforward narrative of the construction of the late Ming Dynasty understanding of martial arts at Shaolin. His analysis, however, is marked by a strong Shaolin bias in placing the monks and the temple in the context of Chinese martial arts history. From Shaolin looking out, particularly with a modern bias, Shaolin is much more central than from the larger history of Chinese martial arts looking in at Shaolin. Kai Filipiak, in his recent book, *Die Chinesische Kampfkunst*, takes a more balanced approach.[10]

A good example of the Shaolin-centered bias is in the consideration of the role of Shaolin monks in the suppression of the *wokou* pirates. A small group of Shaolin monks played a role in several skirmishes with the pirates. Of four known battles they participated in, one was a defeat (blamed on the general's incompetence) and three were victories, the most notable one taking place between 21 and 31 July 1553 at Wengjiagang. One hundred twenty monks from a number of monasteries took part in this running, ten-day fight that ultimately left a hundred pirates and only four monks dead. This was the greatest victory of this force of fighting monks in the campaign, and it was extremely small scale.

While the force itself was composed of monks from a number of monasteries, its leader was from Shaolin, and he earned that place by single-handedly defeating eight monks from a Hangzhou Buddhist temple. This Shaolin monk, Tianyuan, first defeated his opponents with unarmed fighting techniques, following which

the eight monks ran around to the hall's back entrance. Then, armed with swords, they charged through the hall's back entrance to the terrace in front. They slashed their weapons at Tianyuan who, hurriedly grabbing the long bar that fastened the hall's gate, struck horizontally. Try as they did, they could not get into the terrace. They were, on the contrary, overcome by Tianyuan.[11]

This story is used to prove the superiority of Shaolin martial arts over the practice of other monasteries, but it raises some interesting problems that are compounded by the brutality some of the monks displayed while defeating the pirates. One monk, it was reported, killed the wife of an escaping pirate with his iron staff. Tianyuan was clearly an outstanding martial artist; yet we have the spectacle of Buddhist monks deciding to fight physically for leadership. These are not men who have abandoned their egos upon taking up religious vows, but rather men of violence who work for monasteries and dress as monks. They are not just armed with staffs but with swords as well, and they show no remorse in killing an unarmed, noncombatant woman. In manner and skills, they resemble the "fighters' guild" of Hangzhou mentioned earlier.

Shaolin's reputation as a center of martial arts was not first recorded in the Ming Dynasty; it was first created in the Ming Dynasty. The events that precipitated this new reputation appear to be the raids of the *wokou* pirates in the middle sixteenth century. Martial monks including those from Shaolin had taken part in earlier suppressions of other bandits with mixed results. The Shaolin Temple was the direct recipient of imperial patronage in the mid-sixteenth century and government exemption from taxes on its lands. Like any other powerful landowner or institution, Shaolin occasionally put its security force in the service of the state in return for state confirmation of its local power. The temple had been mostly destroyed by the Red Turbans just before the dynasty was founded, but imperial service and patronage had allowed it to rebuild.

Before their recruitment to fight the pirates, and in spite of their previous activities in fighting local bandits and rebels, Shaolin monks were not universally known for their martial arts skills. When Wan Biao, who was responsible for recruiting Shaolin monks to fight the pirates, suggested employing monks in the suppression campaign, three provincial officers ridiculed him for it. These men, it seems, were entirely unaware of the "famous" martial arts abilities of the monks. Wan ended up wagering wine with the three men on the superior combat skills of monks. A nominally unsuspecting monk chosen by Wan was summoned to a banquet where an ambush of eight arms instructors waited to attack him with staffs. The monk evaded their attacks, grabbed one of their staffs, and then proceeded to knock all of them down.[12] This demonstrates that the monks were highly skilled martial artists, but that knowledge of their skills was still limited. All that changed after the pirate suppression despite the minor role played by fighting monks in general and Shaolin monks in particular in the campaigns. Shaolin monks were not a significant military force, yet their reputation as martial artists became a cultural fixture.

Shaolin's reputation for martial arts arose during the sixteenth century, leaving a gap of nine hundred years since the temple was last mentioned in connection with military action. This extremely long gap presents a challenge to those seeking to argue that Shaolin's martial arts tradition goes back to at least the seventh century. Strictly speaking, the available documentary evidence does not even allow us to conclude that martial arts was practiced at Shaolin in the seventh century. It is only in the sixteenth century that we have direct mention of martial arts at Shaolin. The participation of Shaolin monks in a local fight in 621 demonstrated that the temple either had a force of fighters available or raised one after the temple was burned by bandits several years earlier, and after some of the temple lands were seized. In the threatening environment of north China at that time, the monks fortunately ended up on the winning side of the imperial contest. The direct result of their military activity was an imperial letter that protected the temple from undue government impositions during the Tang Dynasty.

Despite Shaolin's proximity to the Tang capital and many visits to the temple by literati who wrote commemorations of those visits, martial arts was not mentioned. Even during the Song Dynasty, when a stellar group of scholars lived at Luoyang in the mid-eleventh century, visited local sites, and wrote on every matter imaginable, no one mentioned martial arts at Shaolin. Indeed, the only arguments to support the idea that martial arts was practiced at Shaolin during these centuries are general ones. First, north China as a whole was generally militarized under the authority of landlords. As a large institution with lands and at least one mill, the temple would have also maintained a commensurate force of tenants or laborers. Like other landlords, the temple authorities would have organized these workers or a separate security force into at least a self-defense militia. Second, temples provided some of the only open space not in agricultural use. Whereas the government might have created training grounds for the army, ordinary people would have turned to temples for martial arts practice space. Third, wandering monks who mixed with merchants and itinerant martial artists often stayed at temples because these places had accommodations for travelers, and because temples were often the site of periodic markets. Fourth and finally, though this is pure speculation, high-ranking elites, including military men, may have "retired" to temples. Retired officials were often given temple guardianships as sinecures to provide them with a salary while out of office. If these general observations were true, then Shaolin would have maintained some practice of martial arts as a part of the larger society.

As a temple in north China, Shaolin would have been part of the general martial arts practice that existed all around it. It might have even had a greater measure of martial arts practice because it was a Buddhist temple where many violent men who claimed to be monks and dressed as monks visited. If we recall the Tang period stories of bandit-monks, it is easy to see how bandit-monks are virtually the same as warrior-monks. These men drank wine, ate meat, and had sex with women – practices alien to true Buddhist monks. A number of Buddhist authorities were deeply troubled by the presence of monks who directly violated Buddhist precepts. We do not know whether there was a sharp break between ordained and trained monks who carefully followed monastic rules in their search for enlightenment and men who simply claimed to be monks, wore monastic robes, shaved their heads, but otherwise did not follow monastic rules. There may well have been a spectrum of behaviors from bandit imposture to enlightened abbot.[13]

The Water Margin offers us an intriguing illustration of all of these issues in the figure of Lu Da, who becomes a Buddhist monk at Mount Wutai. A rough and violent army officer, Lu is forced to flee from his position after killing a man with his bare hands. A powerful local lord of a manor rescues him by providing an ordination certificate for him to become a monk at Mount Wutai. The abbot gives him the name "Sagacious," having already in a trance foreseen that he will transcend his fierce and rough nature and achieve sainthood. Sagacious Lu continued to eat meat, get drunk, fight, and kill people, joining the Liangshan outlaws at the center of the novel, and finally transcending to an enlightened death at the end. Similarly, Wu Song, another of the great heroes of *The Water Margin*, who lost an arm in one of the final battles, chooses to enter a monastery at the end of the book.

This fictional story shows us an environment in which powerful and highly militarized northern manorial lords patronize Buddhist temples, military men become monks for a variety of reasons, and skilled martial artists bring their practice into temples. Rather than see temples as sources or stores of martial arts knowledge, we should see them as collection points. Keeping in mind that martial arts skills were widespread in Chinese society, many monks taking orders would have been trained before they entered a monastery. Similarly, major Buddhist institutions would frequently have been run by men from the upper classes who had become monks. Many of these men, particularly in north China, would have been well-trained martial artists.

Shaolin itself was overrun and destroyed in 1356, just before the founding of the Ming Dynasty. Whatever martial arts were practiced there beforehand were not considered noteworthy by any author. There was, however, an acknowledged tradition of martial arts practiced at Mount Wutai, a connection partly reflected in Sagacious Lu's association with

Wutai. For some reason, perhaps as a result of the 1356 destruction, Shaolin Temple was reconstituted in the early part of the Ming Dynasty with a much more militarized character. Certainly the process of fixing military men in their profession at the beginning of the dynasty must have left an enormous number of former soldiers at loose ends, as some soldiers and their descendants were permanently registered with the army, and others were demobilized and prevented from rejoining the military. It may well be that the ranks of the rebuilt temple were filled with some of the vast multitude of men of violence left once the dynasty was settled. Some monastic authorities were concerned that nearby subsidiary temples housed rowdy, violent men who, though nominally monks, did not follow monastic regulations. These bandit-monks would have been easy enough to recruit and send out as warrior-monks to fight against bandits. Whether they succeeded or failed, the monastery won the appreciation of the government and imperial house.

Shaolin's reputation arose just as *The Water Margin* and *The Romance of the Three Kingdoms* were produced in written form. As an imperially sponsored and tax-exempt institution, Shaolin's fortunes rose with those of the Ming Dynasty. Its good fortune in producing some outstanding fighters in the middle of the sixteenth century established the temple's reputation in print from then on. Even when the temple's armed forces were wiped out at the end of the Ming Dynasty, Shaolin's reputation continued.

BOXING

Any number of boxing styles had existed in China before the Ming Dynasty without attracting particular notice. There were many martial artists skilled at striking or wrestling and sometimes both, without specific names or places attached to their arts. Military manuals before the Ming did not go into detail on the martial arts and usually were more concerned with listing the kinds of weapons available to the army. This changed in the Ming as new manuals, like Qi Jiguang's, and a more general shift in writing topics to include the martial arts began for the first time to list and name unarmed fighting styles. *The Water Margin* in that respect shows its Song Dynasty origins by not naming fighting styles. Its protagonists have specific martial arts skills, like fencing, wrestling, or boxing, but not styles. Style names were either created or at least were recorded for the first time during the Ming Dynasty.

Qi Jiguang lists sixteen styles of boxing in his manual; he does this unself-consciously, indicating that he was merely describing what was available.

The style names must have predated his manual and represent a heavily northern Chinese bias, since he compiled the list while in the north. His list contains styles like "Song Taizu Thirty-Two Positions Long Boxing 宋太祖三十二勢拳," "Six Paces Boxing 六步拳," and "Monkey Boxing 猴拳." By contrast, Zheng Ruoceng's 鄭若曾 list of eleven styles is biased toward southern martial arts and includes many different styles like "Xi Family Boxing 西家拳," "Zhang Fei Divine Boxing 張飛神拳," "Southern Boxing 南拳," and "Northern Boxing 北拳." Even these twenty-seven styles are only an idiosyncratic selection, since more styles are mentioned in other texts. Particularly given the weight that martial arts historians place on Qi Jiguang's discussion of martial arts, it is critical to keep in mind that his survey of martial arts was neither comprehensive nor unbiased. His perspective, intentionally or not, was biased toward northern China.

At the same time, when we compare Qi and Zheng's respective lists of styles we find a number of overlapping names. Zheng's list also has a "Monkey Boxing" as well as a "Zhao Family Boxing 趙家拳," which encompasses a "Zhao Taizu Divine Boxing Thirty-Six Positions 趙太祖神拳三十六勢" within it. Since Zhao was the surname of the Song imperial family, Song Taizu and Zhao Taizu are the same person, but the styles have a different number of positions. There is no way to determine whether these styles were the same or only used the same reference to a historical figure. Similarly, there can be no comparison between the respective "Monkey Boxing" styles. Even were we to assemble a complete list from the extant sources, we would still have only a sample of the many styles practiced during the Ming Dynasty. Unfortunately, we have no way of knowing the total number of styles, nor what their relationship was to each other. The only thing that is clear is that military manuals in the Ming took the time to name at least a few styles.

Some parts of these styles are included in some of the manuals or texts on the martial arts. In some cases the author recorded a chant or song that accompanied the respective positions. This was a mnemonic device for remembering the order of positions, presumably in practicing a martial arts form. Without direct instruction in the forms or the significance of the names, the chants tell us very little. They would, however, have very quickly distinguished those who had been instructed in the complete knowledge of the style by a direct master-disciple transmission from those who had not. Martial arts knowledge was esoteric knowledge and was preserved as such. The skills and knowledge involved were both part of a tradition, whether family or teacher-student, and valuable techniques for self-protection, teaching, or other employment.

Qi Jiguang and other authors were not just assembling these lists of styles out of mere curiosity; they were attempting to find the most functional skills available. Qi complained about the incompleteness of many styles, that they were only good in parts and lacked a comprehensive set of techniques. Most of the authors were also concerned with what they called "Flowery Boxing 花拳," ineffective and overly elaborate styles that only looked nice. Indeed, one of the central issues of the discussion of boxing styles was effectiveness. There was a constant comparison between styles, or anecdotes recounting how someone practiced an ineffective or flawed style. These flowery styles had lost the foundation of boxing and strayed very far from some presumably simple and effective original form.

Although boxing styles varied widely across China, and indeed the terminology for boxing was similarly varied, there was perceived to be a core of effective techniques. Unarmed fighting was not as effective in combat as armed fighting, and that is perhaps why boxing was listed last on the reformulated Ming period list of "Eighteen Martial Arts." From the military standpoint, boxing was not a real battlefield skill. For Qi Jiguang and Mao Yuanyi, boxing was the beginning skill for martial arts training before one took up weapons. It was also useful for developing overall agility with the hands and feet. Anyone expecting to fight on the battlefield would have to be better trained and properly armed. Boxing was recognized as a developmental rather than a functional skill in the army, and Qi dropped it from the later edition of his manual. To practice boxing was therefore more about training the body and mind, despite the quest for practical boxing skills. The practical skills were the genuine or true roots of the art, and thus by definition, more effective in developing the body and mind.

FENCING WITH SWORDS

The single-edged, curved sword remained the basic close fighting weapon of the Chinese military during the Ming Dynasty, and it was widely used in the population at large. Like boxing, the techniques for using the sword were practiced under a bewildering variety of names, with a broad range of effectiveness. The performative aspects of these sword styles sometimes overwhelmed the combat concerns of the practitioner, and it is possible that some stemmed directly from stage traditions rather than the battlefield. Yet unlike boxing, sword fighting was a practical battlefield skill and a practical skill for fighting or self-defense in general.

The origin of these many styles of sword fighting is unclear. Lin Boyuan may be correct in asserting that they developed among the general populace starting in the Song Dynasty but were only infrequently written about before the Ming Dynasty, but this assumption cannot be proven.[14] It is also possible that they developed in the Tang Dynasty or even slightly before that and were simply not written about at all until the Song. Most of the evidence for different styles before the Ming comes from the world of fiction; we find ourselves once again consulting *The Water Margin* and its attendant depictions of fighting for our information. The widespread teaching and practice of martial arts in the Song does argue for diversification of sword fighting styles, if only because of natural regional and local variation. These variations may have been less pronounced before the rise of popular martial arts performances in the Song.

The same men who collected information on boxing styles also collected information on sword fighting styles and other martial arts. They recorded dozens of styles, some with straightforward names such as "Twin Swords 雙刀," and others with more picturesque ones like "Opening Heaven Sword 開天刀," or "Great Peace Sword 太平刀." Overall, however, Qi Jiguang was as unimpressed by the utility of many of these styles of fencing as he was with the boxing styles. Most had a tendency toward elaboration so they would look good when demonstrated. They also differed from strictly military practice because they had developed in response to a different environment. An individual sword fighter trained to defend himself or to fight one-on-one in combat. At most, he trained to fight by himself instead of as part of a formation or larger group of soldiers. An individual fighter would therefore have to be prepared for a larger variety of situations than a soldier. In addition, soldiers would have less time to devote to the dedicated study of the martial arts, particularly of a single weapon, than an individual practitioner.

All the variety and function of Chinese sword practice was a matter of serious consideration because of the *wokou* raids. Many of the pirates were Japanese and were either samurai or practiced Japanese swordsmanship. Two-handed Japanese swordsmanship proved to be far superior to Chinese swordsmanship. Japanese swords were also much higher quality than the weapons issued to ordinary Chinese soldiers. Chinese swords were shorter and were wielded with one hand, meaning they had less reach, less speed, less power, and were more cumbersome. Particularly in the irregular warfare of pirate raids rather than the formation-to-formation combat of regular warfare, Japanese swordsmanship was initially extremely effective. It took some time for the Chinese to recognize, evaluate, and formulate a response to this new problem.

Some Chinese martial artists like Cheng Zongyou learned Japanese fencing from a Chinese martial artist named Liu Yunfeng, whose style

Cheng judged superior to that of another martial artist, Guo Wu, who also taught Japanese fencing; others, like Qi Jiguang approached the matter differently. Qi, as already discussed, stressed better training and the use of spears and other polearms to defeat Japanese swordsmanship. This was entirely effective, overcoming samurai techniques in the same way that Japanese commoners were doing in Japan. Cheng Zongyou recorded the techniques he had learned, though it does not appear that the tradition of Japanese fencing remained in practice in China for very long. This is not surprising, as Japanese fencing was diminishing in importance on the battlefield even in its native land.

FENCING WITH LONG SWORDS

Although during the Yuan Dynasty the long sword enjoyed a partial and idiosyncratic resurgence on the battlefield in the hands of some Mongol troops, it fell out of favor again in the Ming. Just as before, a small number of expert martial artists in the ranks of the army still made effective use of the long sword, but it remained a very specialized weapon. Ordinary soldiers, and even most swordsmen outside of the military, used swords, not long swords. Perhaps because the long sword was no longer an ordinary weapon, it gained a new meaning for literati. It had become, by definition, a refined weapon of ancient pedigree that could only be appreciated or properly wielded by an extraordinary swordsman.

A number of Ming literati are described as "liking long swords and books" and, connected with this, riding horses, practicing knight-errantry, and roaming about. Often these descriptions are used to characterize them in their youth, creating a sense that established scholars and civil officials were bold, heroic men of action. The long sword had become the weapon of the educated man. Scholars could investigate and discuss the early history of the long sword, lament the decline of long sword manufacturing, and trade in long swords as art objects. Literati swordsmen, or at least those interested in the history of long sword fencing, wrote descriptions of this skill.

Ming martial arts scholars determined that there were five or six schools of long sword fencing, creating an esoteric knowledge of the subject for themselves. These schools were traditions of fencing still present in the general population, even though they no longer existed in the military. It seems unlikely that these scholars, who were unable to fully enumerate the styles of boxing or sword fencing, were able to completely survey the extant long sword styles either. They were able to record several mnemonic devices for memorizing principles or motions of the styles, in itself an important consistent practice with other forms of martial arts. They were also able to point out that Chinese long sword practice still included two-handed forms of long sword fighting, though most was one-handed.

The interest of Ming literati in the long sword should be seen as a further step in the evolution of literati engagement with the martial arts. Tang Dynasty men of letters might still practice martial arts without tainting their credentials as Confucian gentlemen. Archery for them still had positive connotations, or at least had not come to be seen as a negative marker of undue interest in martial practice. During the Song Dynasty, literati fundamentally rejected the practice of martial arts, including even archery, as antithetical to their identity as men of letters. Literati were gentlemen who ruled by virtue of their intellects and education-based self-cultivation. Civil gentlemen were morally superior. For some Ming men of letters, at least, fencing with the long sword was a marker of heroic temperament and profound erudition.

SPEAR TECHNIQUES

The spear combined the practical value and importance of the sword with the elaboration and specialization of the long sword. Martial arts manual writers catalogued an extraordinary number of spear styles, including detailed enumerations, descriptions and illustrations of the names, stances, and techniques of those styles. Styles from Shandong and Hebei claimed descent from the famous Song Dynasty Yang family of generals (Yang Family Spear Technique). Shaolin had its own style, as did the Buddhist temples on Mount Emei. Many styles were named for families: Li Family Short Spear, Ma Family Spear Technique, Jin Family Spear, and even a Zhang Fei Divine Spear. As with other martial arts, there was considerable regional variation and many local practitioners.

Spear fighting was a critical martial art for the military, and it garnered a commensurate amount of attention. Soldiers appear to have been given a much more thorough training in spear fighting than was strictly necessary for fighting in formation. They were fully trained in individual combat with the spear, with a basic set of techniques found in all spear fighting styles. One training regimen was designed to provide the complete spear fighting style in one hundred days.[15] Basic training included man-to-man sparring, conditioning soldiers to fight one-on-one.

The Ming military's approach to spear fighting indicates a deeper engagement with the martial arts than we might have assumed. Manual writers were at pains to survey and discuss the available styles of spear fighting because they expected that martial arts training in the spear would be fairly extensive. We don't know why this was the case, or how Ming military training compared to earlier periods. There are two likely reasons for deeper training. First, extensive training in even one weapon would improve the overall fighting capabilities of a soldier. Second, soldiers were expected to fight in more open formations and in a greater variety of circumstances that would require a broader range of spear skills. Particularly for southern Chinese soldiers, who did not have to contend with cavalry, dense formations of spearmen would not have been as necessary or useful.

Outside of the military, spear fighting was widely practiced as well. The nuance and elaboration of the recorded styles shows a deep attachment to the spear. While we are accustomed to seeing cultures fetishize archery or fencing, spear fighting is rare. Men like the late Ming Dynasty martial artist Wu Shu spent three decades studying spear fighting, including Shi Family Spear Technique, Shaolin Spear Technique, Ma Family Spear Technique, Yang Family Spear Technique, Sha Family Spear Technique, and Emei Spear Technique. Wu was not alone in his obsessions, and the very fact that he could travel around the empire studying different forms of spear fighting shows how separate traditions had evolved and taken root. His deep knowledge of the subject he wrote about is also a salutary admonition to those who would do research on the martial arts that they should practice what they study.

The spear was a ubiquitous weapon in Ming China, more important on the battlefield than the sword and at least equal, if not greater, in importance to missile weapons. When the Ming army faced the Japanese in Korea, it was southern troops with their infantry trained in spear fighting that were effective against the Japanese army. Northern Chinese troops with their emphasis on cavalry failed badly. Among the general populace the spear was also widely used. It was a simple and effective weapon that was available everywhere. Not only soldiers but also farmers and villagers called upon to defend their communities would have been armed with and trained to use spears. There was a deep reservoir of spear fighting martial arts throughout the empire. This was reflected in fictional heroes who spoke of being skilled in "spears and staves," and the aesthetics of the spear in theater performances.

STAFF FIGHTING

Spear fighting and staff fighting techniques had many similarities, to the point that some martial artists felt they were virtually identical. Staffs were

naturally even more available than spears and could be carried without
necessarily imputing a martial purpose. One record of staff styles listed
thirty-one, including Shaolin Staff and Zhao Taizu Moving Snake Staff.[16]
Unlike spear fighting, staff fighting was not usually a weapon of the formal
military, nor was it a weapon for community self-defense. Its great value
was for personal self-defense and, as some authorities on the martial arts
argued, as the basis for all martial arts training.

As General Yu Dayou put it: "Using the staff is like reading the Four Books
[the basic works of Confucianism]."[17] He argued that the physical aspects of
staff practice underlay all of the other martial arts. The staff was thus a
fundamental weapon of martial arts practice of much greater importance
than its utility in fighting. For Yu Dayou, staff was more basic than boxing,
and in fact boxing relied upon staff fighting for some of its techniques.

While many different styles of staff fighting were practiced across
China, Shaolin placed special emphasis on its relationship to staff fighting.
There was certainly a long-standing Buddhist association with the staff, as
evidenced by Sagacious Lu in *The Water Margin* using one. Sagacious Lu
actually used an iron staff rather than a wooden one. The staff was
associated with Buddhist authority figures, and in one very famous story
the Buddha himself lent his staff to Mulian so that he could fight his way
into hell and rescue his mother from her suffering there. Given how widespread and varied staff fighting was in China, it is unlikely that any Shaolin
claim to primacy is valid. Although Shaolin emphasized staff fighting in the
Ming, the temple's style was one among a crowded field.

CONCLUSION

Martial arts changed during the Ming Dynasty, but the largest shift was
intellectual rather than in practice. People began to write about the martial
arts in ways they had not before, and that writing led to even more writing
in response. Authors became much more specific in describing the martial
arts, not only surveying the available styles in many categories but also
providing illustrated accounts of specific techniques. Martial arts and
martial artists played important roles in fiction as well, linking performance, theater, novels, and practice in society and on the written page. The
flourishing book industry textualized the martial arts in new and prominent ways during the Ming. This initial literary moment fixed a number of
concepts and myths about the martial arts, like the importance of Shaolin,
in Chinese culture, and shaped our subsequent understanding of the martial arts.

Much of what was recorded had been going on since at least the Song, if not earlier. Local styles of armed and unarmed martial arts were everywhere. Violence and violent men flourished in the absence of a strong government presence, and martial arts were as likely to serve the interest of local thugs as ordinary citizens defending themselves and their communities. Powerful landlords or institutions, including temples, maintained their own security forces to defend and enforce their interests. Sometimes those forces contributed to state security efforts, suppressing bandits, for example, and were rewarded by the state. At other times those selfsame lords or institutions sheltered bandits, men of violence, and other criminals because it suited their own interests. It was often useful to be able to draw upon the large pool of violent men in a conflict. And, of course, the state acted similarly when it recruited soldiers from the floating population of violent men to suppress bandits, bolster its army, or otherwise enforce its interests.

Military martial arts were, as always, the most straightforward of skills and kept a narrow group of weapons – sword, spear, bow, crossbow, and gun – at their core. Boxing and staff skills were useful only as training practices to improve physical endurance, agility, and strength; teach proper stance and balance; and develop the right mental attitude. Practice-fighting with real weapons was much more likely to result in serious injury or death than sparring with staffs or empty-handed. A larger group of more elaborate weapons was available for specialized martial artists, but these were more theatric (and used in theater and fiction) than practical. The "Eighteen Martial Arts" changed in the Ming, by one account, to "bow, crossbow, spear, sword, long sword, mao-spear, shield, fu-axe, yue-axe, ji-halberd, whip, metal tablet, truncheon, shu-spear, fork, claw head, silk corded lasso, unarmed striking."[18] Archery had been restored to its more usual place, and the ordering of spear and sword made practical sense. The gun had been removed, but unarmed striking was added.

Another real change was the connection of long sword fencing with literati spirit. The long sword became the refined weapon of the gentleman or superior martial artist. It was a weapon of skill and subtlety, not raw power. A long sword was truly effective in individual combat or for self-defense in the hands of an expert; otherwise, it was simply a defense weapon appropriate for a gentleman. Having abandoned archery, literati still apparently needed a form of martial expression. At least from the perspective of some biographies, a "heroic" youth practicing long sword balanced a conventional life of literary or bureaucratic service.

There is no particular reason to think that some forms of martial arts suddenly switched their emphasis from effectiveness in combat to self-cultivation during the Ming. If self-cultivation was important in Ming martial arts, it was undoubtedly there beforehand. Not only Buddhists but also Daoists and Confucians had preexisting traditions of meditation unrelated to any martial arts. The long Confucian tradition of self-cultivation through archery practice points to a deep acceptance of the spiritual and intellectual power of the physical practice of martial arts. It did not escape the notice of the educated authors of the martial arts manuals of the Ming that training in fighting had a significant emotional and psychological effect on the practitioner. Men could be made more aggressive or more confident in battle through training. Extensive training in a martial art developed deep and nuanced understandings of physical practice that were valuable in and of themselves. The profound knowledge of physical training could be mentioned, and the gross form of the practice recorded, but true understanding required years or decades of dedicated physical performance under a master.

In many ways the Ming Dynasty was the acme of Chinese martial arts practice before the rapid and revolutionary changes of the succeeding Qing Dynasty. Ming martial arts were rich and varied. Guns were present and important, but hand-to-hand combat with weapons, and archery were all regular and effective components of warfare. There was still an unbroken continuum between the skills of the military and the skills of the ordinary subject. All that would change during the Qing Dynasty, though not before a return of steppe martial arts and values.

9

The Qing Dynasty

The Yuan Dynasty crumbled from internal problems exacerbated by rebellions, but the Manchus, a newly risen steppe polity, destroyed the Ming Dynasty. The Manchus created a new dynasty, the Qing, which presided over a period of incredible territorial expansion in the eighteenth century, followed by a series of stinging military and political defeats at the hands of the encroaching Western powers in the nineteenth century. The Qing court and China itself struggled to formulate an adequate response to the West. This process continued after the dynasty fell in 1911 and a modern nation-state began to emerge. The Qing Dynasty thus straddles two distinct periods of martial arts history: the end of the time in which hand-to-hand combat skills were useful on and off the battlefield, and the beginning of the time in which modern weaponry cast all of those skills in an antiquarian, rather than practical, light. It was that shift that laid the basis for much of our modern understanding of Chinese martial arts.

Guns played an important part in the wars that founded the Ming, and they played a still greater role during the Qing conquest. From as early as the Yuan Dynasty, guns might even be included in the list of Eighteen Martial Arts. European Jesuits at the Ming court were compelled to contribute their knowledge of European gun making to the Ming war effort against the Qing, but the Manchus caught up quickly by capturing Chinese artillery experts trained by the Europeans. Both sides in the conflict fought with all the weaponry of the preceding centuries – swords, spears, bows, crossbows, handguns, and cannon. Military change was incremental, rather than revolutionary.

The late Ming Dynasty was also marked by serious rebellions that did immense damage to local and regional society, particularly in north China.

Caught between the developing threat of the Manchus and serious internal rebellions, the Ming court proved incapable of settling on a coherent strategy. Political infighting at court prevented any faction from pursuing a single policy long enough for it to be effective. The rebellions were nearly destroyed at some points, only to have the commanders impeached or recalled before they could achieve the decisive success that would have yielded valuable political capital. The Ming military itself was blamed in retrospect for its inability to defeat the rebels and fend off the Manchus. Until recently, Ming military rot was traced back to the Wanli emperor's reign, but Kenneth Swope has convincingly demonstrated that in military matters Wanli was decisive and effective.[1] The Ming army performed respectably in Wanli's Three Great Campaigns, showing that, whatever the larger social context, strong political leadership could invigorate the army. Lacking that leadership, however, the army could not act successfully. Even without strong political leadership, some parts of the Ming army were strong and effective.

As the Manchus launched increasingly serious incursions through the Great Wall, Chinese rebels under Li Zicheng stormed across north China, eventually capturing the capital, Beijing, in April of 1644. The Ming emperor, abandoned by his officials, hanged himself at the bottom of Coal Hill. Beijing fell into rebel hands easily, leaving the Ming army posted along the Great Wall caught between defending the border against the Manchus and returning to the capital to restore order and the dynastic fortunes. When the rebels advanced on his position from Beijing, Wu Sangui, the Ming commander, chose to join the Manchus rather than submit to the rebels. Manchu forces tipped the balance in a hard-fought battle between Wu and the rebel's armies. The rebels were routed, falling back through Beijing, pursued by the Manchus. To the surprise of its residents, Beijing was liberated from the rebels by the Manchus who quickly established order under their own authority. Wu Sangui, his fellow commanders, and their troops were sent in pursuit of the remaining rebel armies.

The particular and unexpected events of 1644 dramatically accelerated the Manchus' planned conquest of the Ming. Rather than having to batter their way through the Great Wall and the armies guarding it, the Manchu army added the Ming border army to its own force. This provided an important infantry component to the Manchu army, something that would be necessary to conquer southern China and to hold territory. The Manchu people themselves had been organized along military lines into eight "banners" that formed the basis of social, political, and army life. The cavalry units that formed the core of the Manchu army were drawn from the banners and fought under their respective banner leaders. Banner leaders maintained direct military and political power over their bannermen and their families. Large numbers of Mongols, who had been the Ming's original steppe threat, were also brought into the Manchu system and organized into their own eight banners. The Mongols, like the Manchus, were horse cavalrymen. A third group, Han Chinese, formed another set of eight banners, but they were mainly artillerymen and infantry.

Bannermen were prohibited from practicing a trade or doing manual labor. Ideally, from the perspective of the Qing government, the privileged bannermen would maintain a loyal and effective military force in return for government economic support. By living apart from the subject population in their own garrisons, working and functioning within their particular banner, the bannermen would keep a strong group identity. The system worked reasonably well during the extended period of conquest, but it was beginning to show cracks as early as the Revolt of the Three Feudatories (1673–81). The banners neither produced enough trained soldiers nor enough competent battlefield leaders. The Three Feudatories themselves were the fiefs provided to Wu Sangui and his fellow generals following their efforts in subjugating the Ming empire. They rebelled when it became clear that the Qing government would not permit them to keep their semi-independent authority in southern China in perpetuity.

Chinese soldiers serving in units of the Green Standard Army, so called because they carried green colored pennons or standards, were critical in providing the manpower to defeat the Revolt of the Three Feudatories. Handguns, and particularly cannon, continued to grow in importance during these campaigns. Gunpowder weapons were increasingly critical tools of warfare. Massed cannon could smash through any enemy position given enough time and supplies. Armies needed cannon to succeed, and cannon required a very different set of skills from those used in hand-to-hand martial arts. The shift toward modern warfare that began during the Song Dynasty was far advanced even before Western armed forces appeared in China in the nineteenth century. The Green Standard forces outnumbered the banner forces two to one in suppressing the Three Feudatories; they would go on to handle most of the local security in the Chinese part of the Qing empire during peacetime.

Horse archery and prowess on the battlefield were key components of the Manchu identity. In peacetime, however, there were no battlefields to fight on, and horse archery was difficult to practice for Manchus living within China. Archery and riding were ordinary activities on the steppe but not in China. Bannermen of all stripes who lived in or near Chinese towns and cities were drawn away from the dreary life of the garrison and practicing martial arts of dubious value in peacetime to the more interesting urban Chinese culture. By the late eighteenth century the Qianlong emperor was concerned not only over the loss of Manchu culture but of the Manchu language as well – this despite the Qianlong emperor succeeding in the decades-long struggle begun by his grandfather to destroy the Zunghar Mongols. But perhaps he understood on some level that the great success of the Qing army and its banner cavalry against the Zunghars was really the end of an era.

The Western powers had increased their presence in China from missionaries to merchants over the course of the Qing Dynasty. Western merchants initially paid for Chinese goods like silk, tea, or porcelain with silver bullion. Indeed, at various points, as much as half of all the silver taken by Europeans from the New World went to China. This was a cause for concern among European governments and merchants, as they believed, based upon their prevailing economic theory, that the drain of silver was seriously harming the states exporting bullion. A substitute was found in opium, which the British were able to produce in India in large quantities. It was then the Chinese government's turn to be concerned about the effects of European trade. Opium caused immediate and obvious problems among the Qing population and was very difficult to interdict. The British, who were the most prominent power and major source for opium in the beginning, refused to enforce Qing government prohibitions on the drug, or to restrict their merchants. When the Qing government finally acted, seizing the opium of British merchants and destroying it, the British went to war to receive compensation.

The Opium War (1839–42) revealed both the power of European arms and deep problems in the Qing state. Manchu bannermen and Manchu leadership were completely ineffective in fighting the British. Chinese soldiers were no better, though some Manchu and Chinese soldiers who fought bravely were simply overwhelmed by the advances in European weaponry. The old way of fighting, in terms of weaponry and tactics, had to change if the Qing were to fend off the Europeans. Changing military practice was difficult, particularly since changes in the military structure of the dynasty directly affected the entire social and political structure of Manchu rule. Manchu identity was tied to a particular martial arts practice, horse archery, which European military practice now rendered obsolete. It was less identity threatening to convert Chinese troops to the new military system, but that ran the risk of empowering the Chinese.

The advent of European military practice in China marked a sharp break with the previous milieu for Chinese martial arts. A traditional Chinese army could not stand up to a modern European-style force armed with modern firearms. Archery was now an archaic skill, whether from horseback or on foot, and hand-to-hand combat was unlikely. As firearms improved over the nineteenth century, close combat became less and less important on the battlefield. This was not to say that traditional martial arts were not still useful absent a modern European-style force, but the Qing state had to radically reform its army. Even a vigorous and well-led government would have had difficulty unraveling the previous system of martial arts from society and culture quickly, effectively, and with a minimum of disruption. The Qing government in the nineteenth century was neither vigorous nor well led.

The Qing court's failure of leadership was evident in its inept handling of the Opium War. It continued to be unable to institute needed reforms in the face of the conservative interests of many groups. In a certain sense the relationship between who did which martial arts in Qing society marked out the respective areas of power at the local, regional, and imperial level. The challenge of European weaponry and military practice was not simply to copy it but also to fit it into Qing society. European science and technology as a whole challenged the Qing economy as well as the intellectual basis of the Qing worldview. One of the responses to this European challenge was to portray European technology and science as an external and peripheral knowledge or practice, in contrast to the internal and fundamental Chinese culture. This scheme would allow the retention of Chinese values while the society adopted Western objects and practice.

It was obvious to many concerned people in Qing China, however, that partial modernization or adoption of Western science and technology did not work very well. Western interest in Chinese markets and goods was too intense to allow any gradual or compromise approach sufficient time to work. Western ideas and technology put immense stress on an already sclerotic Qing government, leading to rebellions and growing anti-Manchu and anti-Western sentiment. The Taiping Rebellion (1850–64) was vaguely Christian in its ideology and succeeded for a time in seizing control of large sections of southern China. It was eventually defeated by Chinese forces newly raised in the provinces by Chinese officials outside of the regular channels. The success of these regional Chinese forces was critical to the survival of the Qing regime, but also threatened its foundations. Effective military power was no longer controlled directly by the central government, led by Manchus, or based upon forces of Manchu soldiers.

The final major martial arts event of the Qing before its fall in 1911, was the Boxer Uprising (1898–1901).[2] The Boxers began as a movement in Shandong, spurred on by increasingly difficult economic conditions, to be

丁月華

ILLUSTRATION 21. Theatrical representation of the female hero Ding Yuehua (Moon Flower), wielding a long sword. From *Qixia Wuyi*, 1889.

rabidly anti-foreign and anti-Christian. It was initially based upon groups of martial artists who believed that they could overcome modern weaponry through spirit possession and internal cultivation. Although poorly armed mostly with swords, spears, and some handguns, the Boxers quickly overwhelmed and massacred defenseless Christian missions and churches. They killed thousands of missionaries and Chinese converts before converging on Beijing. The Boxers besieged the foreign diplomats and their families in the foreign legation but failed to capture it. A combined foreign military force fought its way to Beijing and rescued the people trapped in the foreign legation after fifty-five days. Needless to say, neither spirits nor internal cultivation were any protection against bullets and artillery.

The narrative of martial arts history in the Qing Dynasty begins with the remnant Ming loyalists who refused to accept the Manchu takeover of China. These loyalists initiated an anti-Manchu discourse that carried over into discussions of the martial arts. Anti-foreignism shifted the attitude toward martial arts writing, changing the tradition of this type of writing that had begun in the Ming. A certain Chinese chauvinism permeated discussions of the martial arts in direct response to the return of steppe domination. That chauvinism returned at the end of the Qing Dynasty and carried through into the succeeding Republican period. At the same time, the Manchu and Mongol culture of the bannermen reverted to an earlier interest in wrestling and steppe martial arts. Even more so than the Ming, the Qing Dynasty intellectual construction of Chinese martial arts strongly biases the twenty-first-century understanding of Chinese martial arts. It is therefore important to keep in mind how the place and value of the martial arts changed during the Qing Dynasty.

MING LOYALISTS

It was not a simple matter for men to hide their loyalty to the fallen Ming Dynasty. Early in their rule, the Manchus imposed their own particular hairstyle on the men of the Chinese population – the front of the head was shaved, and there was a queue in the back – and used it as an outward demonstration of loyalty to the Qing Dynasty. Confucian notions of loyalty required that men who had served as officials in one dynasty could not be officials in another dynasty. Many literati stretched this concept to include men who had received exam degrees, even if they had not served in government. Of course, many officials did work for the new dynasty, but loyalty to the extinguished Ming Dynasty became something of a fetish for a large number of literati. The Manchus enforced their hairstyle policy ruthlessly, leaving these loyalists with two options. The first was to stay out of cities and towns, living in the countryside away from government authority. Some literati combined this with the long-standing Confucian or Daoist role of secluded hermit. The second option was to become, or at least adopt the raiment of, a Buddhist monk. Since Buddhist monks shaved their heads, the issue of hairstyle was moot.

Buddhism, despite over a millennium of practice in China by the early Qing, was still regarded as a foreign religion. Some people were more troubled by this association than others, of course, but in the tightly censored environment of the early Qing Dynasty, Buddhism could stand in for the Manchus. A foreign religion was equivalent to a foreign people. A Ming loyalist could discuss Buddhism without incurring the wrath of the Qing authorities, while his audience understood that he was really talking about the Manchus. Daoism, on the other hand, was an impeccably Chinese belief system. In either its philosophical or religious form, Daoism posed as the native Chinese counterpart to the foreign Buddhism.

These themes, of Ming loyalty, Buddhist foreignness, and Daoist Chineseness, all came together in the realm of martial arts with the 1669 epitaph for Wang Zhengnan (1617–69) written by Huang Zongxi (1610–95) and the account of Wang's martial arts by his son Huang Baijia (1643–?). This epitaph is the first articulation of an internal school of martial arts in contradistinction to an external school of martial arts. Wang's internal school purportedly originated with a Daoist saint, Zhang Sanfeng. Huang Zongxi's epitaph opens:

Shaolin is famous for its boxers. However, its techniques are chiefly offensive, which creates opportunities for an opponent to exploit. Now there is another school that is called "internal," which overcomes movement with stillness. Attackers are effortlessly repulsed. Thus we distinguish Shaolin as "external."

The Internal School was founded by Zhang Sanfeng of the Song Dynasty, Sanfeng was a Daoist alchemist of the Wudang Mountains. He was summoned by Emperor Huizong of the Song, but the road was impassable. That night he dreamt that the God of War transmitted the art of boxing to him and the following morning [he] single-handedly killed over a hundred bandits.[3]

Huang Baijia's account of the origin of Wang Zhengnan's internal art was somewhat different from his father's:

Wang Zhengnan was a master of two skills: one was pugilism and the other archery. From ancient times great archers have been many, but when it comes to pugilism, truly Master Wang was the foremost.

The external school of pugilism reached its highest development with Shaolin. Zhang Sanfeng, having mastered Shaolin, reversed its principles, and this is called the Internal School of martial arts. Acquiring even a smattering of this art is sufficient to overcome Shaolin.[4]

No author before this time presented or created this kind of dichotomy between respective martial arts practices. Absent the political context, it would just appear that the Huangs were finally putting brush to paper either to describe a centuries-old distinction in styles or were creating a fictitious historical background for a new paradigm. We will discuss these two possibilities later in the chapter. Here it is critical to note Huang Zongxi's background.

Huang Zongxi's father was a prominent Ming official and member of the Donglin faction of Confucian reformers. His father was executed in 1626 on the orders of the dominant eunuch faction at court, which was in a life and death struggle with the Donglin faction. Huang received an exam degree under the Ming and fought against the Qing with Ming holdouts until 1649. He then retired to study and write for the rest of his life, refusing to serve the new dynasty. His many intellectual pursuits would subsequently earn him considerable fame, particularly after some late Qing Chinese reformers like Liang Qichao rediscovered his writings. Huang was a native of Zhejiang, and he returned there after he gave up fighting the Qing.

The facts of Huang Zongxi's Ming loyalism are particularly important when we examine his epitaph for Wang Zhengnan. Douglas Wile has argued that the Huangs, father and son, made a political statement against alien rule through the medium of Wang Zhengnan's biography.[5] Meir Shahar has extended this argument to point out the exact symmetry that Huang Zongxi created with Shaolin and Bodhidarma, the legendary founder of Chan (Zen) Buddhism, by attributing the founding of the internal school to the Daoist saint Zhang Sanfeng. Of course, the illiterate martial artist teaching in Zhejiang was also an interesting reflection of Huang Zongxi himself. Wang is described as refusing to serve after the fall of the Ming, despite repeated requests. Rather than accept the new dynasty, he turned to farming and concealed his skills. The same could have been said of Huang Zongxi.

Of course, Wang Zhengnan did not completely turn to farming. He trained Huang Baijia in the martial arts. And Huang Baijia did not study martial arts with Wang for self-cultivation but in order to fight the Manchus. Thus what Wang's internal school of martial arts in fact was or how it was distinguished from the external school of Shaolin is not explained. In practical terms, it served to train an individual to fight effectively. The military officials who sought to entice Wang into service surely did so because of the effectiveness of his martial arts in combat. His internal style was manifestly more

錦毛鼠白玉堂

ILLUSTRATION 22. Theatrical representation of the hero Baiyu Tang (the Sleek Rat), with his hand on his sheathed long sword. From *Qixia Wuyi*, 1889.

powerful in Huang Baijia's telling because it proceeded from a deeper under-standing of the martial arts than the external Shaolin martial arts. It is worth noting, of course, that Wang Zhengnan had actually served as a military officer under the Ming. He was a professional warrior earlier in his life.

For anti- or non-Buddhist Ming loyalists, Shaolin and Buddhism offered a shorthand for foreigners and the Manchus. Chinese power was internal and concealed, but superior. Internal martial arts was part of a Chinese discourse about identity and political loyalties rather than a transparent description of practice. The Qing Dynasty literature on the martial arts was inflected from its very beginning by the politics of the change from Chinese to Manchu rule. Ming loyalism directly affected the Qing understanding of martial arts. As Chinese scholars in the early Qing wrote about the martial arts and military affairs, they did so in response to a profound anxiety that the Ming had fallen because the literati, who formed the elite of society and led the government at every level, had cut themselves off from everything martial. Ming literati had become too literary and had lost the necessary martial interests to keep their regime strong.

Regardless of the truth of the matter, the neurotic Ming loyalist per-spective on the martial arts and the literati struck directly at the core of Chinese literati identity. During the Qing Dynasty, Manchus and Mongols were clearly more martial, and thus more masculine, than the subject Chinese population. Regardless of how scholars and thinkers tried to cast the relative positions of martial and civil as categories, elevating the civil over the martial, it was clear that martial men were more masculine, steppe people were more martial than Chinese, and civil literati incapable of fighting were likely to be subjugated in any conflict. Brains or moral cultivation might create inner strength, but it was usually beaten by brawn.

INTERNAL VERSUS EXTERNAL MARTIAL ARTS

Wang Zhengnan's internal martial arts, or at least Huang's description of it, left a lasting intellectual mark on the martial arts. While Wang's own art disappeared quite quickly, a permanent link had been established between the internal "school" of martial arts, Zhang Sanfeng, Daoism, and Mount Wudang. It was entirely specious, but it gained credibility with each retell-ing. This was not surprising given that the sort of dichotomy it established between internal and external was completely consistent with other areas of Chinese thought. It took an accomplished philosopher motivated by politics to fit the martial arts into the context of Chinese thought.

The martial arts had hitherto been characterized as a particular kind of skill. Men and women learned the martial arts in order to fight or perform. Some weapon skills, particularly archery for Confucius, were explicitly acknowledged to have the ability to show inner cultivation through the correct demonstration of martial arts etiquette. From the Confucian perspective, the outward expression of the correct rites was directly tied to and affected the inner state of mind of the practitioner. It did not, however, lead to martial prowess. There was an aspect of self-cultivation in this practice, without a separation of internal and external physical development.

Inner strength in the martial arts was a challenging notion because its most basic proof was an external demonstration of power. Wang Zhengnan's power was internally developed and generated but manifested externally. What, in fact, had Zhang Sanfeng reverse engineered from the martial arts he learned at Shaolin (leaving apart the completely mythical/fictitious story itself)? The root or internal aspect of any practice was its true essence. That essence was manifested externally in an obscured or apparently diminished form. A master of something truly understood a particular practice or skill at a level deeper than ordinary people could perceive. This sort of knowledge was a frequent point of discussion in the Daoist philosophical tradition.

A true archer, recalling the anecdote from the *Liezi*, could shoot without regard for his physical circumstances, even standing on the edge of a cliff. A Daoist ruler could establish harmony and prosperity in a state without seeming to do anything. The mistake was to focus on the effects of true understanding rather than trying to achieve the fundamental essence of something. A musician might develop a high level of skill with an instrument without truly understanding music, the instrument he was playing, or even the act of playing that instrument. Yet the route to deeper understanding was to work very hard at playing that instrument or perfecting any other skill. The physical or external practice was a path to the essence of something. It was critical that the practitioner understand that the goal of practice was deeper understanding, not just greater external skill.

There was, therefore, a reasonable consonance between Huang's attribution of internal martial arts to a Daoist tradition. Intellectually, a focus on the internal, mysterious, and profound was superior to the external, vulgar, and superficial, even though it was hard, if not impossible, to distinguish the two in combat. Only those who knew were aware of these things. This also opened up the possibility that someone who did not obviously manifest martial power through his or her physique or strength could nonetheless be a true master. Most military exams, performances of martial arts, or even fictional representations of great heroes used demonstrations of sheer physical strength to mark out the superior warrior. The great fictional hero Wu Song, from *The Water Margin*, displayed incredible strength on a number of occasions. But an internal school of martial arts diminished the obvious physical manifestation of martial arts prowess. A true martial arts master could conceal himself, be physically unimpressive, or even old.

The explicit description of internal martial arts also amplified the pre-existing connection between martial artists and medicine. There were two aspects of this connection. The first was the long-standing, at least since the Song if *The Water Margin* is reliable in this regard, use of martial arts performances in the marketplace to sell medicines. Medicine peddlers used the martial arts not just to attract a crowd to their wares but to prove their own vigorous health. A man who worked on his own health to the point that he could perform impressive martial arts feats clearly understood the workings of the body. His performance validated his medicines. The second aspect was the connection between acupuncture and the martial arts. Some medicine peddlers may have also practiced acupuncture as a broader aspect of medical service, but, as we saw in the Ming, there was also a more general belief that some martial artists could strike someone so as cause a delayed death. This was literally internal martial arts, since the obvious strike seemed to do nothing. A later biography of Zhang Songxi, a putative Ming Dynasty practitioner of the internal art that would be transmitted to Wang Zhengnan, specifically describes him as striking pressure points.[6] Skill of this nature was profound and mysterious.

Wang Zhengnan's epitaph established the discourse of internal versus external martial arts. The originators of Taijiquan (or Tai chi chuan, literally "the Supreme Ultimate Fist," now known for its extremely slow movements) in the nineteenth century adopted Wang's putative emphasis on internal practice. Of course, practitioners of Shaolin martial arts did not necessarily accept their own consignment to the external realm. To further complicate matters, another martial arts discourse developed that was related to the internal/external paradigm: the notion of practicing martial arts for self-cultivation. This particular discourse is extremely powerful in twentieth- and twenty-first-century perspectives on Chinese martial arts, to the extent of badly mischaracterizing the history of Chinese martial arts as a whole.

SELF-CULTIVATION

There is no precise definition of "self-cultivation" so it would seem that some description of what the term means, if only for our current purposes, is warranted. In the context of the martial arts, self-cultivation is a positive physical or mental benefit of practice. These positive effects are the product of the specific training regimen of a martial art. The martial arts were mostly studied to enhance an individual's ability to fight, regardless of the cause to which those skills were applied. This remains the case even today, but a significant number of martial artists beginning in the nineteenth century, or possibly somewhat earlier, gave increasing attention to the other effects of training. Those martial artists wrote about their particular styles in an environment where improved firearms were rendering boxing and hand-to-hand combat weapons less relevant to actual fighting. This shift in emphasis among a certain group of literate practitioners had a disproportionate effect on the overall understanding of the martial arts because, unlike most illiterate martial artists, their accounts of the martial arts were widely disseminated inside and outside China. Consequently, there has been a major effort on the part of martial arts scholars to uncover or recover the tradition of self-cultivation in the martial arts.

Retrospectively, the idea of an internal school of martial arts was critical to the discourse of self-cultivation. Another strand was added with the inclusion of the practices of Daoist "medical gymnastics" (*daoyin* 導引) in some martial arts. Both of these practices strongly associated themselves with the central value of *qi* (vital energy) in enhancing bodily health. For the internal school, this was further extended to developing power and skill in fighting. It was an easy enough next step to see that if medical gymnastics developed one's *qi*, then its practices would be very helpful to martial artists. The historiographical question is whether the later system of practice that relied upon ideas of the internal school and then connected up with medical gymnastics created a false lineage to legitimize itself, or whether it uncovered a progressive development of synthesized practice. Here we again return to the few texts that addressed these issues in the absence of any other evidence for actual practice.

Huang Zongxi and his son's introduction of the idea of an internal school of martial arts highlighted the possibility that there could be something more to martial arts mastery than an outward display of proficient violence. The martial arts might be pursued in the context of self-cultivation, or seeking a deeper understanding of oneself through the practice of the techniques of fighting. If the Huangs' discussion of the internal school of martial arts raised this issue to prominence, it is not clear that this was their intent or even a new idea. The importance of practicing martial arts for self-cultivation, or at least good health, became increasingly important conceptually as better firearms reduced the value of hand-to-hand combat skills on the battlefield. Industrialized warfare rendered most traditional martial arts moot, but many practitioners of those traditional martial arts felt that there was a deeper and abiding value to their traditions. Traditional martial arts benefited the self in some unique way.

It was not a Qing Dynasty idea that some kind of self-cultivation was attainable through the martial arts. As we saw in the early chapters of this book and in the discussion of internal martial arts, Warring States period thinkers thought there was a direct connection between martial arts practice and inner cultivation. Archery in particular had a central role in Confucian public ritual, reflecting the Warring States period origins of Confucian thought. That connection was attenuated and finally broken in practice by the Song Dynasty, at the latest, leaving educated elites without an identity-affirming martial art. Some Confucian thinkers in the Song advocated "quiet sitting" as an appropriate form of Confucian meditation (and some modern writers have classed quiet sitting under the rubric of "Confucian *daoyin*"). In the Ming Dynasty, the long sword became an acceptable gentleman's weapon, and this association continued through the Qing and after.

The long sword became a weapon of the gentleman when it was no longer a regular battlefield weapon. It retained some value for self-defense, but its non-military status allowed educated men to practice its use without associating themselves with thuggish militarism. Still, practicing with the long sword was not discussed in terms of inner cultivation. Some Ming literati practiced with other weapons, including spears and staffs. Men like Wu Shu spent their entire lives pursuing martial arts study without suggesting why they did so. It does not seem entirely unwarranted to suggest that these literati martial artists were seeking some sort of self-cultivation through the martial arts. They self-consciously devoted themselves to finding teachers, often traveling great distances, and spent enormous amounts of time and money on advancing their martial arts skills. Unfortunately, they did not articulate a specific goal. We have even less information regarding the professional martial artists they studied with. For many of those men, at least, studying and teaching the martial arts was a way to make a living.

Daoism has a strong connection to ideas of self-cultivation and some connection to the martial arts, but it seems that the two were not considered together before the Qing Dynasty. Daoist thinkers from the Warring States used examples of martial arts practice in their writings to make philosophical points without necessarily practicing the martial arts themselves. Mount Wudang had a strong connection to martial spirits, with Ming imperial patronage of the Daoist temple on Wudang connected to the True Martial spirit. The Ming imperial house thus patronized both

穿山鼠徐慶

ILLUSTRATION 23. Theatrical representation of the hero Xu Qing (the Mountain Rat), standing in an exaggerated martial pose. From *Qixia Wuyi*, 1889.

Shaolin (Buddhist) and Wudang (Daoist) temples. What tied Daoism, whether religious or philosophical, most closely to self-cultivation was its system of meditation and medical gymnastics. These stances, postures, and movements were designed to enhance the practitioner's *qi* and improve its circulation. This would enhance the practitioner's health, providing for a longer life unencumbered by illness.

Buddhist meditation was perhaps more spiritually focused and less concerned with long life. Given the Buddhist goal of detachment from physical urges and pleasures, this makes some sense. Before the late Ming Dynasty there is no explicit connection between Buddhist meditation and martial arts practiced by Buddhists. Meir Shahar argues that Daoist gymnastics began to enter Shaolin martial arts in the late Ming. Lin Boyuan, in contrast, dates the connection of *daoyin* with the martial arts as a whole to the early Qing Dynasty.[7] Once again, we are faced not just with a question of interpretation but also with the changing nature of the texts involved.

Possibly there was always some kind of connection between the martial arts and meditation. Since we have nothing like Qi Jiguang's direct discussion of the martial arts until the sixteenth century, we are left attributing any number of changes in the martial arts to the Ming or Qing dynasties. Self-cultivation in the purely mental sense was always a part of the martial arts, since a particular mental state was necessary for the effective use of weapons and participation in combat. This was reflected in many Warring States period stories as well as military texts that were concerned with motivating and controlling men in battle. The obvious health benefits of the martial arts were used as a selling point for the medicines sold by traveling peddlers, providing almost a modern American notion of a pill that would have the same health effects as vigorous exercise.

When Shahar, Lin Boyuan, or others connect Daoist medical gymnastics with the martial arts, they are more specifically connecting the martial arts to enhancing one's *qi*. *Qi* is such an all-encompassing and flexible term that it is hard to separate enhanced health or power, mental balance, or long life from enhanced *qi*. Only a very small number of martial artists looked for more out of their training than enhanced fighting skills. At the same time, very few people had the time or access to the training to practice any form of medical gymnastics. There was a superficial resemblance between the postures of martial arts and Daoist medical gymnastics; and much underlying thought could be marshaled to discuss *qi* development, traditional medicine, and philosophical writings in the larger cultural matrix. Both Daoist medical gymnastics and the martial arts grew out of and remained steeped in Chinese culture. It is difficult to parse their relationship in the absence of direct evidence.

The most reliable conclusion we can reach is that among the literate class, only in the late Ming Dynasty did serious attention begin to be focused on martial artists and Daoist medical gymnastics together. Before that, any such practice was not mentioned, even if it did take place. This is an unsatisfying conclusion, of course, but it does suggest a more narrow explanation of the real roots of self-cultivation through the martial arts, and the linking of medical gymnastics to the martial arts. Perhaps it was the literati martial artists themselves who originated these practices. They were the only group who had the leisure, knowledge, opportunity, and interest to participate in these disparate practices. The literati were also the only group who could pursue and intellectually integrate these things theoretically.

At the end of the Qing Dynasty, the value of Chinese martial arts in self-cultivation became wrapped up with a rising discourse of nationalism. Chinese martial arts was not a Western sport but a martial exercise with deep roots in Chinese culture. Some of the urban educated elite sought to find an authentically Chinese martial experience in the martial arts, or argued that it was there. The martial arts were not modern or Western, and these literati needed to find a practical value for this artifact of Chinese culture. Discussions of *qi* and the unequivocal health-promoting benefits of the martial arts stood in sharp contrast to the scientific and modern medical approach to sport. Whatever its earlier place, self-cultivation through the martial arts became firmly based in a nationalist desire to cultivate a truly Chinese self.

SHAOLIN

The Shaolin Temple suffered another episode of destruction at the end of the Ming Dynasty. A local warlord slaughtered most of the monks and looted the temple. The temple thus began and ended the Ming Dynasty in the same way. It recovered much more slowly during the Qing Dynasty and indeed never fully returned to its grand past under Ming imperial patronage. Temple fighters fought in the Ming cause to the end of the dynasty, and the favors the Ming imperial family had lavished on Shaolin left a strong nostalgia for the fallen dynasty. And where Huang Zongxi would use Shaolin as a stand-in for foreigners, in opposition to native Daoists, Shaolin was a highly suspect location for Ming loyalists in the eyes of the Qing government. This was partly due to the reality of Shaolin history and partly to Qing suspicion based on the Shaolin myth.

After the temple and its fighting forces were destroyed, recovery was hampered by the loss of lands and government mistreatment. Qing government officials were not impressed with what they saw at Shaolin, and they were not inclined to assist its recovery. This underlying hostility abated somewhat in the eighteenth century, with some imperial attention and a visit by the Qianlong emperor. But the emperors were careful to support Shaolin as a religious institution and discourage its return as a center of martial arts practice. One of the most important acts in this regard was the destruction of the subsidiary shrines during Qianlong's reign.

The destruction of the subsidiary shrines around Shaolin was probably the most significant anti–martial arts act of the Qing Dynasty. Many temples had tense relationships with their subsidiary shrines. As the power and prestige of a temple brought increased lands and popularity, branches or smaller temples were set up nearby. These subsidiary shrines sometimes deviated significantly from their parent temple's rules and discipline, and even developed their own authority in opposition to the parent when their prestige and popularity grew. In the case of Shaolin, it seems that much of the martial arts activity and disreputable behavior took place in the subsidiary shrines. Many travelers and wandering martial artists, particularly those less interested in Buddhism, might lodge at a subsidiary. As Meir Shahar put it, "Shaolin's was a fluid community of which resident clerics occupied no more than a fraction."[8]

Before the Qing Dynasty, it is impossible to determine the extent to which martial arts activity was centered at the subsidiary shrines. The temple is referred to as a whole, without distinguishing how close the relationship was between the martial monks and the main authorities of Shaolin.[9] Indeed, some amount of ambiguity may have benefited the main temple, allowing it to maintain a security force that intimidated locals but for which the temple could deny full responsibility. The attention of the Qing authorities to this issue clarifies the matter somewhat and suggests an explanation for some of the religious problems of martial monks.

Rather than see martial arts at Buddhist temples and monasteries as unified activities wherein the martial arts grew out of Buddhist practice, it is more accurate to characterize these activities as linked. Before the Ming Dynasty, the martial arts activities of Buddhist monks excited very little attention. This was partly because no one wrote about such practices and partly because there was no perceived conflict in a temple maintaining some trained self-defense forces. Thus the Tang stele commemorating Shaolin's aid to Li Shimin was erected for political defense of the temple, not to make a point of the temple's martial arts practice. It was only during the Ming Dynasty that Shaolin and other temples sent out their martial monks to support the government's authority by combating rebellions and pirates. Once those fighting monks shifted from local self-defense to dynastic defense, the monasteries they came from were transformed into military training grounds. This gained them government support and patronage, but also strongly identified them with the Ming Dynasty.

Some efforts were made to justify these military training activities, along with other forbidden Buddhist practices like eating meat and drinking wine, but there was really no credible way to reconcile such contradictory positions. The reason such disparate activities could co-exist and also why they were hard to control was that they were followed by two separate groups. The resident monks at Shaolin were religious professionals who followed Buddhist precepts; the transient or peripheral population of martial artists concentrated on martial arts and were only marginally involved in Buddhist religious practice. Famous martial artists associated with Shaolin, like Hongji, who was killed fighting against bandits in the late 1630s or early 1640s, simply could not spend their days fighting and killing and act as Buddhist monks. Some might return or truly enter the monastic order after their fighting days were done, something we will see in current practice. Qing efforts to demilitarize Shaolin focused on keeping the resident Buddhist monks and preventing the martial artists from collecting in the monastery.

Shaolin forces suffered multiple military defeats at the end of the Ming Dynasty, and little, if anything, of its martial practice was left by the Qing. When Gu Yanwu (1613–82) visited in 1679, looking for Shaolin's martial arts, he was bitterly disappointed.[10] For Gu, in sharp contrast to Huang Zongxi, Shaolin was a symbol of Ming loyalism, not foreign invaders. In a famous poem, Gu speaks of a deserted place with no martial arts and only a few starving monks left. Having read the Li Shimin stele, Gu assumed a continuous martial tradition from the Sui Dynasty and wished for a new Li Shimin to overthrow the Qing.

Gu Yanwu was not the only visitor to Shaolin to find it deserted and its martial arts gone. Ye Feng (1623–87), Zhang Siming (ca. seventeenth century), and Shen Quan (1624–84) who all visited it independently found the temple destroyed and lamented the loss of a place of Buddhist worship. None of these three visitors was concerned about the martial arts. It was Shaolin as a famous Buddhist temple that was important to them, a point that is frequently overlooked when we concentrate only on its importance to the martial arts. Zhang Siming arrived in 1684, demonstrating that forty years after the Ming fall the temple had still not recovered. Wang Jie (ca. 1620–ca. 1700), the Qing governor of Henan, rousted a few monks living in the ruins to demonstrate their martial arts and declared what he saw "no better than street beggars."[11] Of course, we should not put too much weight on what some monks performed for a powerful and suspicious Qing official. Whatever their actual abilities, they would not have been wise to show great martial arts skills to Wang.

The Kangxi emperor bestowed some of his calligraphy on the temple in 1704, and his son, the Yongzheng emperor, even paid for a large-scale restoration in 1735. Shaolin had thus recovered enough of its Buddhist establishment to host the Qianlong emperor in 1750, but it was still a shadow of its Ming period incarnation. Most tellingly, after a brief stint from 1657 to 1661, no head abbot was appointed until 1999. Without the draw of martial arts and only limited imperial support, Shaolin was much diminished. Some part of its martial arts tradition did remain, however, as the Qianlong emperor saw fit in 1775 to severely admonish the Henan governor for using Shaolin monks in troop training.[12] Buddhism was the only acceptable activity for monks at Shaolin.

In the Qing Dynasty, Shaolin's reputation far outshone its reality. Martial arts styles claimed spurious connections with Shaolin to gain legitimacy. Chinese martial artists and scholars tied themselves to Shaolin as the Chinese source of martial arts, untainted by foreign influence. The authorities, for their part, worried that the many religious uprisings, real or imagined, might somehow gain power by connecting with the Shaolin community. The association of heterodox religious groups, like the White Lotus Sects, with violent uprisings somehow became connected to Shaolin's association with martial arts and the floating population of criminals and marginal groups. Shaolin does not appear to have been actually connected, but various secret societies developed their own mythologies tied to Shaolin. Both officially and in folklore, Shaolin became a center of Chinese martial arts resistance to Qing rule.

TAIJI, BAGUA, XINGYI

Qing records contain dozens and dozens of martial arts styles, and even these records only scratch the surface of what was in practice on the ground. There were probably hundreds if not thousands of "styles" of martial arts practiced in towns, villages, and temples across China. Most of these styles have subsequently disappeared, or wittingly or unwittingly classed themselves under the rubric of some of the main styles currently in widespread practice. Further research into local cultures will no doubt reveal or recover a much greater variety of martial arts styles. Most of these styles contain very similar techniques, whether in boxing, wrestling, or armed combat. When Qi Jiguang developed his *Boxing Classic* (*Quanjing*) within his larger manual of military training, he distilled or derived the techniques from the styles available to him. Qi's manual describes a generic form of boxing that contained the most basic and fundamental techniques without embellishment or theoretical discussion.

The new Qing discourse of internal or soft martial arts created some new styles of martial arts. These styles, most notably Taiji, Bagua, and Xingyi, are widely practiced today and have therefore generated considerable scholarly interest in tracing their origins. Ironically, one of the main reasons these styles are so prominent today is their recent development. These were arts that drew from long-standing traditions to craft styles appropriate to a world of industrial warfare, wherein a martial artist might be an educated, urban worker in need of gentle exercise rather than a tough warrior in the countryside fighting bandits. Yet despite their detachment from the immediate concerns of combat, they remained insistently martial in their overall orientation. Much of what the soft or internal styles claim for themselves in purpose, orientation, and effect can be contradictory. Their histories are therefore similarly challenging. As Douglas Wile pointed out with respect to Taiji:

> The question of Taijiquan's origins is hugely controversial. However, when adjusted for stylistic and ideological partisanship and analyzed strictly on the basis of scholarly methodology, the various accounts differ according to their emphasis on the following conceptual tracers: postures and form, training techniques and combat strategies, and philosophy and legend.
>
> If traced as a distinctive form with specific postures and names, then Taiji's history may be said to begin with Ming general Qi Jiguang's *Quanjing* (Classic of Pugilism), twenty-nine of whose postures are borrowed for the Chen Village art of Henan, possibly as early as Chen Wangting in the seventeenth century, and certainly no later than Chen Changxing (1771–1853) and Cheng Qingping (1795–1868) in the early nineteenth.[13]

In a subsequent book, *T'ai Chi's Ancestors*, Wile goes a long way toward fleshing out the actual documentary evidence for Taiji's background:

> This book [*T'ai Chi's Ancestors*] introduces three sixteenth to eighteenth century traditions that contributed critical genetic material to the construction of taijiquan today....
>
> Qi Jiguang's *Essentials of the Classic of Pugilism* bequeathed its postures and form, Wang Zhengnan's *Art of the Internal School* contributed its philosophy and ideology, and Chang Naizhou's writings share much of the language and theory of the taiji classics.[14]

Wile's approach to the history of Taiji balances between scholarship and the strongly held beliefs of many contemporary practitioners of Taiji (Wile himself is a dedicated Taiji practitioner). Unfortunately, both the scholarship and history of martial arts in China fail to support the myth history of Taiji as many might like. Myths like Zhang Sanfeng's role in the creation of Taiji remain casually accepted and even occasionally aggressively asserted. Rather than apply the "scholarly methodology" in a strict sense, Wile argues thus:

> If taiji's genesis cannot be viewed as a single act of revelation or as an a priori set of perennial principles, this places it squarely in the realm of history and culture. As such, it is susceptible to deconstruction and tracing of influences, but we must go beyond clichés that simply take taiji as a synthesis of martial arts, military strategy, meditation, medicine, philosophy, and the like.[15]

To be fair, Wile's audience is the community of Taiji practitioners who are more interested in what it means to *them*, not what it meant, how it was actually formed, and what its significance was in the context of Chinese martial arts history. Wile's goal is to provide current practitioners with all of the threads that connect Taiji to the fabric of the Chinese past. A more scholarly perspective would see Taiji as less a spectacular artifact of Chinese culture yielded up to the world than as a part of Chinese culture that can, indeed, be deconstructed and traced. It was the product of a time and place and was consistent with other practices of that time and place.

All the aspects of Chinese culture synthesized in Taiji can also be found in other styles. It is a historical accident that Taiji is far more popular outside of China than Bagua, Xingyi, or any number of other internal styles of martial arts. Foreign popularity has enhanced Taiji's status within China, making the study of its history more important. But there is enormous controversy, as Wile notes, about Taiji's history. He is too polite, given his own place in the Taiji community, to explain that the conflict is among Taiji practitioners themselves. Most Taiji practitioners can agree on the tenuous history of Taiji from Qi Jiguang (or even Zhang Sanfeng), through Wang Zhengnan, and on to Chang Naizhou. Most even agree on Chen Family Village as the physical location where Taiji was created. After that, however, the questions of "postures and forms" becomes critical in establishing which style's lineage is the true root from which the others deviate.

Because almost all martial arts in China and outside it share a mostly identical palette of individual strikes, stances, and other techniques, what distinguishes one style from another is which techniques are not used, how techniques are combined, what forms (designated patterns of techniques) one performs, and the emphasis given to certain techniques over others. The internal styles share very similar philosophical, mental, and strategic perspectives, described in similarly broad terminology. The discourse of *qi* weighs heavily on these styles, providing both a connection to Chinese philosophy and medicine and a layer of vague spirituality. External or hard form styles usually shun amorphous discussions of *qi* in favor of clear demonstrations of combat effectiveness.[16]

Xingyi style, which is widely known in China, claims descent from a late Ming–early Qing martial artist named Ji Longfeng. Li's art grew out of, or was originally called, Six Harmonies Boxing (*liuhequan*). He was famous for his spear fighting techniques, and by one account he transformed these techniques into a boxing style. Li justified this on the notion that spear fighting was appropriate for times of turmoil like those he experienced during the Qing conquest, but boxing was more appropriate for defense during peacetime.[17] His students and their students spread Li's art as Xingyi (some say in early incarnations it may have been Xinyi) into Shanxi, Henan, and Hebei provinces. Considerable variation developed among the different branches.

Bagua style, which is also well known in China, is first mentioned in 1774 by a Qing government official who noted that it was practiced by the common people, but its origins are otherwise obscure. Similarly, Plum Blossom Boxing 梅花拳 is first mentioned in a government document in 1813, though it lists a lineage of teachers of the art going back to the Kangxi emperor's reign.[18] Also like Bagua and Xingyi, Plum Blossom Boxing is currently practiced in China in many provinces with a great number of variations. Indeed, the enormous variation within Plum Blossom Boxing along with its lack of even a vaguely historical founder argues that its name traveled further than any particular practice. This is to say that many local styles subsumed themselves under the rubric of Plum Blossom Boxing when it became famous at the beginning of the twentieth century. Plum Blossom Boxing is perhaps most significant for its association with the Boxer Rebellion.

REBELLIONS

One of the peculiar aspects of rebellions or uprisings during the Qing Dynasty was their frequent association with religion or other spiritual beliefs. Why this was so has never been fully explained, but it has engendered a strong association in the communist government of China between religion and rebellion. And since one of the first acts of any group planning to resist government authority is to train in the martial arts, the Qing government (and the communist government) was extremely sensitive to the mixing of religion and martial arts. Rebellion, religiously motivated or otherwise, as a phenomenon has no particular connection to the martial arts, but it does dramatize the place of martial arts in society. Even with the advent of industrialized warfare, the control of any and all means of violence, including traditional martial arts, is of concern to the state.

The most significant rebellion in Qing history was the Taiping Rebellion (1850–64).[19] This Christian-inspired rebellion, fought with both modern firearms and traditional weapons, appeared for a time to threaten the existence of the Qing Dynasty itself. The rebellion's origins in poor and marginal communities within China as well as an avowed ideology of equality led to large numbers of female fighters in the Taiping ranks. As always during rebellion and turmoil in China, the martial arts very quickly spread throughout society. Not only the Taipings but also the many communities in their path trained in the martial arts. The Qing military fought ineffectively at first, revealing deep failures in its martial arts and military training. Indeed, the imperial army never really recovered, and it was regional forces raised from local Chinese that eventually defeated the Taipings. These regional forces returned to the basics of military training, motivating the soldiers, training them in all the necessary martial arts including firearms, and developing discipline.

The Manchu authorities were troubled by the ineffectiveness of Manchu units. As social and economic difficulties plagued the Qing Dynasty in the nineteenth century, some caused and others merely exacerbated by the intrusion of the Western powers, the explicitly racial divide between ruler and ruled reopened. Anti-foreignism easily extended to cover anti-Manchu resentment. As real Manchu military power disappeared, the government was increasingly dependent upon the military power of its Chinese subjects. Most Chinese officials were loyal to the dynasty, despite some suspicions on the part of some Manchus. Yet the goal of the Manchu ruling class became to focus anti-foreignism squarely on the Westerners and away from themselves. At the same time, the government was forced to make a series of concessions to the West after losing repeated military conflicts with them. This was a dangerous game, and it eventually spun out of control.

Beginning in Shandong in 1898, large numbers of "boxers" began violently to oppose foreigners.[20] Christian missionaries used the power of their governments to intimidate the Qing central government to gain influence at the local level. Western immunity from Qing laws was used to shield Chinese Christian converts and influence local courts. What seemed humanitarian work from the missionaries' standpoint was frequently seen as unwarranted and unwelcome intrusions into local society. The missionaries were often openly contemptuous of local customs and extremely aggressive in pursuing their own interests. Up until 1900, despite wishing it could drive out the foreigners, the Qing government generally suppressed the Boxers.

In 1900, following two years of considerable political turmoil at the Qing court, the Dowager Empress Cixi had regained enough support to change course. Cixi was anxious to divert the unrest away from the imperial court and saw the endorsement of the Boxers as an opportunity to drive out the foreigners. At the very least, the two sides, Boxers and foreigners, would weaken each other, thus increasing the power of the imperial court. The imperial army now even helped some Boxer forces. The Boxers massacred many missionaries, and a large force converged on the foreign legations in Beijing. Yet after a fifty-five-day siege, foreign military forces were able to break through to Beijing and raise the siege. Cixi and the court temporarily fled the capital. From then on, foreign governments maintained enough troops in China to protect their citizens.

CONCLUSION

Despite its many military defeats, the Qing Dynasty did begin to modernize its military and bring parts of it up to Western standards. More and better handguns and rifles filtered down to the local level, changing the nature of violence for many ordinary Chinese. As with most societies in the age of guns, however, the Chinese found the martial arts still helpful for the ordinary sorts of violence a person might face. There were significant changes in practice, and these had broader effects within Qing society. Archery, either mounted or on foot, which had been such a marker of steppe identity and even military identity, became completely obsolete. Qing military exams had followed earlier practice and tested archery as a basic skill. Modern firearms and modern tactics rendered the exams archaic.

Internal schools of martial arts like Taiji, Bagua, and Xingyi became more prominent over the course of the nineteenth century in parallel with the growth of modern firearms. This may be a coincidence or an artifact of the source materials written by educated, urban elites. It is entirely possible that martial arts in rural areas were mostly unaffected by the modernization of warfare or that the changes were just an acceleration of the effects that firearms had been bringing to warfare in China for centuries. Guns were not new in China in the nineteenth century. The importance of the internal schools for some writers may have been a reaction to modernization through Westernization rather than the change in battlefield martial arts.

Certainly there was a break in military practice during the nineteenth century, but it seems that the development of internal style martial arts was a product of the early Qing, if not the very end of the Ming Dynasty. Most of the styles can be firmly dated to the eighteenth century, and their claims of earlier genesis are difficult to sustain. It is therefore unwise to connect the two major martial arts developments of the Qing Dynasty – the creation of internal styles of martial arts and the initiation of Western military methods – by default. Modernity, nationalism, and ethnic identity had as much to do with conceptions of the martial arts at the very end of the Qing Dynasty as technology. Indeed, as we shall see in the next chapter, the place of martial arts in post-imperial China was far more a question of politics and ideology than fighting.

10

Post-Imperial China

Many Chinese began to despair over the condition of China well before the Qing Dynasty collapsed in 1911. It had been apparent since perhaps the Opium War (1839–42) that the Qing imperial army was in decline and that Qing military practice had fallen behind Western military practice. Increasing emphasis on Western military technology and techniques brought radical changes to the Qing military, and by the end of the dynasty it had formed completely Western-style armies outfitted with the latest Western equipment. Chinese soldiers, like their Western counterparts, still practiced some hand-to-hand combat skills, particularly the use of rifles with bayonets, but for many soldiers and officers, traditional Chinese martial arts had become obsolete. Rifles and artillery decided battles, not spears and swords.

Of course, this dichotomy was more imagined than real. The Qing army had relied upon cannon and firearms in its wars for centuries. Western military technology had been absorbed into the Qing military as it became available over the course of the nineteenth century, and indeed even before that during the late Ming Dynasty. The break with the past in the martial arts was thus much more psychological or ideological than actual. Western armies were clearly more powerful than Qing armies, and for reasons beyond technology. Focusing on technology, however, allowed the possibility of somehow adopting a material part of Western culture while leaving Chinese or Manchu culture in place. Many, perhaps most, Chinese were convinced of the value, even superiority, of Chinese culture. Few were willing simply to abandon it and adopt Western culture. The military weakness of the Qing Dynasty, and even the subsequent Western-style Republican government's army, as compared with Western armies, was all too clear.

The power of Chinese culture in contrast with its military weakness was explained in several interconnected ways. Some Chinese, like Lei Haizong, blamed Chinese culture itself as too civil and demilitarized. Lei traced this back to the Han Dynasty demilitarization of the farming population at the beginning of the Later Han recovery. It did not matter that this was nonsense; his explanation tapped into a discourse of non-military Chinese culture that has persisted to this day. Chinese culture, in this conception, despite millennia of wars, is distinctively civil, more concerned with poetry and self-cultivation than fighting. Under this rubric, all Chinese activities regardless of how martial they might appear – such as the invention of guns and martial arts practice – only seemed so on the surface. In reality these things were somehow not martial, and that is why the West or steppe people had better armies than the Chinese.

Another line of thought made a clear distinction between Manchus and Chinese, blaming the former for China's humiliation at the hands of the West. The Manchus were corrupt and, because they were conquerors and non-Chinese, could not harness the military potential of the Chinese nation. There was some truth to the idea that Manchu distrust of the Chinese prevented them from fully harnessing the potential military power of the vast Chinese population. But there was no Chinese nation as such during the Qing Dynasty, and it took decades of struggle to form one in the twentieth century. Still, the idea of leaving the failure to modernize and the Qing defeats on the doorstep of the Manchus was very attractive. The new Chinese government could start afresh.

Yet that still left the question of what to do with Western culture. There was no question that Western military practice had to be emulated. To make it truly work, as some argued, required the wholesale adoption of Western culture in every area from politics, to education, to physical culture. The only way for China to become strong was to become Western. The other pole of this debate accepted the need for Western military practice, science and technology, and many other aspects of the West while still maintaining that some core Chinese values and practices were valuable. China, in this argument, could modernize without necessarily Westernizing. Moreover, not only was Chinese culture valuable in and of itself but it also had something to offer the rest of the world.

Chinese martial arts reflected, and continue to reflect, all of these concerns. Advocates for the martial arts fought hard to establish the martial arts as uniquely valuable, and uniquely Chinese. With the influx of Western physical culture in the form of modern sports, there was a perceived need for a distinctly Chinese physical culture. Where did the martial arts fit into the Western categories of physical culture? They were not entirely like boxing or wrestling, or even fencing. The problem was not so much that the Western martial arts were not, in fact, martial arts, but rather that they were thought of as sports. Westerners did connect sports and war, but not necessarily martial arts and war. Playing rugby or other team sports was imagined to build the right character for war, particularly among the upper classes who would lead in war, but the same was not always so for sports like boxing, which had very different class implications in the West.

Even in the late nineteenth century, Western soldiers actually practiced very similar martial arts to those of the civilian world, most obviously shooting with a rifle, but they had largely separated out the respective hand-to-hand combat arts. The modern Olympics present a useful perspective on certain aspects of how Western martial arts developed into sports and also how modern ideas about sports reinterpreted earlier understandings of sports. The ancient Greek games held great religious significance, and many of the competitions were in the martial arts. There were competitions in boxing, wrestling, discus throwing, and javelin throwing, as well as more dual-use activities like running and equestrian events.

In modern times, the French held several Olympic competitions near the end of the eighteenth century, and the Greeks staged an international Olympic competition in 1859. Part of the impetus for the formation of what would become the modern Olympic movement came from the Prussian victory in the Franco-Prussian War (1870–71). One of the most important men driving the Olympic movement in the late nineteenth century was a Frenchman, Baron Pierre de Coubertin. Coubertin believed that the failure of French physical culture was a root cause of France's defeat in the war.[1] It is therefore not surprising that Chinese thinkers and leaders came to believe that sports were important in the "revival" of the Chinese nation. And of course, wrestling, shooting, fencing, and boxing as well as the now apparently demilitarized track and field events like javelin and discus throwing were part of the modern Olympics. Western martial arts were so fully incorporated into the realm of sports that they appeared to be unrelated to the skills of the professional military.

Fencing and other martial arts had continued to be practiced in Europe into the late nineteenth century. In England, the sword had fallen out of use as a true combat weapon and remained neglected, despite the efforts of antiquarian swordsmen like Alfred Hutton, Richard Burton, and Egerton Castle. Fencing was still seriously practiced in Italy, France, and Spain, however, and when Hutton researched past masters, he found fencing manuals going back to the sixteenth century. As a dedicated martial artist, for that is exactly what Hutton was, he struggled to make his art relevant to the late nineteenth-century battlefield. Like much of the discourse on martial arts in China in the same period, he began to emphasize the more general mental and physical improvements that fencing provided the practitioner. The sword was still an archaic weapon from the battlefield perspective, however, and it was unlikely to be available for personal defense in England. The sports versions of the martial arts laid claim to the same ability to improve physical and mental functions, were less dangerous, more widely available, and more socially acceptable. In the West, at least, sports had overwhelmed combat martial arts almost completely by the twentieth century.

Combat martial arts followed a different path in twentieth-century China. Perhaps because China lacked its own tradition of physical culture fully akin to Western sports, it was only with the introduction of Western sports that traditional combat martial arts were challenged to fit into a more modern social order.[2] Chinese martial arts already had a place in Chinese society, in literature, theater, religion, and combat; it was when Chinese society began to shift to accommodate Western modernity that the place or value of combat martial arts was questioned. Its importance in the literary or religious arenas was less severely challenged. New forms and sources of fiction, and Western religion, obviously did not include Chinese martial arts, but these arts continued in places like the theater. And as traditional Chinese theater forms and stories formed the initial sources for the Chinese movie industry – and even popular writers of vaguely Western-style novels – the martial arts continued to live in the world of fiction.

The radical changes in Chinese popular and literary fiction in the twentieth century profoundly impacted the understanding of the martial arts. Particularly as the twentieth century progressed, a national narrative concerning the origin of Chinese martial arts began to emerge through films in particular, but also in popular fiction, that unified practice and origins. Rather than a disparate, dispersed, and widely spread set of responses to combat needs, the martial arts were portrayed as having specific origins, often through a Shaolin or some fictive or historical figure, whose teaching then spread across the "Chinese nation." The variations in the narrative were seen as the natural result of historical divergence from an ideal source. Martial artists trying to sell their skills took up these narratives to attract students and legitimize their own practice. Students decided to take up martial arts after seeing movies or reading books about them. These activities all fed one another, with subsequent movies and fiction reiterating, amplifying, and adding to the earlier mythology.

One of the greatest popular writers of serialized martial arts tales, *wuxia*, is Jin Yong [Louis Cha] (1924–). Jin Yong's tales of superhuman martial artists in imperial China were fully consistent with traditional Chinese stories like *The Water Margin*, and like traditional martial arts tales they took many liberties with historical events and people. He wrote fourteen novels or novellas and one short story between 1955 and 1972, virtually all of which have been adapted for movies, television, or comics. What truly distinguishes Jin Yong's work from earlier Chinese martial arts tales is its exposure and acceptance outside the Chinese language community. Jin Yong took full advantage of the misconceptions about Chinese martial arts and elaborated on them for dramatic effect. Just as in the West, the historical fiction version of the past is far more widespread in the general population than any accurate, but dry, academic account. Jin Yong, born in China and living in Hong Kong from 1947, reflected many of the issues of nationalism, Chinese identity, and the clash between modern values and traditional Chinese ones (thought he is, for the most part, a strong proponent of traditional values). Together with other writers in this genre, Jin Yong created a fictional martial arts world that has profoundly influenced the current understanding of these arts.[3]

At the same time, however, the martial arts, even in the narrow sense of unarmed combat, retained its combat value. The ability of a martial artist to resist state power had political consequences, particularly in a country where firearms were not widely available. Successive modern Chinese governments were concerned, as their imperial predecessors had been, with who practiced martial arts and what kinds of martial arts they practiced. One of the main reasons that arts like Taiji were able to flourish in the twentieth century is because they were not perceived to be combat arts. A noncombat art was no threat to the state. Here we must keep in mind that Chinese government officials were also part of Chinese society, and their understanding of what the martial arts were relied just as heavily on fiction as did the perceptions of any ordinary citizen. Over time, many martial artists similarly came to believe the national or cultural discourse of martial arts that late nineteenth- and early twentieth-century modernizers had pushed on the public. In short, the modern discourse of the martial arts produced a new intellectual and linguistic framework for discussing and understanding Chinese martial arts. This discourse clashed directly with the use of Chinese martial arts for combat.

The progression and history of the Chinese martial arts in the post-imperial period can be usefully divided into three phases. The first phase was the period from after the fall of the Qing Dynasty up until the communist conquest of China in 1949. The second phase began with communist control of China and continued until about 1978, when Deng Xiaoping's political and economic reforms dramatically changed the direction of Chinese culture. The third phase started right after those changes and runs to the present day. In each of those phases the ordinary practice of martial arts based upon the techniques passed from teacher to student struggled to define itself in a rapidly changing political and cultural environment. As so much of China was changing, so too was its physical culture. The martial arts struggled, and still struggle, to find a place in the new society.

THE CHINESE NATION AND REPUBLICAN CHINA

The collapse of the Qing Dynasty began a familiar historic process of post-dynastic warfare as warlords and generals emerged to fight for control of China. With one notable exception, none of the leaders vying for power were interested in founding a new dynasty. It was clear to most people that China needed a new and more modern, if not more Western, form of government. The government of the Republic of China formed in 1912 proved to be a deeply troubled political structure, which struggled to encompass the vast ambitions of a broad range of powerful men. Political and military leaders struggled for power in a milieu untethered from the social and political norms of the previous centuries of imperial rule. The government was both too unstable to provide rewards for the ambitious and too weak to restrain them. It seemed as if anything and nothing was possible.

To these internal political struggles were added cataclysmic external factors. Two world wars radically reshaped the Western presence in China and elevated the importance of Japan in Asia. The Japanese invasion of China completely altered the political and military calculations of the Chinese forces. Politically, China was taken over by foreign ideologies: democracy, fascism, and communism. In the end, it was the latter two that would contend for final control of China after the Japanese were defeated in 1945. The Chinese Communist Party (CCP) defeated the fascist, though nominally democratic, Nationalists (GMD) under Chiang Kai-shek in 1949. Although all sides struggled for political control, the main tool for accomplishing this was war.

Warfare in twentieth-century China was a decidedly modern and Western affair. The best Chinese armies were fully trained and armed with Western weaponry and fought with Western tactics. Less well-equipped and

ILLUSTRATION 24. Two men in Republican period army uniform demonstrating bayonet fighting. From the Jingwu (Pure Martial) Anniversary Book, Republican period.

trained forces roamed the countryside with secondhand, old weapons; unreliable and limited ammunition; and little in the way of military organization. These ragtag units deteriorated very quickly into bands of bandits, and these changed into criminal organizations and groups of petty thugs. At the local level where firearms were still rare, the traditional martial arts were still extremely effective if a fight broke out. The martial arts practiced in towns and villages probably went on mostly unaffected by the political chaos of the time.

The urban environment was more modern and guns were more available in cities. But the problem of where to fit the traditional martial arts into the new Chinese culture was unresolved. For reasons of modernity or Westernism perhaps, a clear conceptual break had formed between Chinese martial arts and firearms. The martial arts comprised unarmed combat and the use of archaic weapons. Firearms somehow stood apart from the martial arts, as if the use of firearms did not require any training. The closest the martial arts came to firearms was in the inclusion of bayonet fighting as a martial art. This conceptual break also separated soldiers from the martial arts. Whereas previously a soldier necessarily learned martial arts to perform his duties, in the modern army soldiers were sometimes trained in the martial arts of unarmed combat or bayonet use as a supplement to their real military skills. As Qi Jiguang had described it in the fifteenth century, unarmed combat was not a battlefield skill but was used only to enhance the men's fitness and agility.

Another new development that owed something to this changed perspective on the martial arts was the appearance of its serious historical study. Men like Tang Hao (1887–1959) pioneered the field of martial arts history. In the attempt to figure out where the martial arts fit into modern Chinese society, it was natural that someone would try to define martial arts. Tang successfully cut through the veil of myths, folklore, and advertising to begin tracking martial arts practice back to specific times, places, and individuals. Not surprisingly, this demystification angered rather than interested many martial artists. The myths of the martial arts were what attracted many practitioners and validated and valorized many martial arts teachers. Placing the martial arts in a historical context undercut their represented world and the heroic narrative that connected them to the swashbuckling heroes of fiction.

The medium of film drew upon the theater traditions of operatic stories, reiterating and amplifying the popular performative traditions of martial arts. Adding to the availability of these heroic stories was the dramatic shift in the written form of Chinese away from the difficult Classical Chinese learned by men studying for the civil service exams to the use of vernacular Chinese. Stories published in newspapers and magazines were more accessible to a broader audience, even if they still drew upon the same classical literature for material, so tales centered on martial artists transferred directly from traditional into modern forms of fiction. The translation of classical tales into modern media was also strongly influenced by the late imperial and early twentieth-century struggle to find a place for the martial arts in Chinese culture. In particular, very late concepts of the martial arts, like the rubric of internal versus external martial arts, were quickly taken up and amplified in the new stories.

Chinese nationalism, mixed feelings about the imperial past, and the continuing anxiety about the place of China and Chinese culture in the now apparently Western-dominated world were all reflected in the new ideas of the martial arts. Both in fiction and in practice the language of internal versus external martial arts exactly paralleled the larger arguments about how deeply to absorb Western culture. Was Western science and physical culture merely external and shallow, as compared to profound, internal Chinese practice? In a martial arts story an old man might manifest dramatic and overwhelming fighting skills based upon internal martial arts. The true power and value of a martial artist who practiced the esoteric internal martial arts was not obvious in his external appearance. Westerners with their larger and more powerful bodies exhibited only external strength.

With the intellectual separation of the martial arts from the military skills of the modern soldier, the place of the martial artist changed profoundly. This change was not only military but also political, social, and geographic. Among the intellectuals and martial artists debating the place of these skills there was much less discussion of the martial arts practiced in rural areas and much more concern with the place of the martial arts in the major cities. Chinese modernity was contested in the major cities by educated elites and some less-educated martial artists. For the most part, the bodies being contested were urban and educated. These urban, educated, white-collar workers were the Chinese vanguard of modernity (if one may expropriate a concept from Lenin), and many martial artists struggled to somehow attach the martial arts to these new Chinese. The other urban group of martial artists was rural men who brought the martial arts with them to their modern factory jobs in the city, and then hired instructors and set up schools in their new environment.[4]

Practicing Chinese martial arts became a way for a white-collar or factory worker to maintain a Chinese body while engaged in a Western lifestyle. This was particularly important for overseas Chinese who struggled to maintain a sense of Chineseness while not actually living in China. There was to be no free market of martial arts ideas, however, as the government saw the control over the martial arts as a way both to impose discipline on society and to control the meaning of Chinese physical culture. This was played out in the conflict between public martial arts organizations, private promoters of the martial arts, and the Nationalist government's assertion of control over the martial arts. The Nationalist government subsequently attempted to reform the diverse practices of the Chinese martial arts into a unified "National Art."

Western influence in China, both economically and intellectually, gave rise to the idea that Chinese (and indeed other Asians and non-Westerners) were physically less robust, disciplined, and manly. The respective economic and military places of Western and non-Western states and cultures in the early twentieth century were a direct reflection of the physical condition and physical culture of the people in those societies. If this was true, then the way to improve a country's economic and military place in the world was by training the bodies of its citizens. This idea may appear fundamentally ludicrous, but through the medium of the modern Olympics it persists to the present in China and much of the world. Physical culture is just that, a culture, and as such it transmits values that cannot be rationally substantiated. Chinese intellectuals and leaders absorbed these ideas most forcefully through Japan, another Asian nation that had already received, absorbed, and transformed itself with Western physical culture. The Chinese word for physical training *tiyu* actually entered Chinese through the Japanese formulation of the term.

All these forces of intellectual change stimulated a vigorous response from at least some urban martial artists. These practitioners and their merchant patrons saw the Chinese martial arts themselves as a way to improve the bodies and spirits of Chinese people. Rather than accept the notion that the martial arts were a part of the problem of backward, traditional China, a number of martial artists took the opposite tack. Their argument was that the martial arts were an expression and means of fostering the disciplined martial body. The problem was that too few Chinese people were practicing the martial arts. For these practitioners, the Chinese martial arts were not only fundamentally valuable Chinese physical culture but also a unique set of disciplines that were a contribution to world physical culture.

Andrew Morris in his outstanding 2004 book, *Marrow of the Nation*, establishes the context of physical culture in Republican period China and discusses some of the specific struggles over the martial arts.[5] Not surprisingly, the political chaos that immediately followed the fall of the Qing Dynasty precluded any direct government action concerning the martial arts. There was certainly no perceived need at the government or national level for action on the question of the place of the martial arts. It fell to private individuals such as the famous Chinese martial artist Huo Yuanjia (1868–1910) and some private businessmen to create a national forum for Chinese martial arts. Huo himself had attempted to prove the superiority of these arts by fighting and defeating Western and Japanese fighters. He was clearly a powerful and effective fighter, and his skills demonstrated that a Chinese martial artist was at least a match, if not more than a match, for any foreign martial artist.

In the nationalistic ideology of modern sports, Huo's individual achievement had the broader effect of valorizing and legitimizing Chinese martial arts and Chinese culture. By itself, however, success in the ring could not spread the practice of martial arts to the Chinese population in general without financial backing. A martial arts teacher might make a living in

ILLUSTRATION 25. Two men in Republican period army uniform demonstrating sword versus bayonet fighting. From the Jingwu (Pure Martial) Anniversary Book, Republican period.

his locality without raising the martial arts to a national level of interest. Largely in response to the new Western sports associations and a more general move toward public associations, the first Chinese martial arts association (the Pure Martial Calisthenics School) appeared in Shanghai in 1910.[6] A number of other urban martial arts organizations sprang up in the major coastal cities shortly thereafter. These organizations and their martial artists tried, and often succeeded, in proving themselves by defeating foreign fighters in public matches. Individual martial skills proved the value and power of the Chinese martial arts, Chinese culture, and the Chinese nation.

Chinese martial artists made considerably less headway against the New Culture modernizers. For these reformers, the martial arts were fundamentally traditional and backward. Rather than accept an entirely marginal place in the larger reforms of national physical culture, some martial artists and martial arts associations adopted new tactics. It is worth noting, however, that the vast majority of teachers and practitioners had nothing to do with these efforts. The first tactic was to include Western sports and other games in the association's activities. The Pure Martial School did this with some success, broadening its appeal while becoming much more of a general sporting association. Pure Martial branches even spread abroad to Southeast Asia. This also reflected the notion held by some practitioners to transform the martial arts into a modern sport, something that had been done in the West and more recently in Japan.

The inclusion of other physical activities at a martial arts association was not necessarily a cynical move to draw in urban youth. The practitioners themselves were also likely interested in doing more than just martial arts all the time. A new world of physical culture had just opened up and they were engaged in finding their own place as well as that of their martial art in it. If the traditional combat martial arts were no longer battlefield skills, then how could they be transformed for the modern world? The problem was retaining something authentically Chinese while updating traditional arts, a problem also being played out in the broader debates about culture.

A second tactic used by martial artists was to simplify martial arts practices into little more than calisthenics. This emphasized the positive physical uses of the practices for promoting health and made it possible for less active people to perform martial arts. One martial arts teacher, Chu Minyi, went so far as to create a new system of Taiji Calisthenics (*Taijicao*) that anyone could perform. Chu had received a medical education in France in addition to his martial arts training in Taiji, and he sought to create a "modern" art explicitly for white-collar intellectuals whose work did not require physical activity.[7] Taiji Calisthenics were even performed as part of the Chinese martial arts demonstration at the Berlin Olympiad.[8] Chu felt that anyone could become proficient in his new art, unlike Taiji, which was extremely difficult to master.

Chu Minyi's new art was also part of the National Art (*guoshu*) movement that began in this period.[9] This was an effort to unify all of China's disparate martial arts into a fixed set of nationally recognized forms. Much of the force behind this effort, if not necessarily the initial idea, came from the Nationalist government. The government decided to wrest control over the martial arts as a whole from the private associations that had been promoting it in order to subsume them within the body politic. This advanced the agenda of many martial artists who wished to incorporate martial arts training into the new public school system and established a place for the martial arts in the modernization efforts for the "New China." Many well-known martial arts teachers joined the new government efforts and established training regimes in their local areas.

Subsuming martial arts training under government control was not, in and of itself, enough to establish it as a National Art. The Chinese government based at Nanjing was recognized internationally as the government of China, but in actuality it did not control large areas of China. At least within its area of control, and as the basis for a future of unified control, the government felt it necessary to establish a system of training for martial arts teachers. This made pedagogical and administrative sense since there needed to be some way to ensure that teachers hired for the schools were competent, but it raised the fundamental question of what those teachers should practice. The need for an established martial arts curriculum coincided with efforts to unify the martial arts into something clearly and eternally Chinese. A further strand of modernization was the inclusion of women in the martial arts curriculum on a somewhat equal basis. In this, again, the government was following the remarkable sexual equality promoted by the Pure Martial School.

In 1928, the Nanjing government established the National Art Research Academy (*Guoshu Yanjiuguan*).[10] It initially established two schools of the martial arts within it, Shaolin and Wudang. Here we see the influence of late imperial concepts of the martial arts based mostly upon literature and theatrical performance. Shaolin represented the Buddhist strand of Chinese martial arts, and Wudang the Daoist strand (including Taiji). Thus the Academy reified the external/internal, Buddhist/Daoist divisions in the late imperial construction of the martial arts as a step toward unifying the whole. This was not done as a self-conscious acknowledgment of the tendentious construction of the split but rather as acceptance of the split that all "experts" and even laypeople accepted as fact. In any event, the teachers hired also believed in the fundamental nature of the split, expressing their "centuries-old differences," as Andrew Morris puts it, by fighting with each other. Like so many other manufactured rivalries, this one was also taken very seriously. Having failed to establish unity on the first try, the Academy was reorganized later in 1928 as the Central National Art Academy with a new structure that did not instantiate the internal/external division in its institutional framework.

The restructured and renamed Central National Art Academy tried to take intellectual control of the martial arts by listing 161 Chinese martial arts and then placing them all under the rubric of National Art. This was a much more ambitious authoritarian gambit than earlier attempts to list the different martial arts, since by listing the arts, they could all be subject to government authority. Ironically, as the Nanjing government did not control large areas of China's Central Plains, including such iconic places as Shaolin, the list could only include well-known styles from those areas and styles present in the area under its control. The list essentially defined what the Nanjing government did and did not control. The Shaolin Temple itself was actually burned down in 1928, further diminishing what was already a much shrunken martial arts center. While the Central National Art Academy drew up plans for martial arts training from the county level up to the national level, along with administrative guidelines and funding for these efforts, other National Art organizations emerged in the areas outside of Nanjing's control.

Despite these limitations, the Central Academy's efforts were a modest success, at least insofar as they promoted martial arts practice under the rubric of government control over a wide area. The students at the Academy itself were trained in many different martial arts, including weapons, archery, and, for the men, bayonet (but not shooting firearms). Women practiced a slightly different curriculum until 1934, when women were no longer admitted. The reason for this was that the female students were being sexually harassed by some of the male instructors. The director's response was not to punish the instructors but to remove the women.[11] Government backing brought many great martial artists into local, regional, and national schools to teach, exposing many more students to their instruction than would have otherwise been the case.

The government and the Academy failed to create a true national physical culture based around the martial arts, despite creating national martial arts exams and competitions. Arguably, in the 1930s there was no "nation" to receive this new culture, only a collection of urban centers and an increasingly marginalized rural hinterland. Political and military power were so fragmented in China even before 1937, when the Japanese army invaded China's eastern seaboard beginning World War II in Asia, that it was simply impossible to use the martial arts as a nation-building practice. In these tumultuous times, most people were far too concerned with survival and the questions of war with modern weapons to have much interest in the martial arts. Because the "martial arts" no longer included battlefield skills, they were of marginal importance to China's twentieth-century wars. Perhaps because they simply ran out of time, China's martial arts did not fully develop into sports for schools and urban workers as they did in Japan. World War II was followed by the Chinese Civil War, and it was only in 1949, with the communist conquest of China, that some semblance of peace returned in China.

1949

The Chinese Communist Party's (CCP) conquest of China in 1949 did not bring in a government sympathetic to traditional martial arts. Chinese communists were ideologically opposed to every aspect of traditional Chinese culture, not just the martial arts, though there was also a tension between the Chinese customs and values that even the most hardened ideologue had grown up with and the demands of communist piety. Like many of the reformers of the Republican period, the communist leadership focused their efforts on modernizing China, understanding "modernize" to mean getting rid of anything traditional. The goal was to build an industrialized state on a par with any in the West, but organized socially and politically along communist lines. This entailed a considerable amount of "Westernization," something that did not unduly trouble the CCP leadership. With Russian help, they would build a new China.

Although the CCP availed itself of the assistance of some martial arts teachers and secret societies practicing martial arts in its struggle to conquer China, many aspects of CCP control were antithetical to the martial arts as they had previously existed in Chinese society. Indeed, the very utility of the martial arts in fighting for control of China argued for the suppression of those skills once China had been conquered. The new government was extremely concerned, particularly in its early years, with preventing internal rebellion. It was one thing to conquer China and still another to control it. The People's Liberation Army (PLA) was stretched quite thin and would soon be involved in the Korean War. The government itself struggled with shortages of trained, reliable officials to staff its own organs of supervision and administration. Even without guns, trained fighters could resist the government at the local level.

The communist government was also vehemently opposed to religion and worked hard to suppress all religious practice in China. There was no room in communism for religion; the new ideology called for reliance upon science and scientific practice. At a minimum, temples and religious institutions were stripped of their lands and thus their wealth. Religious practice was illegal and could be severely punished. Scorn for religion was taught in school and encouraged with propaganda. Places like Shaolin, which had already suffered near total destruction in 1928, now lost all their wealth, patronage, and sources of new monks. Many monks were forced out of religious life and back into society to become productive citizens. The few who remained lived in very circumscribed and poor circumstances. Whatever martial arts training had remained at Buddhist and Daoist temples after the fall of the Qing Dynasty collapsed as the CCP extended its authority throughout China.

The communist government also controlled theater and fiction, using these and other artistic media in its propaganda efforts. Initially, the government was most interested in promoting performances and artistic expression that supported its ideological efforts and spent less effort in suppressing any privately produced entertainment. There were two practical aspects in this: the first was the limited ability of entertainers to reach most of rural China, and the second was the limited power of the government itself. As its control over the country grew, however, the government blocked performances of traditional entertainments. Publishing was quickly controlled by restricting the resources, machinery, and distribution system necessary for book, journal, or newspaper production. Movies were similarly controlled, with private companies in both areas either nationalized or closed down. Particularly with movies, many actors, directors, and companies fled to Hong Kong or Taiwan, where they reestablished themselves. The government also restricted or closed down the venues for performances, shuttering tea-houses and restaurants, and regulating auditoriums.

These efforts culminated in the Cultural Revolution (1966–76), when only certain prescribed plays were permitted. Art and literature were reduced to almost nothing, and traditional martial arts stories were not allowed. The few remaining old monks at Shaolin and other religious institutions were dragged out, beaten, and paraded through the streets in disgrace. Everything traditional or "old" was attacked, and anyone practicing anything declared "old" was marked as a counter-revolutionary and punished. As in so many other aspects of Chinese culture, the Cultural Revolution was the lowest point in Chinese history for the martial arts. If the martial arts were in any way different, it was only as they were understood to be a means of resisting government authority. Much of the Cultural Revolution was carried out with direct physical violence at the local level. In one village studied by Ralph Thaxton, Da Fo village, government authorities were keenly aware of the local traditions of martial arts and were gratified to see that the rigors of overwork and poverty effectively suppressed those traditions. The authorities explicitly sought to keep the villagers unable to rebel by preventing them from training or teaching the martial arts.[12]

The Olympic and modern sports agenda of the late Qing and Republican period modernizers dominated what physical culture remained. Chinese martial arts was not an Olympic sport and therefore could not bring glory to the communist state. To a surprising extent, Chinese physical culture was directed at being Western, with very little effort and very few resources supporting distinctly Chinese culture. The inherent nationalism of the modern Olympic movement, coupled with the

Cold War competition between communist and capitalist countries, was played out in China just as in the rest of the world. International sports was about politics and proving a country's value; domestic sports in China had to serve those goals. Chinese martial arts had no place in that struggle. Some threads of martial arts practice and study may have retained government support, or benign indifference, but enthusiastic support was rare.

If we consider the larger sphere of Chinese culture, however, not just what was occurring within the borders of the People's Republic of China, Chinese martial arts was flourishing in movies produced in Hong Kong and Southeast Asia, spreading awareness of its practices to the rest of the world through that medium. In some cases martial artists who had hitherto restricted instruction in their particular art to a very select group of students began to teach more broadly in order to make a living. Nevertheless, outside the realm of fiction, and really just in film, Chinese martial arts were mostly confined to Chinese communities. A relatively small number of non-Chinese in the West were able to study Chinese martial arts, in stark contrast to Japanese and Korean martial arts.

More than anything else, the cinematic expression of the Chinese martial arts radically changed the place of the martial arts in Chinese culture. Even in modern action movies, the Chinese martial arts gained power and stature. Martial arts was represented in traditional and modern settings, and keyed into the heroic literary images of premodern Chinese warriors. The battlefield had nothing to do with these skills as they became manifestations of inner character on the screen. In sharp contrast, the Chinese martial art most practiced in the West was Taiji, with its distinctive slow movements and focus on "inner" cultivation. This was not wholly a Western phenomenon, however, as the view of the Chinese "nation's" disastrous encounter with modernity was connected with the martial arts. The Chinese imagined themselves a nonviolent, nonmartial people and culture whose representative martial art, Taiji, was really all about internal cultivation and health. In many ways this was the natural culmination of the modern rethinking of the Chinese martial arts.

This pessimistic picture of martial arts practice within the borders of the People's Republic of China necessarily overlooks the continued practice and teaching of the martial arts below the level of government scrutiny. The Chinese government, like all governments, particularly of very large countries, had a limited ability to control culture. It has been extremely effective in doing so, but the government has never been completely successful in destroying traditional culture. The best evidence for this is the resurgence of martial arts practice after the opening up of China in

1978. When the government not only stopped suppressing traditional practices of many kinds but also actively promoted them, all sorts of practitioners reemerged. The traditional arts had been damaged by the first decades of communist rule, particularly the decade of the Cultural Revolution, without being entirely destroyed.

1978 TO THE PRESENT

After Mao Zedong died in 1976, there was some uncertainty as to the direction the country would take. Would it continue on the path set by the Cultural Revolution, or would it turn to a more pragmatic course and rebuild the shattered economy? This question was finally answered in 1978 with the ascension of the pragmatic Deng Xiaoping as the dominant figure in the leadership. Deng was a committed communist, but he was also clear that China was in desperate need of economic growth and political rejuvenation. China reopened its universities and colleges and began rebuilding its economy and society. It also opened up to the outside world, leading to both massive foreign investment in China and an export-led boom in Chinese industry.

These changes did not immediately affect the practice of Chinese martial arts as it had developed since 1949. The limited government-sponsored training centers for martial arts continued as they had, but perhaps with less fear of political criticism. The larger changes had taken place, as mentioned above, outside of China, and with the new openness, those developments began to influence the martial arts within China. Probably the most significant import with respect to the martial arts was foreign movies and media. Hong Kong martial arts films brought an invigorated and exciting performative tradition of Chinese martial arts back to China, and foreigners interested in studying the Chinese martial arts (and who became interested in them as a result of those films) also began trickling in to find teachers. Foreign conceptions of the Chinese martial arts directly affected the Chinese understanding of the martial arts.

During the entire twentieth century the arguments over the place of the martial arts in a modern China had never been settled. Very little attention was paid to these questions while the new nation struggled to define itself politically and economically under communism in opposition to dynastic or traditional China. There were some government centers for martial arts training, and these centers operated under the pre-communist era idea of specific style curricula in national styles. The forms and skills of these styles were usually established by committees of practitioners who all studied variations of the same style. In the same way that the sport versions of martial arts gained set forms in accordance with competition rules, martial arts styles developed set forms so that students could be compared and rated. At the same time, however, many martial arts persisted outside the government system and despite erratic government attempts to suppress them. All this became clear after the government not only stopped suppressing the practice of martial arts outside official centers but also began encouraging its practice. A good example was the effort to renovate the Shaolin Temple and "revive" its martial arts tradition.

The impetus for rebuilding Shaolin was a movie, *Shaolin Temple* (1982), that starred a former mainland Chinese martial arts champion, Li Lianjie (Jet Li). When the Hong Kong movie company went to Shaolin to shoot on location in 1981, the temple was entirely run down and defunct as either a religious or martial arts center. The movie was extremely successful and it attracted Chinese and foreign martial arts students and tourists to Shaolin.[13] Several monks and a number of martial artists claiming some connection to Shaolin's martial arts reestablished Buddhist worship and the teaching of martial arts at or near the temple. While Buddhist worship expanded slowly, martial arts teaching and tourism exploded. Most of the martial arts schools were only near the temple rather than being part of it, and even those martial artists practicing in the official temple training facility had no religious training.

In many respects, the modern legend and movie-based reconstruction of Shaolin recapitulated the martial arts environment of what the temple was probably like at its Ming Dynasty peak. A large and fluid community of martial artists surrounded a community of Buddhist monks who prayed and practiced Buddhism. While thousands of students came to study martial arts in the nearby schools, the monastic population of practicing Buddhists was far more limited. Matthew Polly, an American college student, went to Shaolin in the 1990s and studied martial arts there for two years. His account of that period, *American Shaolin*, reflects both the chaotic relationship of modern China with its traditional past and the confused relationship between Western and Chinese perceptions of the martial arts. The Shaolin Wushu center was built by the Henan provincial government to promote tourism in 1989.[14] At the same time, troupes of Shaolin monks performed around the world. Martial arts, and Shaolin as their exemplar and putative source, became popular, recognizable, and positive representatives of China.

The other great martial arts representative of China is Taiji, though it lacks the site-specific identification of Shaolin. Shaolin has also benefited from hundreds of martial arts movies that perpetuated and amplified the myths of Shaolin's central role. Taiji, on the other hand, is much more widely practiced outside China. Where Shaolin's martial arts is external, Taiji is an internal art. The two martial arts traditions can also lay claim to China's two great religious traditions, Buddhism and Daoism. This modern construction of the place of martial arts and religion in Chinese society is sold both domestically and internationally.

As a living tradition, however, the practice and meaning of martial arts continues to change in China. This has been true in virtually every aspect of the martial arts. Some of these changes amount to revivals of earlier practice, but most highlight the dynamic interaction between popular perceptions and martial arts practice. The martial arts in China now react to foreign and domestic demands, globalization, commercialization, and nationalism. With the partial opening up of the economy and some aspects of society, the government of China now has very limited control over the practice of the martial arts. Martial arts practice has been outside government control in Taiwan, of course, for more than half a century, and in Hong Kong for over a century and a half. Even with Hong Kong's shift to rule from Beijing, the martial arts in the former British colony have been unaffected. The examples of Taiwan and Hong Kong argue that the place of the martial arts in mainland China will eventually stabilize when the society itself stabilizes. As has been true for all of its history, the martial arts follow and reflect the nature of Chinese society. Chinese society in the late twentieth and early twenty-first centuries is in considerable flux, and so is the martial arts.

The lifting of intense government control at all levels of society has allowed the practice of martial arts to return at the local level. Ralph Thaxton's study of Da Fo village charts the reemergence of the martial arts in the post-1978 period. In the absence of martial arts practice in a village previously, at least in the Republican period, known for its martial artists, the communist authorities had been able to enforce government rule through physical beatings and intimidation. As the economy began to improve, however, villagers were able to fight back against the Communist Party officials on several levels. The most direct and immediate response to greater freedom was arson attacks on the homes of party officials and their collaborators, followed in at least one case by cutting down the crops of one of the men who had mistreated the villagers during the Great Leap Forward and the Cultural Revolution. Revenge and counter-intimidation were the main reasons for those acts, but the villagers also turned their efforts to regaining their martial arts skills. Interestingly, one of the first acts in that effort was the rebuilding of temples to Guangong (Guandi, the god of war). This was followed by a return to martial arts training. As Thaxton described it:

> The training had a specific political purpose: villagers took it up to empower themselves in confrontations with Da Fo party leaders so that the latter could no longer place them in threatening situations without paying a price. Between 1985 and 1990, scores of Da Fo families sent two and three sons to train under local martial arts teachers, and they did so for the unstated but understood purpose of hitting back at Bao Zhilong [the communist village leader] and his power network. By 1986 several Da Fo martial artists whose families bore grudges from the Great Leap period were making it difficult for Bao Zhilong to rule the village. They challenged Bao more frequently and occasionally threatened to beat the daylights out of his family members if he attempted to interfere with their affairs.[15]

Bao Zhilong responded to these threats by sending his son to study at the Shaolin Temple Academy for a year. The sixteen-year-old did not learn how to fight effectively, however, and the villagers believed that the teachers had been "imposters." It is difficult to prove the teachers' status one way or the other as the teenager trained with them for only one year. Obviously the Baos seemed to feel that a year of training with a "real" Shaolin martial arts teacher would have been enough to defend against the attacks of embittered villagers seeking revenge for past injustices. Bao Zhilong's authority continued to crumble, and the county police offered little support. He eventually suffered a stroke in 1992, and his chosen successor was also unable to lead in the face of villager resistance.

Thaxton's research has continued, and he has explored the way the martial artists began to form a parallel power structure independent of either the Communist Party or the Chinese state. Ties of teacher-student relationship bind this network together and penetrate into the police force. The fictional touchstone for these martial artists is *The Water Margin*, the Ming Dynasty novel set in the twelfth century. This band of righteous martial arts outlaws now offers a form of real justice in contradistinction to the government.[16] The specific circumstances of Da Fo village, its history of martial arts, its contentious struggle between the Bao family and the Maoist hardliners on the one side and the villagers on the other during the Great Leap Forward, and the villagers' use of martial arts to regain power neatly fit the martial arts into the fictional construction of the twelfth-century bandits. The martial artists in Da Fo appear to be righteous men resisting corrupt government officials, thus connecting the martial arts with righteousness and justice. A weak government response allows this state of affairs to exist, and it is unclear whether better government, at least as perceived by the general population, would eventually diminish the martial artists' influence. It is also unclear whether some of the martial artists' actions may shade more into criminal than righteous behavior.

At least in the case of Da Fo village, martial arts empowers ordinary people in their struggle with a predatory government. The reservoir of martial arts in China, both in the cities and the countryside, is deep and broad, allowing people who feel they need martial arts training to acquire it. A similar process took place when the Shaolin Temple itself was revived. It was not that the temple was able to bring back former martial artists who had previously taught there (if any ever had in the twentieth century) or to find a former Buddhist monk who had practiced martial arts in his youth before taking up religious practice. Instead, martial artists were found to teach at the government-sponsored training center, and other martial arts teachers set up schools nearby, to revive the *tradition* of martial arts instruction associated with Shaolin. Da Fo village had a martial arts tradition from before the communist takeover, and the men who learned martial arts to defend themselves and their family were interested in regaining those skills for functional and practical reasons. They were not focused on reclaiming the specific skills and traditions that had been previously practiced in their country.

Shaolin itself changed dramatically soon after a new head abbot took office in 1999. Most obviously, Yongxin was the first head abbot of Shaolin since the beginning of the Qing Dynasty. He was well connected to the central government and used these connections to have almost all the private martial arts schools, restaurants, and merchandising stalls for tourists removed. The private martial arts schools relocated to the nearby town of Dengfeng, where they thrive on their proximity and connection to Shaolin.

The Shaolin Temple itself now focuses on Buddhism, with a regular traffic in tourists. When Matthew Polly returned to Shaolin in 2003, his old friends among the martial artists had become martial arts instructors. Shaolin itself fed off of its fictional image and continued to reinforce that image with performances for the tourists. Polly remarked that "Shaolin was always unique in having two types of monks: the cultural or Buddhist monks (*wen seng*) and the martial monks (*wu seng*). It seems they now had a third type: the performance monks (*biaoyan seng*)." But his 2003 obser-vations went further: "It was as I had suspected. This new breed had very little connection to the temple. They were extraordinarily skilled martial artists who had basically tried out and won parts in the long running hit musical *Shaolin's Martial Monks.*"[17]

The commercialization of Shaolin's martial arts reputation and the tourist value it included has moved to a new level with the franchising of Shaolin martial arts. In November 2008, Abbot Yongxin made a deal with the authorities in Guandu, on the outskirts of Kunming in Yunnan Province, to take over several newly renovated temples for thirty years, keeping the income from the donation boxes and gift shops. The monks also offered martial arts classes.[18] While some people were deeply disturbed by this turn of events, locals were happy for the tourism business it attracted. Yongxin was capitalizing on Shaolin's fame to spread its influence within China, in the same way that Shaolin monks had been sent to other countries to establish schools.

Shaolin is the most famous "name brand" in the martial arts because of the Hong Kong movie industry, but Taijiquan is more ubiquitous in practice around the world. Taiji's greater practice is due to its earlier export and, at least in the West, its considerably lower threshold of physical fitness. Other martial arts styles famous in China, like Xingyi, are mostly unknown in the West. The plethora of martial arts practiced in the countryside outside of the organizing framework of twentieth-century Chinese governments remain to be discovered. Of course, it is a distinctly late imperial and twentieth-century notion of martial arts being grouped into "styles" that now configures our approach to these physical practices.

Chinese martial arts is also undergoing a shift into sports, with two categories of this competitive version: forms and fighting. The Chinese government has been actively promoting Wushu as an international sport. It had hoped to get Wushu into the 2008 Olympics but was rejected. The Chinese government was particularly bothered by this exclusion because both Judo, a Japanese martial art, and Tae Kwon Do, a Korean martial art, are Olympic sports. The Olympic committee was concerned about the proliferation of marginal sports, which were crowding an already packed schedule of events. At least at the Beijing Olympics, the Chinese government was allowed to stage a Wushu competition external to the official Olympic events.

Sports Wushu grew out of government efforts in 1958 to regularize and organize the martial arts. As had happened under the Guomindang government, the communist government had committees of martial artists unify their own arts into recognized styles, with set forms and practices. This allowed for credentialing teachers and establishing curricula for school physical education programs. Actors like Jet Li established their reputations as martial artists in the Wushu forms competitions. The categories for Wushu forms reified the officially established styles, fixing the "correct" or orthodox forms of those styles. Competitors perfected the execution of those forms according to explicit criteria.

Wushu fixed not only the styles and their forms but also the overarching conception of the martial arts. Hard and soft, or internal and external, styles provide the larger categories for the listed martial arts. All arts are retrospectively mapped onto these divisions. This regularization continues through Shaolin, Taiji, Wudang, and other arts, creating a much neater lineage of martial arts practice than ever existed before. Indeed, further exploration of the martial arts practiced outside these government-sponsored institutions may actually show them to be marginal, at least with respect to the number of practitioners of martial arts in China. With international competitions in Wushu judged by these standards, the Chinese government's version of Chinese martial arts is spreading beyond its own borders.

Wushu competitions also include fighting, or *Sanda* (散打). *Sanda* allows for kicks, punches, sweeps, and takedowns, though not wrestling on the mat. In practice, Wushu fighting is similar to other striking arts, though it appears to be even less practiced outside of China than Wushu forms are. It is certainly a more practical combat art than Wushu forms; competitors wear protective gloves and are divided into weight classes. Indeed, Wushu fighting does not look very different from Thai boxing, Mixed Martial Arts, or even Western boxing. Where Wushu forms look very Chinese in execution and present a distinctly Chinese aesthetic of performance martial arts, Wushu fighting is more generic.

Both aspects of Wushu are now struggling to become more international in their audience and practitioners. Similar to the Chinese martial arts of the Pure Martial School in the early twentieth century, Wushu seems to attract followers by appearing to be an authentically Chinese physical practice with an ancient pedigree. Chinese people, diaspora Chinese, and non-Chinese interested in practicing Chinese physical culture as a means to an authentically "Chinese" experience see Wushu, if not wushu, as quintessentially and distinctly Chinese. At the same time, Wushu seems to be suspiciously modern and competition centered. It is hard to reconcile one of the unified national arts (Wushu) – organized and promoted by the government, performed by professional athletes, taught by professional coaches, and carried out in a sports arena – with the notion of a profound physical culture practiced by ordinary people for self-defense or personal development (wushu). By modernizing and regularizing wushu into Wushu, the Chinese government has assiduously stamped out a living tradition in the expectation of creating an active sport that promotes Chinese culture and the idea of a strong nation.

Many practitioners of Wushu dream of following that most famous of Wushu practitioners, Jet Li, into the movies. The performative emphasis of Wushu forms practice is simply the latest expression of martial arts performance, amplified by the global reach of Chinese martial arts films. Jackie Chan, a martial arts movie star whose fame is equal to or greater than that of Jet Li, trained as a Peking Opera performer, and so his martial arts is also performance martial arts, but of a different lineage. Even so, the distinctly Chinese pedigree of a certain kind of martial arts performance and the commercial possibilities of it have convinced a number of mainland Chinese directors who had previously made dramatic films to also create martial arts movies. Directors like Zhang Yimou and Chen Kaige followed in the footsteps of the Taiwanese director Ang Lee (who directed *Crouching Tiger Hidden Dragon*) to create *Hero* and *The Promise*, respectively. Martial arts films make money in the international box office, and they are also as Chinese as the Western is American.[19] When a Chinese director wants to make an unequivocally Chinese movie that will make money internationally, he makes a martial arts movie.

CONCLUSION

Chinese martial arts in the twentieth century was battered by all the same changes that Chinese society endured in a generally difficult century. This has continued unabated into the twenty-first century as mainland China continues to change at a rapid pace. As a living tradition, martial arts has defied successive governments' attempts to control, direct, and define it, all the while persisting among the Chinese populace. The current government of China would like to define wushu as the officially sanctioned Wushu that is a Chinese cultural treasure, available to the world, but of course always done better by the Chinese themselves. As a direct expression of "Chineseness," Wushu can be properly performed only by a real Chinese person, though foreigners are encouraged to try and be judged by the Chinese. The Chinese government must control Chinese culture, including physical culture, in both the domestic and foreign environments. As the Pure Martial organization found out in the early twentieth century, the Chinese government was not content to allow the private definition of Chinese physical culture.

Government efforts to control the martial arts have only been partially successful. Since martial arts practice is no longer a direct threat to the existence of the central government, the authorities in Beijing are not worried about practitioners leading rebellions. At the same time, farmers in places like Da Fo village are able to use martial arts to challenge, deflect, and undermine local government authority. Not only can the government be effectively challenged with martial arts skills but it can be fully displaced by more admirable local figures who have broken the authorities' monopoly on force. And we should be very clear that the farmers in Da Fo village were not learning Wushu to resist the government. Thus ordinary Chinese continue to define the martial arts in their own way in defiance of the government.

Shaolin, the invented source of Chinese martial arts, is now, more than ever, an arm of the government. The ability of Abbot Yongxin to physically separate most of the martial arts schools from the immediate environs of the temple was based upon his connections to the central government in Beijing. The principal form of martial arts being taught in Dengfeng, where the schools were relocated, is Wushu. This is the government's version of martial arts and the only one that opens up the possibility for a practitioner to teach in public schools as a physical education teacher. Shaolin has once again gained the emperor's patronage, but with patronage comes control.

Of the other modern styles of Chinese martial arts, Taiji seems to be the only one to find international acceptance and to escape government control. Ordinary people can practice Taiji without regard for a strict set of rules for competition and judging. Wing Chun (Yongchun) has also penetrated the foreign market, but it was fortunate in having teachers escape into Hong Kong and Taiwan. The story of Chinese martial arts in the post-imperial era is a narrative reflected and distorted through both domestic and foreign encounters with this particular physical culture. Chinese individuals, governments, and movies have described martial arts in one way, only to have distorted or misunderstood versions of those descriptions come back to them from abroad. And then the process begins again as the individuals, government institutions, and movies respond to those reflected descriptions. At the beginning of the twenty-first century, the practice and meaning of Chinese martial arts is now global.

Conclusion

Chinese martial arts is a living tradition with a very long history. As something alive it continues to change, in both meaning and practice, making simple conclusions about what it is, was, or even should be, impossible. In that respect it is no different from other Chinese practices, where centuries or even millennia of tradition bear strongly on current practitioners. As a physical practice, martial arts keeps the historian at arm's length by the limitations of the textual and archaeological sources. It is usually impossible to prove the continuity of any skill performed over the centuries. At the same time, the legitimacy of tradition, however understood, must compete with the needs or desires to innovate and absorb new techniques. If martial arts was a dead tradition this would not be difficult; the lines would be clear between the past and the present. The struggle to balance out tradition, innovation, and meaning is therefore a positive sign of vitality.

This vitality, however, is a great challenge for the researcher. Throughout this book I have struggled to construct a narrative of martial arts in Chinese culture and society that places specific practices in a broader context. The constraints of space and clarity (not to mention time) frequently forced significant aspects of the history of the martial arts – most obviously religion, theater, and literature – off to the side in favor of more general historical themes. In order to argue for the consistent importance of martial arts, I have spread my coverage more evenly over time at the expense of the availability of sources. Far more can be written about martial arts in more recent periods than in the distant past, but it seemed that apportioning coverage in direct reflection of the source materials might prejudice the reader into seeing martial arts as more important in the modern period than in ancient times. Martial arts has always been important in every society, not only in China, though the specific arts and the categories of practice understood to be "martial" are contested.

Much of the current understanding of Chinese martial arts in the West comes from the particular circumstances of late nineteenth- and early twentieth-century Chinese history, and the representation of the Chinese past in martial arts films. Most Chinese and Taiwanese people share these misconceptions about the history of Chinese martial arts, and indeed Chinese history as a whole. Very few historians, outside of a tiny group of specialists, have read the excellent scholarship in Chinese on the history of Chinese martial arts. It is therefore not surprising that when asked, the average Chinese or Taiwanese person will provide the same list of myths and hearsay that color and distort the understanding of Chinese martial arts. Familiar fabrications – Shaolin is the source of Chinese martial arts, the Daoist Zhang Sanfeng invented Taijiquan, or Chinese martial arts is about peace and self-cultivation, not violence, to name only a few – are repeated so often and so confidently that they appear to be true. They are not, and these misconceptions undermine not only our understanding of the place of martial arts in Chinese history but also the actual practice of martial arts.

A number of nationalisms and orientalisms inform the current meanings of martial arts in China and the world. The individual skill of a martial artist often becomes representative of not simply his or her abilities but also the value of the style practiced and the culture that produced that style. There is an ongoing debate over the relative qualities of the various styles, where they become stand-ins for their country of origin, adding emotional fuel to fundamentally inane comparisons. At the same time, the traditional cast of martial arts and its patina of ancient history attract students interested in connecting with an earlier period. Supposedly ancient practices rooted in discipline, good manners, and spiritual cultivation provide a cure for modern social ills. China as the most ancient of the East Asian civilizations must have the most profound of arts. The older the art, the more hidden are its true powers and value. Although China and Chinese martial arts may sometimes appear old and weak, they are in fact wise and strong. These are comforting myths for some, but myths nonetheless.

China is also a modern country, and its government wishes its distinctive cultural artifacts to be valued like those of other countries. China competes well in international sports but also wants other countries to value and compete in its particular physical culture, Wushu. The rejection of Wushu from the Olympics even after China won the hosting of the 2008 summer Olympics was therefore a galling setback. Japanese and Korean martial arts have been and remain Olympic sports. but China was only allowed to show its growing economic strength and international standing through its competition in Western events. At least in physical culture, Chinese modernization was coterminus with Westernization, but China's physical culture was not accepted as modern, despite the government's best efforts.

MARTIAL ARTS IN ACADEMIA

In his seminal 1999 article, "Academia Encounters the Chinese Martial Arts," Stanley Henning wrote: "In academia, the Chinese martial arts have been conspicuous by their relative absence from scholarly discussion, but when they have made an appearance it has usually been fleeting and in a muddle not much beyond what one sees in the bulk of martial-arts literature on the popular market."[1] Henning detailed the misconceptions espoused by an older generation of sinologists that also occasionally slip into more recent scholarship. Generally speaking, however, martial arts has been ignored by scholars studying China. Despite (or perhaps because of?) the fact that martial arts is one of the most distinctive aspects of Chinese culture for many people, very little research on it has been done. The reason is unclear, but the study of the martial arts touches on a number of academic disciplines.

Military history is an obvious place to start a discussion of martial arts. The field of military history broadened considerably in the late twentieth century, moving onto the battlefield to focus on how men fought other men. This attention to the actual methods of hand-to-hand fighting – in other words, martial arts – became a way to examine critical questions of culture, motivation, and group dynamics among common soldiers. By looking at the armament a given group used, we could see how that group believed combat should take place. When this information was linked to written records, the historian was able to create a fuller picture of the meaning of war, warfare, and combat. Where there is war, there are martial arts, even if they are rudimentary. The particular forms, meanings, and tools of martial arts tell us a lot about a culture. Even the separation between the martial arts of the battlefield and the martial arts of individual self-defense and hunting reveals a culture's construction of the place of violence in society.

Even in times of peace, however, martial arts persisted in all cultures. Violence is often a tool of government, or, in the Weberian sense, a distinctive feature of the state in the form of a monopoly on the licit use of force. Martial arts is simply better trained and executed violence. It enhances the ability to compel others to do one's will, or to resist the compulsion of others. In many places and times certain members of the community (often adult males) are expected to maintain some fighting capability, be it in defense of their family, clan, or larger group. If predatory violence is an accepted fact of life, then it is incumbent upon the individual to be able to defend himself or herself. To others, individuals should not have to be able to defend themselves because they do not accept violence as a fact of life. These are key questions of culture and ideology, which turn on the question of the accepted levels of violence in a community.

The place of violence in a community is reflected most clearly in its laws. Laws delineate how violence can be used, by whom, and under what conditions. A trained martial artist is considered differently under American law, for example, than an untrained party to a fight.[2] Professional fighters are often licensed to compete, and even amateurs must sign liability waivers before participating in amateur meets. Simply to take a class in martial arts a student must usually sign a liability waiver. Where laws intercede to manage the risks of martial arts in the United States, in other societies a student is assumed to accept the risks involved in training (at a minimum) by showing up for class. With respect to weapons, while firearms are regulated and can be licensed in some societies, there is seldom a system for licensing the use of hand-to-hand combat weapons, even for an expert trained in their use. These differences reflect the values and practicalities of different societies.

Attitudes toward violence are also reflected in areas like the construction of gender and fiction. Men and women are socialized into highly gendered relationships with violence, making certain kinds of actions masculine or feminine. Learning martial arts is often similarly gendered, though particular martial arts have different implications. Women seldom practice Western boxing or wrestling, though in recent years a growing number of women are competing in the sport of boxing. Asian martial arts seem to be a more acceptable practice for women in the West because they are perceived to rely less upon sheer physical strength and because there are far more examples of female martial artists in Asian films.

The broad popularity of Hong Kong martial arts films around the world has dramatically reconfigured the representation of combat in Hollywood and other film cultures. Very little remains of the staid fisticuffs of earlier films, except as a counterpoint to the new trend. A trained fighter in a movie must now display East Asian martial arts skills or appear hopelessly inept. While a vestigial American masculine suspicion of elegant techniques over direct power and toughness occasionally manifests itself, the shift appears complete and permanent. This change has empowered women as action heroes (also aided by the Hong Kong gangster films) and raised East Asian men to nearly an equal level of masculinity with Caucasian or African American men. For the most part this has been accomplished through the influx of Chinese, rather than Japanese or Korean, martial arts.

Beyond the direct realm of violence, martial arts has expanded into the realms of self-cultivation and health promotion. Chinese martial arts, usually Taiji, has been used in physical rehabilitation and as a gentle exercise program. The health-promoting effects of Chinese martial arts, particularly "internal" styles, have yet to be subjected to rigorous testing. Many practitioners proceed from a faith in the importance of cultivating *qi*, even in the existence of *qi*, that is difficult to challenge. These practices shade quickly into qigong, opening up a different set of issues separate from martial arts. Even absent the medium of qigong, Chinese martial arts connects with Traditional Chinese Medicine through some practices that use acupuncture points as targets and because martial artists have a regular need for medical care. Indeed, one of the greatest living scholars of martial arts, Ma Mingda, is not only a scholar but also a martial artist and Traditional Chinese Medicine practitioner.

A further only partly explored topic in martial arts is specific to East Asia: the relationship between martial arts and religion. Meir Shahar's book on Shaolin is a beginning point, and several Chinese studies have explored other aspects of Buddhism and Daoism's respective connections to the martial arts, but more certainly needs to be done. Shaolin was not the only Buddhist institution with connections to martial arts, and Daoist institutions like those on Mount Wudang have also manifested some distinctive martial arts traditions. The starting point for any of these topics is to discard the representations of these connections in Chinese fiction and search for historical documents.

Martial arts provides a useful perspective on cultures and societies. In China, martial arts has maintained itself as a distinctive cultural artifact that figures prominently in the society's fiction. Chinese physical culture in the form of martial arts is widely known around the world in entertainment as well as in practice. For scholars, the difficulties in researching martial arts stems not from lack of awareness of the importance of martial arts in Chinese culture but from the belief that there are few historical sources to work from. The material exists, and the door is open to research on a wide variety of subjects through the martial arts.

TO CLOSE

It is challenging to end a book that I hope has opened up more questions and topics than it has resolved. Indeed, I have done little beyond argue that Chinese martial arts has a history. The category of martial arts itself has changed in the last century, and its meaning continues to undergo significant transformation. Chinese martial arts is now an international product subject to globalization, commercialization, and nationalism. The Chinese government still struggles to control martial arts as part of its larger policy of controlling all aspects of Chinese culture – and to define what it is in a universal way. This is impossible, of course, as are the current government's efforts at control in other areas of Chinese culture. Local traditions of Chinese martial arts, both inside and outside China's borders, will continue to exist outside the Chinese government's grasp. Martial arts still resides in the martial artist who gives it meaning through individual practice and teaching.

All cultures have martial arts, yet Chinese martial arts is distinctive. A knowledgeable person can distinguish between the martial arts of Japan, Korea, Thailand, and the Philippines, and perhaps those of a few other cultures, with a fair degree of certainty. Individual arts or styles developed within these cultures are also obviously different. In the West, by contrast, unarmed forms of combat are much more similar across nationalities. Western boxing and wrestling have been made more uniform through sports competitions, which have limited innovation and stifled any large stylistic differences. Asian martial arts, by contrast, is extremely diverse, retaining the markers of its disparate histories.

Fighting arts do not simplify over time to an imagined ideal system of combat in which experience has left only the effective techniques. There are simply too many combat techniques and too many possible combat situations to lead to simplification. Moreover, no individual martial artist can master all the possible combat skills. Despite this diversity, the individual histories of different martial arts mark them. Chinese martial arts remains embedded in and emblematic of the culture and history it came from. It is a historical product, replicated and modified over time, changing but recognizably the same. Politics, fiction, religion, and medicine have all had their role in shaping Chinese martial arts without fixing it into a single, simple practice with a unified meaning. Even grounding the study of martial arts in historical research cannot eliminate the mystery of its effects, its attractions, or its nature. Something is always uncertain. To paraphrase the paradigmatic dialogue of so many badly translated martial arts movies, "Kungfu is very good, but still . . ."

Notes

Introduction

1. Douglas Wile, *T'ai Chi's Ancestors*, New York: Sweet Ch'i Press, 1999.
2. Meir Shahar, *The Shaolin Monastery*, Honolulu: University of Hawai'i Press, 2008.
3. *The Compact Edition of the Oxford English Dictionary*, vol. 3, Oxford: Clarendon Press, 1987, 473 (558).
4. Morohashi Tetsuji, *Dai Kan-Wa Jiten*, vol. 2, Tôkyô: Taishûkan Shoten, 1984–86, 367; Zhang Fangjie, *Far East Chinese-English Dictionary*, Taibei: Far East Book Company, 1992, 148.
5. Luo Zhufeng (ed.), *Hanyu Dacidian*, vol. 2b, Shanghai: Hanyu Dacidian Chubanshe, 2008, 766.
6. The paradigmatic sentence, "His Kung-fu is very good," might be more completely translated as "His technique/skill is very good," or more succinctly, "He is very skilled."
7. Xunzi, Yang Liang (ed.), *Xunzi*, Tokyo: Xunzi Li shi Riben Dongjing shi shu, 1884, ch. 10, 5b.
8. Matthew Polly, *American Shaolin*, New York: Gotham Books, 2007, 6.
9. Matthew Polly, personal communication, 9 January 2010. I wish to express my deepest gratitude to Mr. Polly for his prompt and thorough response to my questions.
10. Wang Guangxi, *Gongfu*, Taibei: Yunlong Chubanshe, 2002, 319–20.

1 From the Stone Age to the End of the Spring and Autumn Period

1. Frederick (Friedrich) Engels, *The Origin of the Family, Private Property and the State*, New York: International Publishers, 1942, 20.
2. Wenwu Chubanshe, *Yinxu Dixia Guibao: Henan Anyang Fu Hao Mu*, Beijing: Wenwu Chubanshe, 1994, 142.
3. Jia Lanpo et al., "Report on Excavations of Shiyu Paleolithic Sites in Shanxi," *Journal of Archaeology*, 1 (1972), 51–2, cited in Yang Hong (Zhang Lijing, trans.), *Weapons in Ancient China*, Rego Park, NY: Science Press New York, 1992, 9. I have been unable to locate the original article. Stephen Selby gives a somewhat later range of 20,000–10,000 years, see Stephen Selby, *Chinese Archery*, Hong Kong: Hong Kong University Press, 2000, 6.

4. Yang Hong, *Weapons*, 4.

5. Mark Edward Lewis, *Sanctioned Violence in Early China*, Albany: State University of New York Press, 1990, 27.

6. The association of hunters and martial artists is evident in several characters from the sixteenth-century novel, *The Water Margin (Shuihuzhuan)*. See Shi Nai'an and Luo Guanzhong, *Shuihuzhuan*, Beijing: Zhonghua Shuju, 1997, and in English translation, Shi Nai'an and Luo Guanzhong, Sidney Shapiro (trans.), *Outlaws of the Marsh*, Beijing: Foreign Language Press and Bloomington: Indiana University Press, 1981. Additionally, bandits, those other regular anti-establishment martial practitioners, often lived in the mountains or wilds where they would have hunted for sustenance.

7. The other two were the ancestral temple and stables. All of these together linked the three activities of sacrifice, warfare, and hunting. See Mark Edward Lewis, *Sanctioned Violence in Early China*, 19. There is no indication of whether the military storehouse included a manufacturing facility, or whether the weapons stored there represented all or most of the weapons provided for the army in times of war.

8. *Zuozhuan Zhu*, Lord Zhao year 1, pp. 1211–12, cited and translated in Lewis, *Sanctioned Violence in Early China*, 43.

9. Lewis, *Sanctioned Violence*, 23.

10. Lewis, *Sanctioned Violence*, 127.

11. Wenwu Chubanshe, *Yinxu Dixia Guibao: Henan Anyang Fu Hao Mu*, Beijing: Wenwu Chubanshe, 1994, 119.

12. Yang Hong, *Weapons*, 58.

13. This discussion of the chariot follows Edward L. Shaughnessy, "Historical Perspectives on the Introduction of the Chariot into China," *Harvard Journal of Asiatic Studies*, 48 (1988), 189–237.

14. Some Chinese scholars have argued for the presence of cavalry in the Shang dynasty. The evidence of one tomb may indicate horse-riding, but, particularly in the absence of other such tombs, it does not demonstrate that the occupant fought from horseback.

15. Shaughnessy, "Historical Perspectives," 214.

16. Shaughnessy, "Historical Perspectives," 231.

17. Lewis, *Sanctioned Violence*, 228.

18. Lewis, *Sanctioned Violence*, 226.

19. James Legge (trans.), *Shi jing*, New York: Paragon Reprint, 1967, 286–7.

2 The Warring States Period

1. Confucius (Edward Slingerland, trans.), *The Analects*, Indianapolis: Hackett, 2003, 86.

2. Lewis, *Sanctioned Violence in Early China*, Albany: State University of New York Press, 1990 51.

3. While it seems likely that Confucius, Mencius, and Xunzi were actual historical figures, Laozi, Sunzi, and Zhuangzi were probably not. The texts attributed to any of these figures all have complex histories. For the sake of convenience, I will

discuss the texts respectively attributed to these figures as if they were the authors, without further parsing of their authorial layers.

4. I use the translation "noble man" following Paul Goldin's discussion of the term *junzi* 君子, literally "the son of a lord." See Paul Goldin, *Rituals of the Way*, Chicago: Open Court, 1999, vii–viii.

5. Confucius, *Analects*, 12.

6. Yang Hong, *Weapons in Ancient China*, Rego Park, NY: Science Press New York, 1992, 110.

7. Yang Hong, *Weapons*, 180.

8. An example of the magical qualities of bows and arrows was the mulberry bow and six arrows provided for boys at birth. The arrows were to be fired in the four directions and up and down to drive off evil spirits and protect the boy from harm.

9. The first historical mention of crossbow use in a battle is in the *Shiji* account of the battle of Maling (341 BCE). Sima Qian, *Shiji*, Taibei: Dingwen Shuju, 1999.
   Bronze crossbow trigger mechanisms have been found from the Warring States Period. It is possible that earlier mechanisms were made from less durable material and simply disintegrated over time.

10. Confucius, *Analects*, 23. And Zhu Xi's comment on the passage that follows.

11. Confucius, *Analects*, 24 and fn 10.

12. Confucius, *Analects*, 19.

13. Mencius, *Mencius* (D. C. Lau, trans.), New York: Penguin, 1978, [2A7] 83.

14. *Mencius*, D. C. Lau (trans.), [5B1] 150–1.

15. Lieh-tzu (Eva Wong, trans.), *Lieh-tzu*, Boston: Shambala, 2001, 58.

16. This discussion of strength and weight lifting follows Liu Gengguo, *Zhongguo Gudai Tiyu Shihua*, Beijing: Wenwu Chubanshe, 1987, 68–70.

17. Ruan Yuan (ed.), *Liji*, in *Shisanjing Zhushu*, vol. 5, Taibei: Yiwen Yinshuguan, 2001, 17.344. Legge translates 角力 as "trials of strength." Han dynasty sources make it clear that these are paired contests, and included strikes as well. The section in the *Liji* on music mentions the inclusion of weaponry in a number of locations: "The combination of those modulated sounds, so as to give pleasure, and the (direction in harmony with them of the) shields and axes, and of the plumes and ox-tails, constitutes what we call music." James Legge (trans.), *Li Chi*, New York: University Books, 1967, 92, and, "By the bells, drums, shields, and axes, they introduced harmony into their seasons of rest and enjoyment." Legge, *Li Chi*, 97.

18. "怒，搏闵公，絕其脰。" Gongyang Gao and Ruan Yuan (eds.), *Gongyang Zhuan*, in *Shisanjing Zhushu*, vol. 7, Taibei: Yiwen Yinshuguan, 2001, 7.91.

19. Liu Xiang (ed.), *Xinxu* 新序, section 8 (Yiyong 義勇), http://www.gutenberg. org/cache/epub/23945/pg23945.html

20. See Fan Ning's commentary, 1st year of Duke Xi: "搏，手搏也。" Ruan Yuan (ed.), *Guliang Zhuan*, in *Shisanjing Zhushu*, vol. 6, Taibei: Yiwen Yinshuguan, 2001, 7.70.

21. Zuo Qiuming and Ruan Yuan (eds.), *Zuozhuan*, in *Shisanjing Zhushu*, vol. 6, Taibei: Yiwen Yinshuguan, 2001, 16.272.

22. Chapter 86 of the *Shiji* contains the biographies of the "Assassin-Retainers" in Burton Watson's translation, 45–67, Ssu-ma Ch'ien (Sima Qian) (Burton

Watson, trans.), *Records of the Grand Historian*, New York: Columbia University Press, 1958; Sima Qian, *Shiji*, Taibei: Dingwen Shuju, 1999, 86.2515–38.

23. Sima Qian (Watson, trans.), *Records*, 67.
24. Mencius, 62.

3 The Qin and Han Dynasties

1. Sima Qian, *Shiji*, Taibei: Dingwen Shuju, 1999, 7.295–339. The title of this book has been translated as *Records of the Grand Historian* by Burton Watson (New York: Columbia University Press, 1969) and *The Grand Scribe's Records* by William Nienhauser (Bloomington: Indiana University Press, 1994–). I have used parts of both translations in the text, citing each work as appropriate, but the reader should be aware that both refer to the same work, the *Shiji*.
2. Mark Edward Lewis, "The Han Abolition of Universal Military Service," in Hans Van de Ven (ed.), *Warfare in Chinese History*, Leiden: Brill, 2000, 41–42. For Wang Mang's rebellion see Hans Bielenstein, "Wang Mang, the Restoration of the Han Dynasty, and Later Han," in Denis Twitchett and Michael Lowe (eds.), *The Cambridge History of China*, vol. 1, Cambridge: Cambridge University Press, 1986, 223–90.
3. Most famous or infamously by Lei Haizong, in the twentieth century, who attributed the demilitarization of Chinese society and consequent military weakness of China in the nineteenth and twentieth centuries to this change. Lei Haizong, *Zhongguo wenhua yu zhongguo zhi bing*, Changsha: Yuelu Shushe, 1989 (First edition 1939). For a broader discussion of this issue, as well as further instances of the demilitarization of China, see Hans Van de Ven's introduction in Hans Van de Ven (ed.), *Warfare in Chinese History*, Leiden: Brill, 2000, 1–32.
4. Sima Qian (Watson, trans.), *Records of the Grand Historian*, 326.
5. Sima Qian (Nienhauser, trans.), *The Grand Scribe's Records*, 328.
6. Sima Qian (Nienhauser, trans.), *The Grand Scribe's Records*, 333 [modified]; Sima Qian, *Shiji* 86.2538.
7. Sima Qian (Watson, trans.), *Records of the Historian*, 158.
8. Zhang Chunben and Cui Lequan, *Zhongguo Wushushi*, Taibei: Wenjin Chubanshe, 1993, 94.
9. Sima Qian, *Shiji* 87.2559.
10. Modified translation from Nienhauser, *The Grand Scribe's Records*, 179.
11. Sima Qian (Nienhauser, trans.), *The Grand Scribe's Records*, 180.
12. Ban Gu (Homer H. Dubs, trans.), *History of the Former Han Dynasty*, Baltimore: Waverly Press, 1938–55, 34.
13. Ban Gu, *History of the Former Han Dynasty*, 63. Watson, *Records of the Grand Historian*, 83. Xiang Bo had previously drunk a toast of friendship with Liu Bei, after which Liu had declared himself loyal to Xiang Yu. When Xiang Bo returned to Xiang Yu, he argued that Liu had actually served Xiang's interests and it would not, therefore, be right to attack him. Fan Ceng believed, on the contrary (and ultimately correctly), that Liu Bei was a fundamental

threat to Xiang Yu's interests and convinced Xiang Zhuang to try to assassinate Liu.

14. Ban Gu, *History of Former Han Dynasty*, 91.
15. Sima Qian (Watson, trans.), *Records of the Grand Historian*, 206.
16. Ban Gu, *History of the Former Han Dynasty*, 120.
17. Ban Gu, *History of the Former Han Dynasty*, 127.
18. Ban Gu, *History of the Former Han Dynasty*, 143.
19. Zhang Chunben and Cui Lequan, *Zhongguo Wushu Shi*, 106.
20. Ban Gu, *Hanshu*, Taibei: Dingwen Shuju, 1997, 6.194 and 6.198.
21. Ban Gu, *Hanshu*, 96b.3928.
22. Ban Gu, *Hanshu*, 68.2961. Here I have followed Jin Zhuo's 金灼 gloss of the term *hu* as "neck" in his notes to the *Hanshu*. Several alternative readings suggest themselves, however, if we read *hu* as either "blind" or "barbarian." Meng Kang 孟康 explains the term as a kind of "hidden" or perhaps "surreptitious" turn, which is close to the "blind" meaning; see his note in *Hanshu* 68.2962. Alternatively, given the close connection with the steppe, a technique called "throwing the barbarian" might not be beyond reason either.
23. Wei Shou, *Weishu*, Taibei: Dingwen Shuju, 1998, 109.2828.
24. See the comment in Fan Ye, *Houhanshu*, Taibei: Dingwen Shuju, 1999, 28.3624.
25. See Sima Qian, "Letter to Ren An." *Hanshu*, 62.2725–2736.
26. Zhang Chunben and Cui Lequan, *Zhongguo Wushu Shi*, 110.
27. Note 9 in Zhang Chunben and Cui Lequan, *Zhongguo Wushu Shi*, 111.
28. Ban Gu, *Hanshu*, 54.2451.
29. Sima Qian, *Shiji*, 117.2999.
30. Zhang Chunben and Cui Lequan, *Zhongguo Wushu Shi*, 115.

4 The Six Dynasties

1. To this list we can also add "China's Dark Ages" mentioned by Albert Dien. See Albert Dien, *Six Dynasties Civilization*, New Haven: Yale University Press, 2007, 1. For a more general history of the period in English, see Mark Edward Lewis, *China between Empires: The Northern and Southern Dynasties*, Cambridge, MA: Harvard University Press, 2009. Lewis prefers the term "Northern and Southern Dynasties."
2. Guojia Tiwei Wushu Yanjiuyuan Bianzuan, *Zhongguo Wushushi*, Beijing: Renmin Tiyu Chubanshe, 1996, 106.
3. Albert Dien, "The Stirrup and Chinese Military History," *Ars Orientalis*, 16, (1986), 38
4. On local fortifications, see Albert Dien, *Six Dynasties Civilization*, 15–45.
5. Albert Dien, *Six Dynasties Civilization*, 1.
6. Cited in Albert Dien, *Six Dynasties Civilization*, 6.
7. Lin Boyuan, *Zhongguo Wushushi*, Taibei: Wuzhou Chubanshe, 1996, 132–3.
8. Liu Xi, *Shiming*, ch. 23 (Explaining Weapons), *China Text Project*, 14 June 2011. http://ctext.org/shi-ming/shi-bing: "A spear eighteen feet long is called a 'shao,' it is said that, wielded from horseback, this shaoshao is effective at killing."
9. Pei Songzhi, *Sanguozhi* (*Weishu*), Taibei: Dingwen Shuju, 1997, 17.519.

10. Pei Songzhi, *Sanguozhi* (*Weishu*), 1.2.
11. Pei Songzhi, *Sanguozhi* (*Weishu*), 18.544.
12. Pei Songzhi, *Sanguozhi* (*Weishu*), 1.35.
13. Pei Songzhi, *Sanguozhi* (*Weishu*), 8.239.
14. Pei Songzhi, *Sanguozhi* (*Shushu*), 36.943. I must emphasize that this story is recorded in the historical records of the Three Kingdoms. Not surprisingly, it also appears in the fictionalized account of the period.
15. Fan Xuanliang, *Jinshu*, Taibei: Dingwen Shuju, 1995, 103.2694.
16. Pei Songzhi, *Sanguozhi* (*Weishu*), 16.510.
17. Fan Xuanliang, *Jinshu*, 103.2683.
18. Fan Xuanliang, *Jinshu*, 109.2827.
19. Pei Songzhi, *Sanguozhi* (*Weishu*), 2.89
20. Pei Songzhi, *Sanguozhi* (*Weishu*), 11.340.
21. Pei Songzhi, *Sanguozhi* (*Weishu*), 12.367.
22. Pei Songzhi, *Sanguozhi* (*Shushu*), 35.914.
23. Pei Songzhi, *Sanguozhi* (*Wushu*), 54.1267.
24. Pei Songzhi, *Sanguozhi* (*Weishu*), 1.8
25. Shen Yue, *Songshu*, Taibei: Dingwen Shuju, 1998, 18.506.
26. Fan Xuanliang, *Jinshu*, 25.771.
27. David Graff, *Medieval Chinese Warfare, 300–900*, London: Routledge, 2002, 114.
28. For an example of this, see the Daoist swordsman in *Chinese Ghost Story* (*Sien nui yau wan*), Dir. Siu-Tung Ching, Perf. Leslie Cheung, Joey Wang and Ma Wu, Cinema City Film Productions, 1987.
29. Pei Songzhi, *Sanguozhi* (*Wushu*), 60.1379 (notes, citing the *Baopuzi*).
30. Ge Hong, *Baopuzi*, Taibei: Xinwenfeng Chuban Gongsi, 1998, 50/13.263.
31. Wei Shou, *Weishu*, Taibei: Dingwen Shuju, 1998, 15.375.
32. For Yi Huan, see Wei Shou, *Weishu*, 32.991; for Er Zhuzhao, see Wei Shou, *Weishu*, 75.1661.
33. Sima Guang, *Zizhi Tongjian*, Taibei: Taiwan Zhonghua Shuju, 1966, 154.6b.
34. Shen Yue, *Songshu*, Taibei: Dingwen Shuju, 1998, 72.1880.
35. Lin Boyuan, *Zhongguo Wushushi*, 154–5.
36. Sima Guang, *Zizhi Tongjian*, Taibei: Taiwan Zhonghua Shuju, 1966, 66.2a.
37. Fan Xuanliang, *Jinshu* 96.2515.
38. "The Ballad of Mulan" translated by William H. Nienhauser in Wu-chi Liu and Irving Yucheng Lo (eds.), *Sunflower Splendor: Three Thousand Years of Chinese Poetry*, Garden City, NY: Anchor Books, 1975, 77–80.
39. Sima Guang, *Zizhi Tongjian*, Beijing: Guji Chubanshe, 1956, 157.4882, cited and translated by David Graff, 107.
40. Graff, *Medieval Chinese Warfare*, 107.

5 The Sui and Tang Dynasties

1. David Graff, *Medieval Chinese Warfare, 300–900*, London: Routledge, 2002, 161.
2. Li Yuan's mother and Yang Guang's mother were sisters, making the two emperors first cousins.
3. Graff, *Medieval Chinese Warfare*, 169.

4. Graff, *Medieval Chinese Warfare*, 176.

5. Wei Zheng, *Suishu*, Taibei: Dingwen Shuju, 1997, 1.24.

6. Liu Xu, *Jiu Tangshu*, Beijing: Zhonghua Shuju, 1975, 2.30–31.

7. Ouyang Xiu and Song Qi, *Xin Tangshu*, Beijing: Zhonghua Shuju, 1975, 40.1325.

8. A *bu* or double pace was 5 Chinese feet. A Tang foot was 11.8 inches or 30.3 centimeters. I am grateful to David Graff for correcting me on this issue and preventing an embarrassing error.

9. *Tang Liudian*, 16.7b in *Siku Quanshu*, Hong Kong: Chinese University of Hong Kong & Digital Heritage Publishing Ltd., 1999–.

10. I translate these terms with some trepidation. The "defense sword" comes from the meaning of *zhang* as a barrier, and because it was used for personal defense. The "cross sword" comes from the meaning of *heng* as "crosswise" rather than its meaning of "east-west" as opposed to north-south. The "divided sword" comes from the meaning of *mo* as the raised path between fields running east-west, and from its more symmetric division between blade and handle.

11. I have translated this as "Long Blade" to avoid confusion with my translation of the term *jian* as Long Sword. "Long Sword" would be a more direct translation.

12. Li Quan, *Taibai Yinjing*, 4.13b in *Siku Quanshu*, Hong Kong: Chinese University of Hong Kong & Digital Heritage Publishing Ltd., 1999–.

13. Zhang Yu, "Madam Gong Sun," in Barbara Bennett Peterson (ed.), *Notable Women of China*, Armonk, NY: M. E. Sharpe, 2000, 209–11.

14. Duan Chengshi (Carrie E. Reed, trans.), *A Tang Miscellany*, New York: Peter Lang, 2003, 108–9.

15. Jacques Gernet (Franciscus Verellen, trans.), *Buddhism in Chinese Society: An Economic History from the Fifth to the Tenth Centuries*, New York: Columbia University Press, 1995.

16. Huijiao, *Gaoseng zhuan*, Beijing: Zhonghua shuju, 1991; Daoxuan, *Xu Gaoseng zhuan*, 2 vols., Shanghai: Guji chubanshe, 1995 and 1999; Zanning, *Da Song Gaoseng zhuan*, Taibei: Shangwu yinshu guan, 1983.

17. Bernard Faure, "Relics and Flesh Bodies: The Creation of Ch'an Pilgrimage Sites," in Susan Naquin and Chün-Fang Yu (eds.), *Pilgrims and Sacred Sites in China*, Berkeley: University of California Press, 1992, 156.

18. Heinrich Dumoulin, *Zen Buddhism: A History*, New York: Simon and Schuster Macmillan, 1994, 92–3.

19. Faure, "Relics and Flesh Bodies," 156–7. Quote modified from Wade-Giles to Pinyin Romanization.

20. John Kieschnick, *The Eminent Monk*, Honolulu: University of Hawai'i Press, 1997, 62.

21. Meir Shahar, *The Shaolin Monastery*, Honolulu: University of Hawai'i Press, 2008, 21–2.

22. Du You, *Tongdian*, Beijing: Zhonghua Shuju, 1988, 18.451. Lin Boyuan has slightly misquoted this as "恐人忘戰" rather than the correct phrase "恐人之忘戰." See Lin Boyuan, *Zhongguo Wushushi*, Taibei: Wuzhou Chubanshe, 1996, 187.

23. Jonathan Skaff, "Barbarians at the Gates? The Tang Frontier Military and the An Lushan Rebellion," *War and Society*, 18, no. 2 (2000), 23–35.

6 The Five Dynasties and Ten Kingdoms and the Song Dynasty

1. For the relationship of *The Water Margin* (*Shuihuzhuan*) to actual Song history, particularly the role of martial arts instructors, see Paul Jakov Smith, "*Shuihu zhuan* and the Military Subculture of the Northern Song, 960–1127," *Harvard Journal of Asiatic Studies*, 66, no. 2 (December 2006), 363–422.

2. Li Tao, *Xu Zizhi Tongjian Changbian*, Beijing: Zhonghua Shuju, 2004, 117.2746; Zeng Gong, *Nanfeng Xiansheng Yuanfeng lei gao*, Taibei: Taiwan Zhonghua Shuju, 1971, 51, and Toghto, *Songshi*, Taibei: Dingwen Shuju, 1998, 348.11032, respectively.

3. Li Tao, *Xu Zizhi Tongjian Changbian*, 134.3198–7, cited in Paul Jakov Smith, "*Shuihu zhuan* and the Military Subculture of the Northern Song, 960–1127," *Harvard Journal of Asiatic Studies*, 66, no. 2 (December 2006) 382.

4. Zeng Gongliang, *Wujing Zongyao* (*Complete Essentials from the Military Classics*), vols. 3, 4, and 5 in *Zhongguo Bingshu Jicheng*, Vol. 6, Beijing: Jiefangjun chubanshe, 1992.

5. Hua Yue, *Cuihui Beizheng Lu*, in *Zhongguo Bingshu Jicheng*, Beijing: Jiefangjun chubanshe, 1992, vol. 6, 681.

6. Hua Yue, *Cuihui Beizheng Lu*, 686.

7. For Song efforts to procure horses, see Paul Smith, *Taxing Heaven's Storehouse*.

8. Xu Dong, *Huqian Jing* 虎鈐經, in *Zhongguo Bingshu Jicheng*, Beijing: Jiefangjun chubanshe, 1992, vol. 6, 175.

9. Wenying, *Xiangshan Yelu*, Beijing: Zhonghua Shuju, 2007, 2.39–40.

10. Confucius (Edward Slingerland, trans.), *The Analects*, Indianapolis: Hackett, 2003, 23.

11. Wang Pizhi, *Shengshui Yantan Lu* in *Shengshui Yantan Lu/Guitian Lu*, Beijing: Zhonghua Shuju, 2006, 9.113.

12. Ouyang Xiu, *Guitian Lu*, in *Shengshui Yantan Lu/Guitian Lu*, Beijing: Zhonghua Shuju, 2006, 1.9–10.

13. Lieh-tzu (Eva Wong trans.), *Lieh-tzu*, Boston: London: Shambala, 2001, 58.

14. According the *Songshi*, Archery Societies were an old or preexisting practice in Hebei. Toghto, *Songshi*, 190.4725.

15. Su Shi, *San Su Quanshu*, vol. 12, Beijing: Yuwen Chubanshe, 2001, 214.

16. Toghto, *Songshi*, 190.4725.

17. *Songhuiyao Jigao*, Taibei: Xinwenfeng Chubangongsi, 1976, *Bing* 7999.7/6b; Li Tao, *Xu Zizhi Tongjian Changbian*, Beijing: Zhonghua Shuju, 2004, 20.449.

18. Meng Yuanlao, *Dongjing Menghua Lu*, 4.1a, "Juntousi" in *Siku Quanshu*, Hong Kong: Chinese University of Hong Kong & Digital Heritage Publishing Ltd., 2004.

19. Wu Zimu, *Mengliang Lu*, 20.15a, "Jiaodi" in *Siku Quanshu*, Hong Kong: Chinese University of Hong Kong & Digital Heritage Publishing Ltd., 2004.

20. Lin Boyuan, *Zhongguo Wushushi*, Taibei: Wuzhou Chubanshe,1996, 210.

21. Toghto, *Songshi*, 194.4853: "In the imperial army [those] paid more than five hundred cash a month train in martial arts (*wuji* 武技) every day; [those] receiving less than three hundred cash, sometimes do labor and sometimes practice."

22. Meng Yuanlao, *Dongjing Menghua Lu*, 2 (Dongjiaolou jiejian), and 5, (Jingwa jiyi), in *Siku Quanshu*, Hong Kong: Chinese University of Hong Kong & Digital Heritage Publishing Ltd., 2004.

23. Li Fang, *Taiping Guangji*, 85.20a in *Siku Quanshu*, Meng Yuanlao, *Dongjing Menghua Lu*, 2 (Dongjiaolou jiejian), and 5 (Jingwa jiyi), in *Siku Quanshu*. Hong Kong: Chinese University of Hong Kong & Digital Heritage Publishing, 2004.
24. Wu Zimu, *Mengliang Lu*, 20, "Jiaodi." In Meng Yuanlao, *Dongjing Menghua Lu*, 2 (Dongjiaolou jiejian) and 5 (Jingwa jiyi) in *Siku Quanshu*, Hong Kong: Chinese University of Hong Kong & Digital Heritage Publishing Ltd., 2004.
25. Sima Guang, *Sima Wenzheng (Wengong) Ji*, Taibei: Taiwan Zhonghua Shuju, 1965, 3.13b–14a.
26. Lin Boyuan, *Zhongguo Wushushi*, 223.
27. *Jinhua Xianta Chuan*, 12, cited in Lin Boyuan, *Zhongguo Wushushi*, 217.

7 The Yuan Dynasty

1. Marco Polo (Ronald Latham, trans.), *The Travels of Marco Polo*, London: Folio Society, 1990 (reissue), 80.
2. Marco Polo, *The Travels*, 82.
3. "殺鬼招鬼" reading "zhao" as a verb "to target," rather than "to call up," as Selby translates it. My presumption here is that it is the spirit or ghost that is the target of the arrows. Stephen Selby, *Chinese Archery*, Hong Kong: Hong Kong University Press, 2000, 239.
4. The Mongols classed northern Chinese as *Hanren* and southern Chinese as *Nanren* or *Jiangnanren* because they perceived the people of the north and south as culturally and politically separate.
5. Song Lian, *Yuanshi*, Taibei: Dingwen Shuju, 1998, 13.276.
6. Song Lian, *Yuanshi*, 5.91.
7. Song Lian, *Yuanshi*, 9.181.
8. Song Lian, *Yuanshi*, 15.321.
9. Song Lian, *Yuanshi*, 28.619.
10. Song Lian, *Yuanshi*, 29.658.
11. Zhang Qiyun (ed.), *Zhongwen Dacidian*, Taibei: Zhongguo Wenhua Daxue Chuban Bu, 1993, vol. 9, 839, defines this as "the same as a *jian* 簡," which is a bamboo slip used for making notes, and that it is one of the eighteen martial arts.
12. She noted her skill with the Peach Blossom Spear: "For twenty years there was no match for me in the world with the Peach Blossom Spear." Toghto, *Songshi*, Taibei: Dingwen Shuju, 1998, 477.13850.
13. *Yuandianzhang*, cited in Lin Boyuan, *Zhongguo Wushushi*, Taibei: Wuzhou Chubanse, 1996, 275.
14. Song Lian, *Yuanshi*, 2.619.
15. Marco Polo, *The Travels*, 270–2. Polo dates the contest with the visiting prince to 1280.
16. Bi Yuan, *Xu Zizhi Tongjian*, Taibei: Taiwan Zhonghua Shuju, 1965, 207.22.
17. For Li Quan's biography see Toghto, *Songshi*, 476.13817–477.13851.
18. Toghto, *Songshi*, 476.13817.
19. Toghto, *Songshi*, 476.13818.
20. Han Rulin 韓儒林 (ed.), *Yuanchaoshi* 元朝史, Beijing: Renmin Chubanshe, 1986, 4.

21. I owe this particular insight to Michael Brose, who provided me with a timely, precise and erudite discussion of the Mongol treatment of northerners and southerners. The discussion that follows benefits directly from his helpful comments.

8 The Ming Dynasty (1368–1644)

1. Kathleen Ryor, "Wen and Wu in Elite Cultural Practices during the Late Ming," in Nicola DiCosmo (ed.), *Military Culture in Imperial China*, Cambridge, MA: Harvard University Press, 2008, 219–42.
2. For the development of the Great Wall, see Arthur Waldron, *The Great Wall of China*, Cambridge: Cambridge University Press, 1992.
3. Kenneth Swope, *A Dragon's Head and a Serpent's Tail*, Norman: University of Oklahoma Press, 2009.
4. My use of this term follows David Robinson, *Bandits, Eunuchs and the Son of Heaven*, Honolulu: University of Hawai'i Press, 2001, 2.
5. James Tong, *Disorder under Heaven*, Stanford: Stanford University Press, 1991, 7, cited and quoted in Robinson, 177 fn. 14.
6. Robinson, *Bandits*, 5.
7. Robinson, *Bandits*, 5.
8. Robinson, *Bandits*, 84–5.
9. Meir Shahar, *The Shaolin Monastery*, Honolulu: University of Hawai'i Press, 2008.
10. Kai Filipiak, *Die Chinesische Kampfkunst*, Leipzig: Leipziger Universitätsverlag, 2001, 66–92.
11. Quoted and translated in Shahar, *The Shaolin Monastery*, 70.
12. Shahar, *The Shaolin Monastery*, 82–3.
13. For a Japanese comparison see Mikael S. Adolphson's discussion of the warrior monks in Japan, *The Teeth and Claws of the Buddha*, Honolulu: University of Hawai'i Press, 2007.
14. Lin Boyuan, *Zhongguo Wushushi*, Taibei: Wuzhou Chubanshe, 1996, 300.
15. Lin Boyuan, *Zhongguo Wushushi*, 315.
16. Wang Qi, *Xu Wenxian Tongkao*, 166 (Conglun Junji), cited in Lin Boyuan, *Zhongguo Wushushi*, 310.
17. Lin Boyuan, *Zhongguo Wushushi*, 317.
18. Lin Boyuan, *Zhongguo Wushushi*, 319.

9 The Qing Dynasty (1644–1911)

1. Kenneth Swope, *A Dragon's Head and a Serpent's Tail: Ming China and the First Great East Asian War, 1592–1598*, Norman: University of Oklahoma Press, 2009.
2. Here I have chosen to follow Joseph Esherick and Paul Cohen's terminology, calling it the "Boxer Uprising" rather than the "Boxer Rebellion." Joseph Esherick, *The Origins of the Boxer Uprising*, Berkeley: University of California Press, 1987; Paul A. Cohen, *History in Three Keys: The Boxers as Event, Experience, and Myth*, New York: Columbia University Press, 1998.

3. Huang Zongxi, "Epitaph for Wang Zhengnan," translated in Douglas Wile, *T'ai Chi's Ancestors*, New York: Sweet Ch'i Press, 1999, 53. I have modified the Romanization of the translation for consistency.

4. Huang Baijia, "Art of the Internal School," translated in Douglas Wile, *T'ai Chi's Ancestors*, 58. Romanization modified.

5. Douglas Wile, cited in Meir Shahar, *The Shaolin Monastery*, Honolulu: University of Hawai'I Press, 2008, 177.

6. "Biography of Zhang Songxi," in the *Ningbo Prefectural Gazetteer*, translated in Douglas Wile, *T'ai Chi's Ancestors*, 69.

7. Lin Boyuan, *Zhongguo Wushushi*, Taibei: Wuzhou Chubanshe, 1996, 355.

8. Shahar, *The Shaolin Monastery*, 185.

9. A stele erected in 1677 referring to seventy Shaolin monks fighting rebels around 1640 indicates that while the bulk of them came from Shaolin monastery, some came from the subsidiary Yongtai shrine. Shahar, *The Shaolin Monastery*, 185188.

10. Shahar, *The Shaolin Monastery*, 185182.

11. Shahar, *The Shaolin Monastery*, 185187.

12. Shahar, *The Shaolin Monastery*, 185190–91.

13. Douglas Wile, *Lost T'ai-chi Classics from the Late Ch'ing Dynasty*, Albany: State University of New York Press, 1996, xv–xvi. Romanization converted to pinyin for consistency.

14. Wile, *T'ai Chi's Ancestors*, 1. Romanization modified.

15. Wile, *T'ai Chi's Ancestors*, 1–2. Romanization modified.

16. The designation "external" seems only to be used by internal stylists to characterize pejoratively noninternal styles. Some noninternal styles do accept and even embrace the designation "hard" as a pragmatic approach to fighting. Hard stylists contrast their practical and effective martial arts against the wooly-minded and ineffective soft styles.

17. Tang Hao, *Zhongguo Wuyi Tujie Kao*, "Liuhequan Pu," Shanghai (no publisher), 1940, ch. 1.

18. Lin Boyuan, *Zhongguo Wushushi*, 361.

19. For a history of the Taiping Rebellion, see Jonathan Spence, *God's Chinese Son: The Taiping Heavenly Kingdom of Hong Xiuquan*, New York: W.W. Norton, 1996.

20. For an overview of the Boxer Rebellion see Joseph Esherick, *The Origins of the Boxer Uprising*, Berkeley: University of California Press, 1987, and Paul Cohen, *History in Three Keys: The Boxers as Event, Experience, and Myth*, New York: Columbia University Press, 1997.

10 Post-Imperial China

1. David Young, *The Modern Olympics: A Struggle for Revival*, Baltimore: Johns Hopkins University Press, 1996, 68.

2. Since at least the late twentieth century an enormous number of books in Chinese have been published on the history of physical education in China. The martial arts are always included in these histories, but the category itself is a modern, Western import.

3. There is a considerable scholarship on Jin Yong in particular. Classical Chinese tales of martial artists have also, of course, been studied extensively. For Jin Yong, see John Christopher Hamm, *Paper Swordsmen: Jin Yong and the Modern Chinese Martial Arts Novel*, Honolulu: University of Hawai'i Press, 2006; the most recent work on the rise of the modern Chinese martial arts novel is Margaret Wan, *Green Peony and the Rise of the Chinese Martial Arts Novel*, Albany: State University of New York Press, 2010; on the development of Chinese vernacular fiction (with particular reference to the *The Water Margin (Shuihuzhuan)*), see Liangyan Ge, *Out of the Margins: The Rise of Chinese Vernacular Fiction*, Honolulu: University of Hawai'i Press, 2001. In addition, many of his works have been translated into English, for example, Louis Cha (John Minford, trans.), *The Book and the Sword*, Oxford: Oxford University Press, 2005; and Jin Yong (Olivia Mok, trans.), *Fox Volant of the Snowy Mountain*, Hong Kong: Chinese University Press, 1996.
4. Lin Boyuan, cited in Andrew Morris, *Marrow of the Nation*, Berkeley: University of California Press, 2004, 186.
5. Morris, *Marrow of the Nation*.
6. Here I disagree with Morris's assertion that "once-disparate bands of itinerant performers and teachers suddenly exposed in China's cities to *wushu* schools and artists from other regions, began to mature and coalesce into a 'community' of martial artists" (186). This community long predated the late Qing interest in public associations.
7. Morris, *Marrow of the Nation*, 223–5.
8. Morris, *Marrow of the Nation*, 227.
9. I have translated the term *guoshu* 國術 as "National Art" rather than Andrew Morris's "National Arts" to emphasize the intent to create a unified Chinese martial art that encompassed all of the disparate arts into one, all-embracing framework. The term in Chinese is, of course, ambiguous with regard to number.
10. Morris, *Marrow of the Nation*, 204.
11. Morris, *Marrow of the Nation*, 210.
12. Ralph Thaxton, *Catastrophe and Contention in Rural China*, Cambridge: Cambridge University Press, 2008, 315.
13. Matthew Polly, *American Shaolin*, New York: Gotham Books, 2007, 57.
14. Matthew Polly, *American Shaolin*, 6.
15. Thaxton, *Catastrophe and Contention*, 316.
16. Professor Thaxton kindly allowed me to read some of his unpublished research.
17. Polly, *American Shaolin*, 356–7.
18. Andrew Jacobs, "Town Asks Kung Fu Monks for Tourism Blessing," *New York Times*, 1 January 2009.
19. It is an interesting parallel that non-Chinese have been able to make Chinese martial arts movies as well as or better than Chinese directors, in the same way that the iconic spaghetti Westerns were shot by non-Americans.

Conclusion

1. Stanley Henning, "Academia Encounters the Chinese Martial Arts," *China Review International*, 6, no. 2 (Fall 1999), 319.
2. Carl Brown, *American Law and the Trained Fighter*, Black Belt Communications, 1983.

Bibliography

Adolphson, Mikael S. *The Teeth and Claws of the Buddha*. Honolulu: University of Hawai'i Press, 2007.

Ban Gu. *Hanshu*. Taibei: Dingwen Shuju, 1997.

Ban Gu (Homer H. Dubs, trans.). *History of the Former Han Dynasty*. Baltimore: Waverly Press, 1938–55.

Bi Yuan. *Xu Zizhi Tongjian*. Taibei: Taiwan Zhonghua Shuju, 1965.

Bielenstein, Hans. "Wang Mang, the Restoration of the Han Dynasty, and Later Han," in Denis Twitchett and Michael Lowe (eds.), *The Cambridge History of China*, Vol. 1. Cambridge: Cambridge University Press, 1986.

Brown, Carl. *American Law and the Trained Fighter*. Black Belt Communications, 1983.

Cha, Louis (John Minford trans.). *The Book and the Sword*. Oxford: Oxford University Press, 2005.

Chang, K. C. *Shang Civilization*. New Haven: Yale University Press, 1980.

Cohen, Paul A. *History in Three Keys: The Boxers as Event, Experience, and Myth*. New York: Columbia University Press, 1998.

Confucius (Edward Slingerland, trans.). *The Analects*. Indianapolis: Hackett, 2003.

Daoxuan. *Xu Gaoseng zhuan*. 2 vols. Shanghai: Guji chubanshe, 1995 and 1999.

Dien, Albert. "The Stirrup and Its Effect on Chinese Military History." *Ars Orientalis* Vol. 16 (1986), 33–56.

Dien, Albert. *Six Dynasties Civilization*. New Haven: Yale University Press, 2007.

Du You. *Tongdian*. Beijing: Zhonghua Shuju, 1988.

Duan Chengshi (Carrie E. Reed, trans.). *A Tang Miscellany*. New York: Peter Lang, 2003.

Dumoulin, Heinrich. *Zen Buddhism: A History*. New York: Simon and Schuster Macmillan, 1994.

Engels, Frederick (Friedrich). *The Origin of the Family, Private Property and the State*. New York: International, 1942.

Esherick, Joseph. *The Origins of the Boxer Uprising*. Berkeley: University of California Press, 1987.

Fan Ye. *Houhanshu*. Taibei: Dingwen Shuju, 1999.

Fan Xuanliang. *Jinshu*. Taibei: Dingwen Shuju, 1995.

Faure, Bernard. "Relics and Flesh Bodies: The Creation of Ch'an Pilgrimage Sites," in Susan Naquin and Chün-Fang Yu (eds.), *Pilgrims and Sacred Sites in China*. Berkeley: University of California Press, 1992.

Filipiak, Kai. *Die Chinesische Kampfkunst*. Leipzig: Leipziger Universitätsverlag, 2001.

Ge Hong. *Baopuzi*. Taibei: Xinwenfeng Chuban Gongsi, 1998.

Ge Liangyan. *Out of the Margins: The Rise of Chinese Vernacular Fiction*. Honolulu: University of Hawai'i Press, 2001.

Gernet, Jacques (Franciscus Verellen, trans.). *Buddhism in Chinese Society: An Economic History from the Fifth to the Tenth Centuries*. New York: Columbia University Press, 1995.

Goldin, Paul. *Rituals of the Way*. Chicago: Open Court, 1999.

Gongyang Gao, Ruan Yuan (ed). *Gongyang Zhuan*. In *Shisanjing Zhushu*, Vol. 7. Taibei: Yiwen Yinshuguan, 2001.

Graff, David. *Medieval Chinese Warfare, 300–900*. London: Routledge, 2002.

Guojia Tiwei Wushu Yanjiuyuan Bianzuan. *Zhongguo Wushushi*. Beijing: Renmin Tiyu Chubanshe, 1996.

Hamm, John Christopher. *Paper Swordsmen: Jin Yong and the Modern Chinese Martial Arts Novel*. Honolulu: University of Hawai'i Press, 2006.

Han Rulin (ed.). *Yuanchaoshi*. Beijing: Renmin Chubanshe, 1986.

Henning, Stanley. "Academia Encounters the Chinese Martial Arts," *China Review International* Vol. 6, No. 2 (Fall 1999), 319–32.

Henning, Stanley. "Ignorance, Legend, and Taijiquan." Journal of the *Chen Style Taijiquan Research Association of Hawai'i* Vol. 2, No. 4 (1994), 1–7.

Henning, Stanley. "General Qi Jiguang's Approach to Martial Arts Training." Journal of the *Chen Style Taijiquan Research Association of Hawai'i* Vol. 3, No. 2 (1995), 1–3.

Henning, Stanley. "On Politically Correct Treatment of the Myths in the Chinese Martial Arts." Journal of the *Chen Style Taijiquan Research Association of Hawai'i* Vol. 3, No. 2 (1995), 17–21.

Henning, Stanley. "Chinese Boxing: The Internal Versus External Schools in the Light of History and Theory." *Journal of Asian Martial Arts* Vol. 6, No. 3 (1997), 10–19.

Hua Yue. *Cuihui Beizheng Lu*, in *Zhongguo Bingshu Jicheng*, Vol. 6. Beijing: Jiefangjun Chubanshe, 1992.

Huijiao. *Gaoseng zhuan*. Beijing: Zhonghua Shuju, 1991.

Jacobs, Andrew. "Town Asks Kung Fu Monks for Tourism Blessing." *New York Times*, 1 January 2009.

Jia Lanpo et al. "Report on Excavations of Shiyu Paleolithic Sites in Shanxi." *Journal of Archaeology*, Vol. 1 (1972), 39–60.

Jin Yong (Olivia Mok trans.). *Fox Volant of the Snowy Mountain*. Hong Kong: Chinese University Press, 1996.

Keightley, David N. *The Ancestral Landscape*. Berkeley: Institute of East Asian Studies, University of California, 2000.

Kieschnick, John. *The Eminent Monk*. Honolulu: University of Hawai'i Press, 1997.

Legge, James (trans.). *Li Chi*. New York: University Books, 1967.

Legge, James (trans.). *Shi jing*. New York: Paragon Reprint, 1967.

Lei Haizong. *Zhongguo wenhua yu zhongguo zhi bing*. Changsha: Yuelu Shushe, 1989 (First edition 1939).

Lewis, Mark Edward. *Sanctioned Violence in Early China*. Albany: State University of New York Press, 1990.

Lewis, Mark Edward. "The Han Abolition of Universal Military Service," in Hans Van de Ven (ed.), *Warfare in Chinese History*. Leiden: Brill, 2000.

Lewis, Mark Edward. *The Early Chinese Empires*. Cambridge, MA: Harvard University Press, 2007.

Lewis, Mark Edward. *China between Empires: The Northern and Southern Dynasties*. Cambridge, MA: Harvard University Press, 2009.

Li Fang. *Taiping Guangji*, in *Siku Quanshu*. *Siku Quanshu*. Hong Kong: Chinese University of Hong Kong & Digital Heritage Publishing, 2004.

Li Quan. *Taibai Yinjing*, in *Siku Quanshu*. *Siku Quanshu*. Hong Kong: Chinese University of Hong Kong & Digital Heritage Publishing, 2004.

Li Tao. *Xu Zizhitongjian Changbian*. Beijing: Zhonghua Shuju, 2004.

Lieh-tzu (Eva Wong, trans.). *Lieh-tzu*. Boston: London: Shambala, 2001.

Lin Boyuan. *Zhongguo Wushushi*. Taibei: Wuzhou Chubanshe,1996.

Liu Gengguo. *Zhongguo Gudai Tiyu Shihua*. Beijing: Wenwu chubanshe, 1987.

Liu Xi, *Shiming*, ch. 23 (Explaining Weapons), *China Text Project*, 14 June 2011. http://ctext.org/shi-ming/shi-bing.

Liu Xiang (ed.). *Xinxu* 新序. E-Gutenberg. 16 June 2011, http://www.gutenberg.org/cache/epub/23945/pg23945.html.

Liu Xu. *Jiu Tangshu*. Beijing: Zhonghua Shuju, 1975.

Loewe, Michael. *Everyday Life in Early Imperial China*. New York: G. P. Putnam's Sons, 1968.

Luo Guanzhong (Wu Xiaolin, ed.). *Sanguo Yanyi jiao zhu*. Taibei: Liren Shuju, 1994.

Luo Guanzhong (C. H. Brewitt-Taylor, trans.). *Romance of the Three Kingdoms*. Rutland, VT: C. E. Tuttle, 1959.

Mencius (D. C. Lau, trans.). *Mencius*. New York: Penguin, 1978.

Meng Yuanlao. Dongjing Menghua Lu, in *Siku Quanshu*. Hong Kong: Chinese University of Hong Kong & Digital Heritage Publishing, 2004.

Morris, Andrew. *Marrow of the Nation*. Berkeley: University of California Press, 2004.

Nienhauser, William H. (trans.). "The Ballad of Mulan," in Wu-chi Liu and Irving Yucheng Lo (eds.), *Sunflower Splendor: Three Thousand Years of Chinese Poetry*. Garden City, NY: Anchor Books, 1975.

Ouyang Xiu. *Guitian Lu, in Shengshui Yantan Lu/Guitian Lu*. In *Tang-Song Shiliao Biji Congkan*. Vol. 6. Beijing: Zhonghua Shuju, 2006.

Ouyang Xiu and Song Qi. *Xin Tangshu*. Beijing: Zhonghua Shuju, 1975.

Pan Ku (Homer H. Dubs, trans.). *The History of the Former Han Dynasty*. Baltimore: Waverly Press, 1938.

Pei Songzhi. *Sanguozhi*. Taibei: Dingwen Shuju, 1997.

Peterson, Barbara Bennett (ed.). *Notable Women of China*. Armonk, NY: M. E. Sharpe, 2000.

Polly, Matthew. *American Shaolin*. New York: Gotham Books, 2007.

Polo, Marco (Ronald Latham, trans.). *The Travels of Marco Polo*. London: Folio Society, 1990 (reissue).

Qi Jiguang. *Jixiao Xinshu*. In *Zhongguo Bingshu Jicheng*, Vol. 18. Beijing: Jiefangjun chubanshe, 1992.

Robinson, David. *Bandits, Eunuchs and the Son of Heaven*. Honolulu: University of Hawai'i Press, 2001.

Ruan Yuan (ed.). *Guliang Zhuan*. In *Shisanjing Zhushu*, Vol. 6. Taibei: Yiwen Yinshuguan, 2001.

Ruan Yuan (ed.). *Liji*. In *Shisanjing Zhushu*, Vol. 5. Taibei: Yiwen Yinshuguan, 2001.

Ryor, Kathleen. "Wen and Wu in Elite Cultural Practices during the Late Ming," in Nicola DiCosmo (ed.), *Military Culture in Imperial China*. Cambridge, MA: Harvard University Press, 2008.

Schlütter, Morten. *How Zen Became Zen*. Honolulu: University of Hawai'i Press, 2008.

Selby, Stephen. *Chinese Archery*. Hong Kong: Hong Kong University Press, 2000.

Shahar, Meir. *The Shaolin Monastery*. Honolulu: University of Hawai'i Press, 2008.

Shaughnessy, Edward L. "Historical Perspectives on the Introduction of the Chariot into China." *Harvard Journal of Asiatic Studies*, Vol. 48 (1988), 189–237.

Shen Yue. *Songshu*. Taibei: Dingwen Shuju, 1998.

Shi Nai'an and Luo Guanzhong. *Shuihuzhuan (The Water Margin)*. Beijing: Zhonghua Shuju, 1997.

Shi Nai'an and Luo Guanzhong (Sidney Shapiro, trans.). *Outlaws of the Marsh*. Bloomington: Indiana University Press, 1981.

Shi Yukun. *Qixia Wuyi*. Shanghai: Shanghai Guji Chubanshe, 1990.

Shi Yukun (Song Shouquan, trans.). *The Seven Heroes and Five Gallants*. Beijing: Foreign Language Press, 2005.

Siku Quanshu. Hong Kong: Chinese University of Hong Kong & Digital Heritage Publishing, 2004.

Sima Guang. *Zizhi Tongjian*. Taibei: Taiwan Zhonghua Shuju, 1966.

Sima Guang. *Zizhi Tongjian*. Beijing: Guji Chubanshe, 1956.

Sima Guang. *Sima Wenzheng (Wengong) Ji*. Taibei: Taiwan Zhonghua Shuju, 1965.

Sima Qian. *Shiji*. Taibei: Dingwen Shuju, 1999.

Sima Qian (Burton Watson, trans.). *Records of the Grand Historian*. New York: Columbia University Press, 1969.

Sima Qian (William H. Nienhauser et al., trans.). *The Grand Scribe's Records*. Bloomington: Indiana University Press, 1994–.

Skaff, Jonathan. "Barbarians at the Gates? The Tang Frontier Military and the An Lushan Rebellion." *War and Society*, Vol. 18, No. 2 (2000), 23–35.

Smith, Paul Jakov. *Taxing Heaven's Storehouse: Horses, Bureaucrats, and the Destruction of the Sichuan Tea Industry, 1074–1224*. Cambridge, MA: Harvard University Council on East Asian Studies, 1991.

Smith, Paul Jakov. "*Shuihu zhuan* and the Military Subculture of the Northern Song, 960–1127." *Harvard Journal of Asiatic Studies*, Vol. 66, No. 2 (December 2006), 363–422.

Song Lian. *Yuanshi*. Taibei: Dingwen Shuju, 1998.

Songhuiyao Jigao. Taibei: Xinwenfeng Chubangongsi, 1976.

Spence, Jonathan. *God's Chinese Son: The Taiping Heavenly Kingdom of Hong Xiuquan*. New York: W.W. Norton, 1996.

Su Shi. *San Su Quanshu*, Vol. 12. Beijing: Yuwen Chubanshe, 2001.

Swope, Kenneth. *A Dragon's Head and a Serpent's Tail*. Norman: University of Oklahoma Press, 2009.

Tang Hao. *Zhongguo Wuyi Tujie Kao*. Shanghai: (no publisher), 1940.

Thaxton, Ralph. *Catastrophe and Contention in Rural China*. Cambridge: Cambridge University Press, 2008.

Toghto. *Songshi*. Taibei: Dingwen Shuju, 1998.

Tong, James W. *Disorder under Heaven*. Stanford: Stanford University Press, 1991.

Xunzi, Yang Liang (ed.). *Xunzi*. Tokyo: Xunzi Li shi Riben Dongjing Shi Shu, 1884.

Van de Ven, Hans. "Introduction" in Hans Van de Ven (ed.), *Warfare in Chinese History*. Leiden: Brill, 2000.

Waldron, Arthur. *The Great Wall of China*. Cambridge: Cambridge University Press, 1992.

Wan, Margaret. *Green Peony and the Rise of the Chinese Martial Arts Novel*. Albany: State University of New York Press, 2010.

Wang Guangxi. *Gongfu*. Taibei: Yunlong Chubanshe, 2002.

Wang Pizhi. *Shengshui Yantan Lu*, in Shengshui Yantan Lu/Guitian Lu. In *Tang-Song Shiliao Biji Congkan*, Vol. 6. Beijing: Zhonghua Shuju, 2006.

Wei Shou. *Weishu*. Taibei: Dingwen Shuju, 1998.

Wei Zheng. *Suishu*. Taibei: Dingwen Shuju, 1997.

Wenwu Chubanshe. *Yinxu Dixia Guibao: Henan Anyang Fu Hao Mu*. Beijing: Wenwu Chubanshe, 1994.

Wenying. *Xiangshan Yelu*. Beijing: Zhonghua Shuju, 2007.

Wile, Douglas. *Lost T'ai-chi Classics from the Late Ch'ing Dynasty*. Albany: State University of New York Press, 1996.

Wile, Douglas. *T'ai Chi's Ancestors*. New York: Sweet Ch'i Press, 1999.

Wu, Zimu. *Mengliang Lu*, in *Siku Quanshu*. Hong Kong: Chinese University of Hong Kong & Digital Heritage Publishing, 2004.

Xiaowuyi. Shanghai: Shanghai Guji Chubanshe, 1990.

Xu, Dong. *Huqian Jing* 虎鈐經, in *Zhongguo Bingshu Jicheng*, Vol. 6. Beijing: Jiefangjun chubanshe, 1992.

Yang Hong (Zhang Lijing, trans.). *Weapons in Ancient China*. Rego Park, NY: Science Press, 1992.

Young, David. *The Modern Olympics: A Struggle for Revival*. Baltimore: Johns Hopkins Press, 1996.

Zanning. *Da Song Gaoseng zhuan*. Taibei: Shangwu yinshu guan, 1983.

Zeng Gong. *Nanfeng Xiansheng Yuanfeng lei gao*. Taibei: Taiwan Zhonghua Shuju, 1971.

Zeng Gongliang. *Wujing Zongyao (Complete Essentials from the Military Classics)*. Vols. 3, 4, and 5 in *Zhongguo Bingshu Jicheng*, Vol. 6. Beijing: Jiefangjun chubanshe, 1992.

Zhang, Chunben and Cui, Lequan. *Zhongguo Wushushi*. Taibei: Wenjin Chubanshe, 1993.

Zhang Qiyun (ed.). *Zhongwen Dacidian*. Taibei: Zhongguo Wenhua Daxue Chuban Bu, 1993.

Zhongguo Bingshu Jicheng Bianweihui. *Zhongguo Bingshu Jicheng*. Beijing: Jiefangjun chubanshe, 1991–.

Zuo Qiuming, Ruan Yuan (ed.). *Zuozhuan*. In *Shisanjing Zhushu*, Vol. 6. Taibei: Yiwen Yinshuguan, 2001.

Index